PAVLODAR

NUR-SULTAN ★

KARAGANDA

N

A

ALMATY

SHYMKENT

BISHKEK ★

KYRGYZSTAN

TASHKENT ●

KOKAND

KHUJAND

OSH

TAJIKISTAN

CHINA

NBE ★

TAN

PAKISTAN

xmas 2021.

To my best bvd.

x Stella

RED SANDS

By the same author

SAMARKAND & BLACK SEA

Praise for *Black Sea*:

'Eden's blazing talent and unabashedly greedy curiosity will have you strapped in beside her … If Sybille Bedford or Patrick Leigh Fermor had included a few recipes in their accounts of their journeys, you'd know exactly where to shelve this gem.'

THE NEW YORK TIMES

'Her prose at its best reminds me of Lawrence Durrell's travel writing: taut, colorful, opinionated and full of zest.'

EDWARD LEE, AUTHOR OF *BUTTERMILK GRAFFITI*

'She captures people, history, and the ineffable soul of cities with astonishing, almost novelistic precision … I can't remember any cookbook that's drawn me in quite like this.'

HELEN ROSNER, ART OF EATING JUDGE

RED SANDS

Reportage and Recipes Through Central Asia
from Hinterland to Heartland

CAROLINE EDEN

photography by Theodore Kaye and Ola O. Smit

Hardie Grant

QUADRILLE

Publishing Director and Editor Sarah Lavelle
Copy Editor Tamsin English
Designer Dave Brown
Head of Design Claire Rochford
Photographer Ola O. Smit
Location Photography Theodore Kaye
Illustration Ivana Zorn
Props Stylist Tabitha Hawkins
Food Stylist Pip Spence
Head of Production Stephen Lang
Production Controller Nikolaus Ginelli

Published in 2020 by Quadrille, an imprint of Hardie Grant Publishing

QUADRILLE
52–54 Southwark Street
London SE1 1UN
quadrille.com

Cataloguing in Publication Data: a catalogue record for this book is available
from the British Library.

text © Caroline Eden 2020
photography © Theodore Kaye with the exceptions of pages 19, 20, 45, 55,
87, 89, 95, 105, 111, 113, 122, 125, 134, 145, 153, 165, 166, 187, 207, 215,
217, 231, 232, 241, 243, 245, 255, 263, 271, 279 and 281 © Ola O Smit
2020; and pages 10, 65, 68, 70, 72, 74, 76, 79, 80, 83, 106, 141, 156, 160
and 209 © Caroline Eden 2020
design © Dave Brown 2020

ISBN 9781787134829

Printed in Italy

CONTENTS

For J.E.K., of course.

'I look back as through a telescope, and see,
in the little bright circle of the glass,
moving flocks and ruined cities.'

– Vita Sackville-West

'Food is as revealing as money and sex,
and is revealed more often.'

– Sybille Bedford

PRELUDE AND SETTING

In the shattered rear-view mirror, the land was pink from the rising sun. The fractured looking glass rendered the desert view, mainly sand dunes, scrub and small hills, broken and repetitive. On the road, between the cities of Bukhara and Khiva – some stretches good, others badly potholed – there was a sense of slowly evaporating, of being dwarfed by the Kyzylkum ('red sand') Desert.

Life's usual urban markers – glass, advertising, people and concrete – had vanished. Every mile crossed felt acute because, even in the safety of a car, deserts trigger intensities: uneasy mirages of lost directions and fears of supplies running short. But, despite imagined terrors, deserts also excite awe.

When Freya Stark flew over here in the 1960s, she admired the watery path of the life-giving Amu Darya (or the Oxus River, as it is historically known), skirting this parched expanse, and she welcomed its geography into her breast. Looking down, she thought of warrior-rulers Genghis Khan and Tamerlane riding the riverbank on 'small, strong horses, before they began to build where they destroyed' but she dreaded the ominous inch and lurk of the Kyzylkum Desert that spans Uzbekistan and Kazakhstan: 'The desert fear creeps even into the shiny surfaces of the aeroplane', she wrote in a newspaper dispatch. Like the sea, a desert landscape is all waves and ripples and movement. Not dead, but alive. Here, sand, blown by hot sticky summer breezes and by bitterly cold wintry winds, forms barchans, tall crescent-shaped dunes. Above fly eagles and bats, and below snakes zigzag past the smashed shells of too-slow steppe tortoises.

At some point during this six-hour drive, I don't recall when exactly, a flat-roofed structure appeared. In front of the rough, squat building a group of men reclined on a steel tapchan, a raised platform for tea drinking, topped with a thinly padded floral mattress, and upon that, a small table on four legs where cups, spoons and teapots glinted. A desert café: an island of comfort in a sea of saffron-coloured scrub and sand.

Out of the yawn-scented car, into the sun and onto soft-as-felt sand. Right foot, left foot, right foot; boots gradually shifting the hot grains. The sun's glare forced my eyes downwards until they met a hard-backed beetle emerging from its hole. Right-angled legs appeared one by one as it scuttled upwards and out, exposing its shiny bullet-shaped body to the sun. 'Not a scorpion,' I said out loud, to no one. Desert salt, carried on the dry wind, brushed skin and gritted teeth.

Walking past the lounging men, through thick grey shashlik smoke corkscrewing up from the grill, I went into the kitchen to order what I could smell (for there wouldn't be anything else). Inside the walls of the clay tandoor were roundels of non bread, each one slowly baking and expanding until golden on top, chewy in the middle and crispy underneath. What smell in the world is more innocent, more primevally reassuring, than that of bread? No smell. Nothing is more soothing than the scent of bread.

The kitchen was as ordered and sand-whipped as it was clean. A red Russian weighing scale stood on a steel table and next to it were empty rice sacks used as makeshift soufreh, traditional squares of clean material used to prepare food upon. Alongside, a blue and white teapot, a handle-less teacup called a piala, and a wooden chekich bread stamp. Dense heat hung over it all and a small team worked in silent rhythm: a woman dressed in a red and gold tunic ferried plates and cutlery to the men outside; a chef in a paisley bandana pushed and pulled non bread out of the tandoor and outside, by the tapchan, a man fanned the cubes of lamb with one hand while turning the skewers with the other. Glossy caramel chunks of fat, threaded between the meat, glowed as the signature notes of Central Asian cooking – meat and bread – puffed and travelled on the wind out to the desert. Behind the kitchen lay the skeleton of a rusting Russian truck, baked by the sun. Stripped of any value, it had no roof, no windows and no wheels. Ruinously pretty, it looked like a piece of art that had been carefully wedged in the sand by a band of guerrilla artists.

I joined the men outside. The skin around their eyes was heavily lined, as if carved from redwood, and their demeanour was contagiously languid, suited to the heat. With their settled-in postures and sun-faded clothes it looked as though they'd been here an age already, and were happy to be here another more. In a busy world, the quiet desert has its pleasures.

First from the kitchen came green tea, steaming in a stout teapot decorated with Persian-style birds. Then bread, still warm and good to chew, a plate of raw onion rings, a canister of salt, and lastly the juicy, fatty shashlik threaded tightly onto the rough-hewn metal skewers. We ate, and we ate together, anchored on the desert tapchan, our hunger collectively divided and divided again. The time – an hour or so – passed cordially, carefree. It was early autumn but the heat still oozed. Shashlik smoke quivered in the middle distance, mixing and melding with the desert's glow, vibrating up from the sand, creating mirage-like waves. I split open a watermelon with a penknife, and placed dripping crescents of it onto a spare plate. Red water bled out from sugary wet flesh, quickly reducing and fading into a dry pale-pink stain. We ate it, then I wiped my hands on my jeans, stood up, and left.

Setting is all, of course, and desert romance has a tendency to spill into memories like sand into boots, but that roadside meal in the Kyzylkum Desert – shashlik, bread, raw onion rings, salt and melon – eaten five or so years ago, had authority. Requiring very few tools, it was good and it created no waste. And, it was at that desert café that I considered whether I'd ever eaten anything, anywhere, so simple yet so harmoniously in tune with its extreme environment. So entirely suited to its surroundings. And, I concluded that I had not.

FOOD AS PASSPORT, FOOD AS ANCHOR

This book takes its name from the Kyzylkum Desert, straddling Uzbekistan and Kazakhstan, spread out between two legendary rivers, the Amu Darya (Oxus) and Syr Darya (Jaxartes), famous in world literature and history.

Known in the past as Transoxiana and Turkestan, Central Asia today consists of five modern republics, Kazakhstan, Kyrgyzstan, Tajikistan, Uzbekistan and Turkmenistan, the last not included in this book as reporting freely there is problematic. Independent since the USSR collapsed in 1991, today each country balances its own economic challenges with pressures from Russia, China and the west while negotiating nation-building, religious reawakenings, and a history that collectively takes in the Silk Road, Alexander the Great, powerful khanates and nomadic empires.

That lunch in the Kyzylkum Desert sparked the idea for this book. And that same desert forms a centre point within these pages, but the stories and journeys recollected here – drawn from a six-month trip to Central Asia split between spring and autumn of 2019 – travel far beyond its sandy edges.

My mission for this book is twofold: firstly, to preserve on paper something of these countries as they rapidly develop and open up further to the world. To record them before further changes come and more disappears for good via bulldozers, the march of globalisation and increased tourism. And, secondly, to reveal a unique and different portrait of Central Asia, using food as an agent, device and theme.

Two writers whose books I carried on these journeys knew the value of the everyday and ordinary. How the seemingly mundane can be telling, and even magical, if you pay attention to it.

Isabella 'Ella' Robertson Christie was a formidable and sharp-eyed traveller, born in 1861 close to my adopted city of Edinburgh. She came not once, but twice to this region, in 1910 and 1912, publishing her adventures in 1925 in *Through Khiva to Golden Samarkand*, a book I kept with me always. Her musings provided constant reminders to travel unhurriedly but deliberately, to observe quietly and to examine life both high and low. To indulge a hunger for the world but to go slow and stay busy by simply 'being there'.

What sets Ella Christie's work apart from better-remembered writers of this region, such as Peter Hopkirk and Sir Fitzroy Maclean, are her commonplace observations and her motivation. Rather than setting out to spy, break records or gain accolades, she took pleasure in observing and noting the domestic and commonplace – cooking, clothing and workshops – in great detail. But that's not to say she wasn't tenacious. Travelling across the Caspian Sea into Turkmenistan and on by train, cart and even steamer on the Oxus River, she headed into Uzbekistan to the notorious slave-trading town of Khiva. Some historians believe she was the first western woman to reach it. On her journeys, she described ice lollies sold in an Uzbek bazaar, made by chiselling down a block of 'frozen snow' and pouring raisin syrup over the chips; of being pinned down by fear in her carriage out on the steppe by thoughts of a black spider called a karakurt, capable of killing a camel in three hours; and eating eggs cooked by spirit lamp.

Before setting off, the Foreign Office issued her with a personal warning: should she contract plague in Central Asia, she ought to 'hang a red cloth over the window.' But Christie knew such government advice was iffy. 'No thought was given as to where red cloth was to be obtained, if there would be any windows over which to hang it.' Christie made a note of this guidance, and went anyway.

John Wardell recorded his years living in Kazakhstan in a fascinating and well-written book entitled *In the Kirghiz Steppes* (historically, the Kazakh steppe was referred to as 'Kirghiz'), sadly little-read today. He'd arrived in 1914, on his 25th birthday, to mine copper for the tsar, having left London 16 and a half days earlier. He witnessed Kazakhstan on the eve of industrialisation, and delighted in the seasons changing. He catalogued the flora: yellow irises, marigolds, wild sage and bitter lemony southernwood, and noted 'horses' hooves bruising the herbs so that the air is redolent with perfume.' These are far from impossible images. On my own journey through the Kazakh steppe in early summer red poppies stretched blazing and livid for hundreds of miles and I crushed strongly scented wild mint and thyme underfoot. Wardell's book, also carried with me, was a physical reminder of the value of recording the present, of noting people, places and countries at a time of development and transformation.

For *Red Sands*, written ten years on from my first ever visit to Central Asia, we start on the springtime shores of the Caspian Sea, way out west, in the largest country in the region, oil-rich Kazakhstan. Then it's on through steppe, desert and mountain cradle, via burgeoning and unsung cities, until we end in Tajikistan, in autumn, in the knot of the Fergana Valley, shared by three countries: Uzbekistan, Kyrgyzstan and Tajikistan. This valley has suffered bloody ethnic violence in recent history, but it is the heartland of Central Asia, home to a multitude of ethnicities and wonderful produce, traditions and hospitality. Autumn, when the markets are abundant, is the time to be there.

And, just as journeys, writers and books need rhythm, the pattern of mealtimes provides an escape and a break, a relief and stability on the road, the assurance of a drink, a meal, and a rest at the table. Navigate this trek, complete this border crossing, finish this drive, and then there will be breakfast, lunch or dinner. A canteen or a café. Or a bar session. On these long journeys, the tempo of food and mealtimes became a mental rudder, routinely forming the basis of reflections, meetings and revelations. Sitting at the dastarkhan (literally 'tablecloth'), the covered table set low to the ground, as is common throughout Central Asia, vast mealtimes proceed as they have done for centuries. Freshly baked non bread will be torn and handed around, a plate of warm flaky samsa will be set down, a platter of plov placed in the centre, endless cups of tea will be ferried back and forth, all alongside salads and many bowls of seasonal fruit. In the spring, cherries and strawberries, and in the autumn, melon – always melon – for they are the best in the world.

As with my previous book, *Black Sea*, the recipes here, which I hope some readers might try, are emblematic. Edible snapshots, if you like. They are intended to complement the stories, offering a multisensory way to enjoy the journey, shining further light onto the words and adventure, much in the way photographs do. Some recipes are inspired by literature, others by imagination, but most are based on meals eaten in situ. They are memories; interpretations of what I ate and enjoyed in restaurants, on trains, in homes and in kitchens. Some dishes written about here are likely to have been what you've eaten, too, in Central Asia or will eat, if you visit. Often they have originated in other countries of the former Soviet Union – so in Kazakhstan I frequently ate Russian and Georgian food, while in Kyrgyzstan mealtimes were sometimes made up of Uzbek and Dungan dishes, which is how many Central Asians eat. This is a region full of borders, invisible and visible, secure and insecure. Given the wide multicultural mix we will see that there is no one Central Asian cuisine; rather, within each country there is an eclectic blend. Crossover dishes – plov, manti, laghman, shashlik – are served in all four countries featured in this book.

Each essay is named after a man-made space, structure or building because the artificial environment – often mixing Islamic-tsarist-Soviet design and histories – is as uniquely Central Asian as natural desert plateaus, steppe grasslands and mountains. If I think of Central Asia, it is factories, mosques, canteens, sanatoriums, that come to mind first. All provide unique settings from which to tell stories.

There are parallels, too, between travelling curiously – especially to a new place – and trying out a recipe. Both require hope, patience and a plan. Both require a willingness to be defeated and a willingness to learn. Both embrace otherness: other times, other lives, other places and other ideas. Both require persistence, concentration and patience but also offer the delirious state of being neither here nor there – a feeling of floating on a friendly sea, enrolling just enough of the senses to be lost in the project. Both suggest the possibility of transformation. There will likely be a degree of success; there will likely be some failure.

Then, there is the return. A treasured recipe, one familiar, practised and therefore personal, is like a journey to a favourite place. A revisiting, a rebound, a retreat. A homecoming, even. With recipes, as with travel, first we find ourselves urged and curious, seeking something new. And then, if what we find pleases us, it tempts us again, and we return. We often find ourselves in the thick of it before starting out: by imagining, forecasting and dreaming of the sensory pleasures that lie ahead, in detail and in Technicolor, until we can almost smell the ingredients, smell the sunshine. There is much joy to be had in the planning. And there is need for flexibility, too. To 'travel' rarely means going in one direction. To suit seasons, whims and border crossings, for this book I travelled forwards most of the time, but sometimes I backtracked, zigzagging into different corners. As the great traveller, and visitor to Samarkand in the 1930s, Rosita Forbes, once wrote, 'No journey is given to one complete like an egg.'

Travel and cookery raise another shared and compelling question: why this particular destination over another? Why this recipe, and not that one? After all, there are thousands to choose from. Yet we find ourselves somehow summoned, somehow called upon. We find ourselves *invited*.

PART ONE

SPRING

MICRO-DISTRICT

Touching down in Central Asia

AKTAU, WEST KAZAKHSTAN: A cool morning breeze washed over Aktau's esplanade, slapping waves against the city's pale cliffs, the same cream colour as the bones, fish teeth and fossils that litter the bottom of the Caspian Sea. Aktau, meaning 'white mountain' in Kazakh, takes its name from this marine bluff. I walked the promenade, watching the Caspian shoreline breathing in and out, mind wandering to the quintet of countries that share its lake-like border: Kazakhstan, Turkmenistan, Iran, Azerbaijan and Russia – lands of carpets, palaces, mosques, desert oases and frozen taiga. Yet, Aktau is located in Europe, geographically if not politically and culturally, as here we are west of the Urals. Curious, but then Aktau, at the far edge of western Kazakhstan, is a city of edited geography, and of simulated environments.

Addresses and street names here, for the micro-districts, or mikrorayons, that make up the city, are mainly wordless and clueless, instead all numerical dots and dashes. Reading like phone numbers they make for difficult navigation through a maze of identical grid-like Soviet-era eight-storey apartment blocks, each with a number roughly painted on the side. If your address reads 5-30-15, that is the fifth district, 30th building, 15th apartment.

Quiet and closed off, the numbered blocks gave little away as I walked on. Only the seaside shrubs appeared alive, shaking gently. I stuck my nose in. The spindly branches were teeming with butterflies, a whisking, whirring blur of orange and black wings. A kaleidoscope of what looked like 'painted ladies' with their forewings marked with white spots and hind wings with black. Thousands of them, skimming and fluttering, landing and resettling. Were they migrating? They congregated on every living branch, only avoiding the glossy Floridian-style king palms, spaced out along the boulevard, each one perfect and identical. Pretend and man-made, therefore ignored by the butterflies. Fake plastic trees on the Caspian Sea.

By an 11-storey block, with the city's small gear-stick-shaped lighthouse atop its roof, a string of grand villas cut off the rest of the city from the sea. Banking the sand, these newly built mansions, some with their own shashlik sheds, were likely built on oil-dollars. The martial orderliness and manufactured landscape of Aktau makes it hard to imagine the wilder outskirts where red wolves occasionally menace scrubby villages, attacking chicken sheds and livestock, and oil fields stretch for miles. Out there, some still speak of the time, 20 years ago, that a newly born lamb brought a mullah running to decode the animal's unusual fleece. On one side of the lamb the word 'Allah' appeared, and on the other side 'Muhammed'.

Before Ukrainians and Russians built the city in the late 1950s, only a few seekers and merchants passed through here: Scythian tribes, fishermen, wandering saints. And hunters, too, prepared to hack it out in climatic extremes for fatty Caspian seals – the littlest seals in the world – highly valuable for their fur and oil. English merchant Anthony Jenkinson, dispatched by England's Muscovy Company, left for Central Asia in 1558 and travelled for four months from Astrakhan – Russia's 'Caspian capital' – ravaged at the time by both plague and famine (so bad that parents were selling children for bread) taking a boat down the Volga River and then on to the Caspian Sea dodging pirates and storms, until he arrived on the Mangyshlak Peninsula, right here. The first Englishman to sail the Caspian Sea.

'During the time of our navigation wee sett up the redd crosse of S. George in our flagges, for honour of the Christians, which I suppose was never seen in the Caspian Sea before.' Then he went into 'wild fields' and on to the Uzbek trading city of Bukhara. No one lingered long around here because the desert oases deep in the barren plateaus were spread too far apart. Still today, Aktau and its surrounding plains of oil fields exude loneliness.

Today, Kazakhstan is still marginal in most minds, if it is familiar at all. But it matters. And the word that we use to describe the Caspian Sea matters, too. During the era of the Soviet Union, it was classified as a lake, but following the collapse of the USSR things became complicated. Slightly larger than Germany, and containing billions of gallons of oil and natural gas reserves, if it is officially termed a lake then it is divided between states. Seas, though, are governed by The United Nations Convention on the Law of the Sea, and the rights to their minerals, divvied up according to the size of coastlines. Therefore, Iran, with the smallest slice, calls the Caspian a lake, while the Kazakhs call it a sea. Leaders of the countries surrounding the Caspian Sea often debate what lies below, arguing how best to strip, exploit and monetise nature.

Close to the promenade, a gigantic seated statue of Taras Shevchenko, national hero of Ukraine, looks out to sea. A group of students read books under the shade of his huge arms. Exiled to the eastern bank of the Caspian Sea by Tsar Nicholas I, the moustachioed poet rose from Ukrainian serfdom to become prophet and promoter of Ukrainian independence and language. Ukrainians celebrate him by marathon poetry readings. In 2014, on what would have been the 200th anniversary of Shevchenko's birth, a group read out his *Kobzar* book of poems 45 times, for 456 hours.

Aktau's weird geography has edited the great poet, too. The town was known as Shevchenko until 1991, but all that remains of him now is this statue, perhaps because he wasn't very fond of this region: 'A desert without any vegetation: only sand and stones. When you look around, you feel so forsaken that it makes you want to hang yourself', he wrote.

Today, this part of Kazakhstan has a slightly lawless, wild west reputation. Money swills around as freely as oil does, and crime syndicates abound. The isolation helps. People here are far removed from the watchful eyes of the new capital Nur-Sultan and the old one, Almaty. It is obvious that there is money here. You can eat caviar or steak, or smoke a hookah with a pink Caspian sunset view in a beachfront restaurant staffed by expensively dressed Russians. You can drink in a vitamin bar and you can sip single malt whiskey.

FIRST SETTLERS AND SHASHLIK EATERS

I didn't want the flash and glitter of Aktau's face-control restaurants but I did want a decent dinner. A new restaurant, serving dishes from Azerbaijan across the Caspian Sea, had opened and I have a thing for food from that country. I flagged a car down, driven by a man from Dagestan (Aktau has a 30 per cent Russian population) and we eased through the nameless mikrorayons until we came to Barashka Dine & Drink, located out on a limb, sandwiched between an industrial string of shopfronts and garages. An unusual setting, I thought, heart sinking. But inside, the gritty exterior slipped away. In front of an open kitchen, scatterings of kilim cushions – the sort interior designers would fight over – lined benches and in the centre of the room, a giant 1950s samovar from Turkmenistan. Jars of pickles glowed neon, filling niches on exposed brick walls. This is Emil Akperov's restaurant, a Kazakh citizen, born here in Aktau, with Azeri heritage, who has worked in kitchens at celebrated restaurants in Vancouver. He told me it had not occurred to him to open Barashka anywhere but Aktau, next to where his father once had a 70-seater shashlik restaurant called Albina (which explained the unorthodox location).

'I was born here so my food is Russian and Kazakh but mainly it is Azeri-style. Growing up we had Azerbaijani plov, with saffron rice, raisins, and dried apricots. Rice and lamb cooked separately. Mum is a great home-cook.' His mother would cook dolma only in baby grape leaves, so today he does the same, growing his own here in this challenging environment.

As we spoke many good things arrived at the table. Qutabs, flatbreads filled sparingly with lamb, and others with greens, dusted with lemony sumac, thin and blissfully melting. A plate of unpeeled whole stubby salty cucumbers, eaten as if they were apples. The shashlik eaters, his dad's diners, now come here and Akperov travels across the Caspian Sea, to Baku, to collect the best Azeri-centric ingredients.

'This is Baku in Aktau, and what I can bring in, I do. I bring chestnuts from Baku's Green Bazaar, for the plov. I bring in the sour flavours of kizil [dogwood], pomegranate molasses and sumac for salads. I fly directly from Aktau, it's really close.'

Akperov's grandparents came to Shevchenko from Ağstafa, a town that was once just a railway station – it still has a train at the centre of its coat of arms – close to the Armenian border. Lured by higher wages, they arrived here in the 1960s as 'first settlers' when the city, newly named Shevchenko, was being built. They arrived willing to do the jobs that needed doing. His grandfather was a train operator, as a man from Ağstafa might well have been; his grandmother, a nurse. From here, his grandfather moved around the USSR, at one point, working on infamous permafrost-ridden BAM (Baikal-Amur Mainline), in Far East Siberia. Dubbed by Soviet leader Leonid Brezhnev as 'the construction project of the century' the idea was to surpass the engineering feat of the tsarist-era-built Trans-Siberian Railway. BAM promised to be a triumph of Soviet man over nature. In reality the project – to link the west of Lake Baikal in Siberia to the Strait of Tartary in the Pacific Ocean, across some of the most inhospitable permafrost land on the planet – was vastly underused. Many intended 'boom towns' along the route ended up little more than ghost towns.

More plates arrived from the kitchen: tangy yogurty suzma, not thick but silken, with faint traces of dill. A dip-like mangal salad of aubergine, red onion, bell pepper, tomato and garlic, all grilled as the name suggests. A punchy sour salad of tarragon, tomato, purple basil, red onion and kizil molasses, which was exquisite.

On the menu there is also bozbash, lamb meatballs in a broth, and hasselback potatoes, a habit from Canada but here cooked with lamb tail fat, Central Asian-style. Kebab-wise, it was sturgeon, lamb or chicken. Quail, popular in Azerbaijan, did not work ('the locals didn't like it'). Sumac is an entirely new flavour for Aktau, as are chestnuts. 'Local tomatoes and cucumbers are good – we grow our own. Eggplants. Purple basil. All summer long we use these ingredients.'

'And, caviar?' I asked.

'It's in the endangered red book, yet people buy it from unofficial sources around Fort Shevchenko [further north up the coast].'

For a long time, caviar was food for poor peasants and it is still dirt-cheap here but you probably wouldn't want to eat it. Much of the world's best 'real' caviar, that is what was once wild and not farmed, came from here, but larger Caspian sturgeon – osetra, beluga and sevruga – are all grossly overfished, damage inflicted by Caspian caviar mafia and driven by poverty around the Ural River Delta. Illegal trade was once ten times the legal trade and when a ban on the international trade in caviar was imposed in 2006 prices went up and farms were set up around the world, from Israel to China, even in Abu Dhabi. Oil pollution, which reduces both food and oxygen in the clear-looking water has affected the migration routes of sturgeon. Caviar is far from straightforward.

Barashka, where the bill at the end is small and the cooking superb, was one of the biggest surprises of all my time eating in Central Asia. But then sometimes the most interesting cooking is found in the most unexpected of places. Thanks to the internet and cheap flights, finding the genuinely unforeseen has become harder as much of the world that was once faraway, is now familiar. But that cannot be said for Aktau. And, for now, it cannot be said for Kazakhstan, either.

Emil's Lamb Plov with Chestnuts, Apricots and Watercress

Aktau is a long way to travel, but Emil Akperov's restaurant, Barashka, is your reward. If you've no immediate plans to visit, try making this light plov at home, inspired by Emil's own recipe. Topped with mellow-flavoured chestnuts, peppery watercress and sweet golden apricots – which have their origins in Central Asia – unlike many other plovs and pilafs, here the rice and meat are cooked separately. You could substitute lamb with game birds such as partridge or quail.

SERVES 2 GENEROUSLY

300g/1½ cups basmati rice, rinsed

500ml/2 cups vegetable stock

½ tsp saffron threads soaked in 3 tbsp of warm water

3 tbsp olive oil

1 large onion, finely diced

½ tsp fine salt

2 tsp ground cumin

90g/½ cup unsulphured dried apricots, halved (if these are hard, plump them up

by soaking them in boiling water when you begin the recipe)

180g/1 cup cooked and peeled whole chestnuts

Knob of butter

250g/9oz lamb leg, diced into 2–3cm/1in cubes

A couple of handfuls of watercress

Freshly ground black pepper

Put the rice into a large saucepan, for which you have a lid. Pour in the stock and the saffron-infused water (not the threads) and bring to a boil. Cover with the lid and reduce the heat, simmering for 6 minutes.

Remove the saucepan from the heat, take the lid off and, using the handle of a wooden spoon, make several holes in the rice to allow steam to escape. Then put the lid back on and allow it to steam for a further 10-15 minutes.

Heat 2 tablespoons of the olive oil in a frying pan over a medium-low heat and add the onion. After 5 minutes, add the salt and cook for a further 20 minutes until tender. Once golden, add the remaining tablespoon of oil and stir in the cumin, apricots and the chestnuts, gently crumbling them into rough halves with the wooden spoon as you stir. Next, add the butter and then the lamb and cook for about 12 minutes until browned and the juices have been absorbed.

To plate up, spoon the rice into a disc shape, then lay the lamb, chestnuts and apricots in a wide strip across the centre. Season with black pepper and arrange the watercress around the edges.

Caspian Anchor

Bright-orange sea buckthorn berries, protected by long sharp thorns, grow around coastal areas of Central Asia, especially the Caspian Sea and Issyk-Kul in Kyrgyzstan. Used in tea, jam, cocktails and juices, they add a fresh mouth-puckering sharpness.

This bracing sour cocktail is just the thing for hot afternoons. Sea buckthorn juice – a pain to find, admittedly – is sold online and is stocked in some healthfood shops, or you may be able to forage your own along coastlines in late summer and autumn.

MAKES 1 COCKTAIL

FOR THE SIMPLE SUGAR SYRUP

15ml/1 tbsp water

15g/1 tbsp granulated sugar

(If you like you can make more than this recipe requires but keep to the 1:1 ratio of sugar and water)

2 ice cubes, crushed

40ml/2 ½ tbsp vodka

50ml/3 tbsp sea buckthorn juice

To make the syrup, combine the sugar and water in a small saucepan and slowly bring to a boil, stirring all the time until the sugar dissolves. Remove from the heat and allow to cool.

Add the crushed ice to a tall glass and pour over the vodka. Top with the sea buckthorn juice and sugar syrup and stir vigorously.

OIL FIELD

Following pilgrims to desert mosques

MANGYSTAU, WEST KAZAKHSTAN: Woolly, gamey smells surged and billowed from a trio of foaming cauldrons. Fiery logs spat underneath them and steel ladles leant against pots, ready for scooping out the chunky meat – most of a sheep whose soft russet pelt lay discarded in the nearby slaughterhouse. For now, the mutton was left to bubble along as the cooks filed around a corner, carrying enamel buckets of water for the samovars, laying plastic tablecloths along thin, low-slung tables, each the length of a London bus. Whitewashed and primeval, this holy desert kitchen is where cooks prepare mutton, noodles, rice and fried bread for pilgrims who have travelled hundreds of miles to pray at the underground mosque complex of Beket-Ata. Located deep in the outlandishly remote desert steppe of western Kazakhstan, the subterranean shrine-like mosque stands alone, isolated and sheltered inside a windblown sandstone cliff.

Those who come here – tens of thousands a year – bring their own food to donate to the kitchen. The rich carry live animals, meat and sacks of rice and the poor take everything else: chocolate bars, packets of biscuits, pots of cream, jugs of milk, oil and animal fat, golden discs of shelpek bread, dried spaghetti. Survival food. On arrival, they pray and swap stories of the terrible roads that brought them here, and they speak of their reasons for coming: arthritis, heart problems, infertility, money worries. Then, together, they eat. Noodles and rice. Bread and tea. Metaphysical mutton. The journey is the pilgrim's cradle, the food on arrival, the comfort. That much I understood.

Born in 1750 into a family of Kazakh warriors, Beket-Ata was a clairvoyant, astronomer and physicist who became a revered sufi. Four desert mosques in this country bear his name, but it is here, in the Oglandy Valley, that he is buried, in Kazakhstan's spiritual heartland, Mangystau, a desert region of labyrinths, mountain plateaus, necropolises and hideouts. Out here, mystical importance is heaped upon sky, fire and earth, mountains and stone. Before Islam was gradually adopted in Central Asia between the seventh and eighth centuries, Kazakhs widely followed shamanism and animistic traditions. Much of this landscape is poorly mapped, and it makes up a considerable swathe of what is, in most minds, an enormous and unfamiliar territory. To get to Beket-Ata, I had set off from Aktau, on the shores of the Caspian Sea, a five-hour drive away.

THE EARTH IS HARD, THE HEAVENS FAR

Two silver stars twinkled their last in the sky and then, as dawn broke, I bundled my morning bones into the four-wheel-drive. I couldn't see, or hear, the Caspian

Sea but I could smell and taste its mineral brininess on my tongue. Yuri, my driver, was born in Grozny, Chechnya. He wore blue jeans, belted tight on his belly, and a neat silver moustache that bristled above a row of gold teeth, which held a toothpick. An air of preparedness radiated from him. Spare water, blankets, a flask of tea, a cool-box of water and jerricans of petrol, were packed neatly underneath the back seat. Gaffer tape, spare phone chargers, a knife and crepe bandages were stored in the glove compartment. A framed Orthodox saint, Nicholas, hung from the rear-view mirror alongside 'praise be to God' written in Cyrillic. On the wing mirrors, Arabic script warned that oncoming vehicles might be closer than they appear. One window didn't open, neither did one door. The clock had 500,000 kilometres on it.

'This is a real desert car. I shipped it from Dubai.' Yuri said, starting the engine.

We left Aktau's shoreline and its clinging marine air, driving through the scrappy outskirts of the city, travelling into the desert interior, a vast untamed spiritual geography. A rising morning light ascended from the wide steppe, silvery and gossamer-thin, the sort you only get in deserts and at sea. It felt a world within itself. Yuri's hands relaxed onto the faux-fur steering wheel as we entered Karagiye, meaning 'Black Jaw', a 25 mile-long karst depression that sits 130 metres below sea level, the lowest point in Central Asia and the former Soviet Union according to a rusty road sign. Through this trench go snakes, hares and vultures but I saw only blown-over electricity pylons, laid horizontal at awkward angles like slain steel dinosaurs. This is the only place for miles around, I was told, where mushrooms grow.

Herds of two-humped Bactrian camels occasionally appeared, nodding and swinging in a stately manner across the steppe, rugs of matted fur dangling from their tall, half-ton bodies. The reddish-brown ones looked as though they had bloody steaks hanging from their flanks. We stopped the car and I got out to photograph them. Behind me, Yuri pulled a lighter out of his pocket and smoked the first of many cigarettes.

Click, fizz, suck, puff.

I marvelled at the camels' long eyelashes, their humps filled with fat and the knobbliness of their knees. How humanly interested they seemed in us. Yuri stared hard at a uranium mine in the distance. During the day camel milk – shubat – is sold by villagers on the roadside who cover their faces in sun-protecting white muslin balaclavas. At night, the camels are a peril to drivers as they kneel their huge bodies onto the road, to sleep.

The journey flung up one horizon after the next. Stony deserts surrounded golden-hued hills and buff-pink ridges, and white chalk ascents met cliffs of dove-grey clay. Wind-carved faces appeared in eroded mountainsides and small green oases proved the existence of water. And then, suddenly, movement. Teams of horses – brown, chestnut, black – would go galloping past, kicking up long trails of dust on the desert steppe. Not wild, their flanks clearly branded, but free to roam great distances. The foals were young, still fluffy.

Apart from winter, when ground blizzards blow hard, every week carloads of Kazakhs make the journey to Beket-Ata. In front of us, a Russian-made off-road Bukhanka van stopped and a man jumped out, went into the steppe and collected handfuls of discus-shaped camel dung.

'Free fuel, why not?' Yuri smiled, flashing me his golden incisors.

We edged into the small town of Zhanaozen built on oil in the 1960s, driving through city gates flanked by a steel monument with two hearts at its centre, rusted by the desert wind, hinting, accidentally, at its dark history. It is the only place to stock up on supplies and so at a little shop, we stopped. The scene was pure Kazakh spaghetti western. The road, dusty and sand-whisked, had just a few male lurkers on it, not in Stetsons and cowboy boots, obviously, but maroon boiler suits. Oil worker uniforms. I went inside the shop while Yuri leant on the car.

Click, fizz, suck, puff.

Dried brown scaly fish, laid out in a greasy cardboard box, sat on the counter, their mouths open as if desperately gasping for air. Behind them, a wall of vodka bottles with labels reading 'Taiga' and 'Status'. Two women manned the shop, both unsmiling. Their eyes were on my hands as I picked up packets of pasta and crisps. Clashes involving striking oil workers here in 2011 left at least 17 dead, and outsiders still aren't welcome here. Only journalists come, asking questions, probing, reminding. I paid for a bag of corn puffs, pasta, a packet of chocolate-filled croissants, some form of boudoir biscuits and a bottle of Coca Cola. Yuri started the engine and we wobbled out of town.

A gas station on the outskirts of Zhanaozen had its windows blacked out with posters depicting a grinning, white-toothed, gym-fit couple in bed, in a Manhattan-style loft apartment, eating a stack of blueberry pancakes and drinking coffee from a cafétière. It felt a cruel hallucination. There are no loft apartments in Zhanaozen, or blueberry pancakes. Here, 'the earth is hard, the heavens far', as a Central Asian saying goes.

TEA, SYMPATHY AND NODDING DONKEYS

From Zhanaozen we entered the black, oily heart of Kazakhstan: the Ozen oil fields with their pumps, jacks and nodding donkeys that bow rhythmically to the ground, like animals at a waterhole, going all day and all night. A sign on the road showed the direction of Turkmenbashi, 500 kilometres away in Turkmenistan, on the Caspian Sea, proving the loneliness of this nook of the world.

Legend has it that Alexander the Great's horsemen struck oil by accident when pitching tents by the Amu Darya river, east of here. Sometimes, newspapers report oil wells being 'abandoned', with Kazakh police chasing the owners who have disappeared due to business disputes, leaving oil spewing. Passion for profit dominates but there is something mesmerising about oil fields – their remoteness, their moving parts, what you cannot see beneath the surface. In Azerbaijan, across the Caspian Sea, there are crude oil sanatoriums where miraculous black baths are taken, believed to help muscular, dermatological and skeletal conditions.

We pulled over and took a jerrican of water out from under the back seat and drank it fast, dehydrated.

'No fresh water here or in Shevchenko,' Yuri said, using the old Russian name for Aktau. It hardly rains during the hot months so locals used to hoard ice and snowmelt in reservoirs, Yuri explained.

'In Shevchenko, 70 per cent of all drinking water is purified from the sea, the other 30 per cent comes from underground,' Yuri said in his cigarette-smog growl. That is what happens if you drop a city – built on uranium-mining dreams – in a desert. We followed rough tracks to the underground mosque complex and former cave of the Sufi follower Shopan-Ata, who inspired Beket-Ata. If you go on a pilgrimage to Beket-Ata the rule is that you must stop here first, an hour west. We parked and headed in.

Click, fizz, suck, puff. Another cigarette went under heel.

A female Kazakh caretaker, with high cheekbones and a neat floral bandana fixed over greying hair, ushered us down a path, past a revamped courtyard paid for by an oil company, and into a resting room. Yuri muttered, 'salaam alaikum', as the three of us removed our shoes and stepped inside. Round as a yurt, the room had many of the trappings of a nomad's tent. On the walls, willow trellis, embroideries, tassels, geometrical felt designs, and in the very centre of the curved roof, a reimagined tunduk (the opening you find at the top of a yurt to let smoke out and light in), except here, instead of a hole, hung a huge, bling-y chandelier. The floor was a chequerboard of bloodstone red rugs. A samovar sat at the head of the dastarkhan, tended to constantly by female volunteers who filled enamel teapots, already with milk inside, and then passed them down the low-to-the-ground tables. Lightly fried Kazakh shelpek bread had been torn into pieces and was scattered across the tablecloths; it looked as though it had dropped from the heavens, falling through the imaginary tunduk. The dastarkhan tables stretched through the centre of the room, ending at a large framed poster depicting crowds of hadjis circling the Ka'bah, the huge black granite cube and the heart of Islam, in the holy city of Mecca. A visual bond connecting the Muslim brotherhood, and the world of pilgrimage. Two very different forms of religious wayfaring characterised here in this make-believe yurt: Shopan-Ata's tiny underground mosque, large enough for a couple of dozen people to enter at one time, and Saudi Arabia's multi-billion-dollar global hajj attracting several million people a year in a stunning logistical feat. Just as those who travel to Mecca make sacrifices and travel long distances, those who come here, to this sacred ground, also strive and struggle to arrive, hoping that their journey too will be transformational.

Placing my donation of pilgrim food on the table: a packet of dried pasta, two large flatbreads and some dubious-looking chocolate-filled croissants that I'd bought from the forlorn Zhanaozen shop, I padded in socks over the soft rugs to sit down next to a woman dressed in a leopard print headscarf. Pouring me tea, she said: 'The Kazakh tradition is to give and be given to, and to eat together.'

She told me about her daughter who had moved to New York, and her fears that she would not return to her mother and the oil town of Zhanaozen. We shared the shelpek bread, doughnut-soft and chewy. Another woman, Kausar, told me she had travelled 1,400 miles in the hope that by praying here, her leg, mangled from a botched operation, would recover, or the symptoms would ease.

'Most come here hoping for money,' the first woman chipped in. I asked how much and the responses came in unison, a neat and cool 'one million tenge', around $2,500. No questions were asked of Yuri and me, the non-Muslims, we were simply welcomed as guests, as fellow pilgrims. The atmosphere was one of solemn patience, gratitude and recognition. Back outside, women pulled buckets up from a well.

'The sinful pull up an empty bucket, the pure, one full of water,' one elderly woman said as she huffed and yanked.

Click, fizz, suck, puff. Yuri lit up.

Under cauliflower clouds we washed our hands at an outside faucet, little shards of soap littering the trough, before walking up a short gravel path to where Shopan-Ata is buried in an underground mosque. In the bleak desert steppe, a string of gangly camels walked in caravan formation past a giant city of the dead, hovering on the plains, one of many such burial places in the Kazakh wilderness. Some lie deep in the silent steppe joined by no track; others, next to the roadside, are close enough for detail. Built to honour ancient warriors, chieftains and shepherds, these ancestral village-size cemeteries display vast funerary architecture: Egyptian-looking pyramid mausoleums; dome-topped mazars boxed in by picket-like fences; piles of stones not unlike the cairns at the summits of Scotland's Munros; altars and columns carved with precious things once owned, from horses to cooking utensils, swords to banners and towering statues of rams.

In his book, *In the Kirghiz Steppes*, John Wardell wrote of witnessing such grave sites: 'these tombs are architectural triumphs . . . even when old and weather-worn.' One mass grave, he noted, was 'in the shape of a huge horseshoe, and consisted of about twenty graves', emphasising the importance of horses to nomads. The view was so enormous I began to hallucinate the curvature of the earth.

I added my own shoes to the pyramid of sandals and sneakers and, crouching behind the pilgrims with whom we'd had tea, followed them through a hobbit-like round wooden door that had been cut into the limestone hill. Ducking, one by one we entered the grotto-like underground mosque, ushered in by the mullah's helper. I focused on the feel of the soft rugs underfoot, inching my way, giving my eyes time to adjust to the dim light. Gradually colours and patterns formed on the rugs and the walls appeared white as salt and honeycombed as a bath sponge. Inside, men and women were separated and the mullah, once satisfied that enough of us were present, began softly reciting in Arabic. A thin shard of sunlight poured in through a hole in the roof, lighting the Qur'an. Everyone held their palms up to their faces, eyes closed, quietly breathing in the stale air. Next, his disciple, a young boy, delivered his lines. I wondered if they understood the Arabic words, or just knew them by rote; my guess was that the pilgrims did not know the meaning at all, but simply accepted them and trusted the power of the deliverer. This was low-voltage worship. Private fears freed for a moment through togetherness and ritual. The dim light and silent steppe outside provided peace, the cave afforded spirituality and tradition.

Male pilgrims peered around a curtain to see Shopan-Ata's tomb but we women were ushered into another subterranean den, the burial place of Bibi Han, his wife. At Shopan-Ata, there was a collective air of an ancient truth being recognised, one that maybe we all shared, but have perhaps lost over time. We returned to the car. Beket-Ata was only an hour away now, on rough roads. I'd read that the Kazakh pilgrims hope for a challenging course, welcoming spine-jarring bumps and car-thrashing tracks. For to suffer is to be rewarded. A shame, then, that a parallel tarmac road was being built. Once that was completed the only way to suffer would be to walk.

METAPHYSICAL MUTTON, MESSIANIC MUTTON

A magnetic force seemed to propel and pull us on; Yuri's car travelling only on gritty tyre tracks that had gone before us. To get back to Aktau mostly in daylight, avoiding the worst of the no-rules driving and possible camel collisions, meant travelling at speed. We bounced along, dwarfed dramatically by the ramparts of mountains above us. The landscape was overwhelming and eventually I became grateful for wide plains, just steppe, heaven and earth. Then, axles nearly destroyed, we arrived at Beket-Ata. Yuri stopped the car, parking it next to dozens of other dusty pilgrim vehicles.

Click, fizz, suck, puff.

It was a Saturday and therefore busy. I left Yuri to rest with his perfectly packed lunch of boiled eggs, sausages, cucumbers, a little canister of salt and bread, and walked through the gates flanked by lions and giant urns on pedestals. It became obvious that there was an unspoken system in play. Pilgrims arrive just after lunchtime, and then they have tea, bread and biscuits. Afterwards, they walk to the mosque and back, which takes a couple of hours up and down a steep path of steps. Then, some have a nap on the floor cushions and rugs off the dining hall before everyone feasts from the mosque kitchen, the food prepared by volunteer cooks using donated ingredients, as at Shopan-Ata. Some pilgrims stay overnight, bedding down on a sleeping mat in a 'hospitable room' for free, leaving a donation in the morning.

Following a mother and daughter who wore sweaters emblazoned with the words 'I'm too good for you' and 'born in the 90s', I walked into the main courtyard. The girl threw scraps of food to a roaming dog as we went – the creature, so far from any village, also entirely dependent on pilgrim donations. Outside the kitchen, two male chefs hovered, squatting on their haunches. I went inside. The sheep, prepared at the on-site slaughterhouse, bubbled in the cauldrons. I asked what they were preparing.

'Plov is for weekends like today when it is very busy. Usually we feed 400 or so but at the busiest times we feed 1,500. In the week, when it is less busy, it's beshbarmak – Kazakh noodles.'

I left the mutton bubbling, and followed the crowds down the mountainside path towards the mosque. Yuri was waiting. I didn't have long. Overtaking pilgrims to save time meant stepping off the trail and onto the dirt, purple pebbles shifting, dust puffing up, clay and sand formed over many years, earth powdered by countless footsteps of past walkers. How many pilgrims have trodden this holy pathway? These old tracks felt far more tangible than walking on concrete or asphalt. I let a little of the spiritual dirt in, the holy soil spinning around my ankles and falling gritty between my toes. Pavilions – shady stopping points – were where the unfit and elderly wheezed and puffed. Everywhere, people sat on benches staring at the vast moonscape of gargantuan cliffs and pink-hued chalk hills carved by the wind, lit by bleak desert sunlight. The landscape was holy, too, and appreciation of it a vital part of the pilgrimage. Those who came tended to want three things: to obtain a blessing, to be closer to God, and to relax and have a day out with friends. During the Soviet period it was necessary to dress up pilgrimages to religious sites as secular tourism or sightseeing. Today, circling piles of stones and places once exposed to the soul of a saint may not be in line with scriptural Islam, but no one doubted the air of spiritual power here.

A large crowd huddled at the opening to the mosque cut into a steep hill. I left my shoes in a pile and joined the throng. After an hour I hadn't moved an inch, mainly because many pilgrims pushed their way to the front, skipping the wait. As the imam recited passages from the Qur'an inside, those outside, held their palms up in prayer, too. I estimated it could be several more hours before my turn came, as only ten faithful were allowed in at a time. As I waited and waited, I became acutely aware of my alien awkwardness. I felt voyeuristic. My personal pilgrimage

was to see the landscape, to take the journey and to see the desert mosque kitchen at work. I'd been lucky enough to join in with the prayer ritual at Shopan-Ata. I put my shoes on, and returned up the path.

Back at the kitchen, the chefs smiled and lifted the cauldron lids to show me how the plov was coming along. Now with added onions and carrots, the mutton smell was tempting. Beyond, in the desert scrubland, dusk was starting to colour the mountains. It was time to go. In the car, lines from Dorothy Hartley's 'Vicarage Mutton' from *Food in England* ran through my mind: 'Hot on Sunday, Cold on Monday, Hashed on Tuesday, Minced on Wednesday, Curried on Thursday, Broth on Friday, Cottage pie Saturday.' Mutton, mutton, mutton. Messianic mutton. Moral mutton. Mutton madness. Mutton used in all ways, on all days. But I could never have imagined mutton cooked this way, so far from the man-made world.

The road was no less biblical than before, but it already felt less foreign. As we rounded one mountain, a deep pool appeared, like a mirage at first, and in the shallow water stood at least 30 horses, all soaking their hooves, knee deep. We stopped. But on the car-door slam, the horses – tan, white and black – all regally turned their backs to me, the foals following suit. They stood collectively with their eyes closed, noses to the wind, stock-still, sensing foreign presence, but not fearful enough to run. I imagined what their lives are like at other times of the year, in the marrow-melting summer months and during the long frigid winter. Only the camel – a sort of super-camel that Kazakhs created by breeding two-humped Bactrians with the one-hump dromedary, to make a hybrid that is tough in cold conditions (like Bactrian breeds), but good for producing milk (like dromedaries) – made eye contact.

Abay Qunanbayuli, Kazakhstan's great poet, wrote of horses on the steppe:

'And herds of horses in pasture frolic
In the frost or drowsy, droning heat.'

This is a land, and a people, tied to livestock. If a favourite horse died, nomads would mourn it as they would a family member. The year was planned around the grazing of horses, following historic routes to pasture, following the seasons, migrating together. 'How are your legs?' one herder or horseman might ask the other – the sentiment being, if your legs are good to ride, then all is well.

We went back through the oil fields again. The sun dipped further, throwing bright-orange sunset rays across oil-slick puddles. They glimmered like tin foil.

It could be western Australia, it could be Texas. Was the oily scent of naphtha soaking into the car interior? Could I taste it? Of course not, I was tired, imagining things. Desert mind tricks in the black, oily heart of Kazakhstan.

Headlights flashed fast and erratic in the darkness, evidence of gauntlet-style dangerous driving. As we neared Aktau, we were run off the road by racing cars, before becoming accidentally sandwiched in a police convoy. I paid for the night-time desert miles with shot nerves. Finally, we made it back to the city and the sea.

Click, fizz, suck, puff.

We unloaded the car in the dark and I said goodbye to Yuri with a hug. I was grateful for his coolness and safe driving, and for his company. The Caspian Sea glinted in the distance. The occasional boat was still out at sea and the waters were as calm and peaceful as the underground mosque complexes with their hushed rug-filled caves, convivial resting rooms and generous mosque kitchens.

At Mangystau's desert mosques, there are no heaven-reaching pencil-shaped minarets to prick the sky, no grand stone arches, no golden dome crowns. How different and quiet compared to the Gothic spires that shoot up from Cologne Cathedral, the grand temples of Angkor and the vaulted arcades of Istanbul's Sultan Ahmed Mosque. Instead, all is dark. All is inwards. Underground and low voltage. More organic, less man-made. Out there, so far from the concrete familiar, nature is sacred and divine, positioned not in the background but at the very fore.

The next day I left to fly east. It felt natural to set out on the long journey ahead from the far western frontier of Kazakhstan, travelling through the ninth largest country in the world. It also felt almost impossible to comprehend so many miles in one nation. Kazakhstan is so huge that the brain can easily get lost in the mere idea of it. And what can be more thrilling than that?

KONDITOREI
Finding unexpected pleasure

PAVLODAR, NORTHEAST KAZAKHSTAN: Almost 2,000 miles northeast of Aktau, ice floes – some the size of garage doors, others small as paperbacks – nudged like chess pieces on the Irtysh River past the city of Pavlodar. Drifting from the snowmelt and glaciers of the Altai Mountains, locals say that this week-long phenomenon happens just once a year after the ice detaches and splits, moving northwards and joining Russia's Ob river system that floods into the Arctic Ocean.

I'd arrived just in time. A large piece of driftwood had wedged in the narrow-necked river beach providing a seat, and so I sat and watched as the translucent islands jostled along. Each one making its own journey and each one making its own unique chiming noise – *ping, pop, snap, crack, crunch, clap*. A symphony of xylophone-like sounds stirred in the air, like a hundred wooden pencils running along a row of half-filled milk bottles. I felt an urge to contain the notes, to somehow bank them, but I had no recording device and anyway the frigid air, radiating bitterly from the floes, had numbed my hands rendering them useless. Instead, I simply watched, drifting into what psychologists would call a 'plateau experience', a kind of serene blissfulness.

The river is wide and in mid-winter, when the mercury plummets to –25°C, it is frozen solid but in the warmer months it is alive, rushing and full. John Wardell, the British copper miner, had to cross it with all of his belongings in early summer but the wild current sent him and his team hopelessly off-course: 'We crossed the Irtysh the next day in a large boat manned by six rowers and a helmsman, and the voyage took seven hours. At this point the river was about ten miles wide . . .'

Pavlodar, its appearance described by friends as 'basically, Siberia', appealed. I'd arrived with no set plan except a desire to explore this unsung city, to indulge the thrill of the new, to see another side of Kazakhstan, different from the larger, better-known cities of Almaty and the capital, Nur-Sultan. Germans have a word for this sort of inclination, sehnsucht, which roughly translates as a desire for the unknown, a craving for otherness, other places, and other ideas. It is a vaguer word than their fernweh, a longing for faraway places.

I'd travelled by plane and train from the shores of the Caspian Sea, covering the same distance as London to Marrakech all the while remaining within Kazakhstan's borders. The train from Nur-Sultan, had gone through a landscape so unbroken, open and wide, that you could probably watch a car drive away on it all day. Once, a stunning construction broke the monotony: a Soviet-era grain silo the size of an airport. 'Bread, the wealth of the people!' read huge red letters on its facade, bookended between two yellow sheaves of wheat. It seemed to rise, like a golden loaf, straight out of the steppe. Working, or abandoned? I couldn't tell.

Pavlodar was chilly and Siberian-fresh. Despite spring breaking in, snow showers were forecast for tomorrow and on the opposite side of the river, away from the city, winter had killed off all colour. Clusters of reeds crowded around leafless trees, swampy snowmelt pooled at the bases of their trunks, rich breeding grounds for biting insects that will hatch and fly and plague and bite people as soon the weeks swing into summer. For now, the sun's weak tangerine glow, so gladly received by every living thing, provided a short window of comfort before the mosquitoes would begin to torment. I joined the strollers on the wide naberezhnaya (embankment – so much slinkier in Russian somehow), the watery Kazakh sun ably warming hands, backs and faces; muscles, joints and bones. Dropping shoulders. 'The sayings and sallies of spring poke through the pages of winter's volumes', wrote the Russian poet, Velimir Khlebnikov.

Away from the icy water, the temperature rocketed upwards, an odd phenomenon of two seasons battling it out in the same city. Winter in its death throes, spring bursting in. The ice floe show had been a welcome curiosity but there were other unexpected things in Pavlodar, too.

Just beyond the naberezhnaya, thin legs of sunlight strobed through a stand of birch trees, creating a tunnel of vertical lights, from the treetops to the dirt. Blinding and magnetic, the rays shone off the white branches, suggesting warmth. Kneeling down among them, and looking up through the gangly trunks, felt like a Kazakh version of hanami, the Japanese ritual of getting high on sakura blossoms. Pink blooms have drama, but there is a purity found in the creamy white-blistered birch bark against a cloudless navy-blue sky. Attractively severe. I wanted to lay below them, flat, and to stare freely but I was too aware of myself, too English to give it a go.

To get a handle on the city, I walked on. Ladas, oozing cheap cough-inducing benzene from their exhausts, went puffing by, wheezing metaphors for the old Russian literary greats who've had streets named after them here: Lermontov, Tolstoy and Dostoyevsky, all crossing Pavlodar's main drag, Lenin Street. Under a string of run-down Soviet-built tower blocks, a purposeful-looking Sunday farmers' market was getting going without the promotional bunting, tote bags or advertising fluff found in the west. Gruff men from the Russian-Kazakh border, dressed in yellow pinnies over their camouflage fatigues, heaved bucket-size tubs of honey from vans to tables, standing ready with a wooden swab for tastings. Taking one from a giant calloused hand, I licked the stick. The honey was grassy yet dense, tasting intensely of the greenness and herbs of the land. Vans popped open their boots, showing off green Kazakh apples, figs from Turkey and dried apricots from Uzbekistan. On trestle tables, pyramids of canned horsemeat.

WINTER CHERRIES AND CHEKHOV

Further up the bank, past the Mashkhur Jusup Mosque with its turquoise shuttlecock dome, the service at the Blagoveshchensk Cathedral, by Karl Marx Street, was getting going. Outside, beggars with missing limbs, stumps wrapped in plastic against the cold, wheeled, stumbled and shuffled between the churchgoers. The blind went along with their heads tilted back, arms outstretched. One man, wearing peasant galoshes, wore a desperately sad coat, so ragged and torn that it looked like it had been through a shredder. The scene was a Russian novel tableau. Tenge notes were dropped into begging boxes and buckets as parishioners walked towards the golden cupolas, carefully dressed for God in their best suits, dresses, bonnets and jewellery. In each hand, an unlit thin sickly yellow candle. Inside, elderly women dressed in furry booties, wobbled towards saints, dipping their heads gently, silently, to the gilt-framed paintings. Wardell had had concerns about such piety, 'Certain devotional habits struck westerners as repulsive and likely to transmit disease. One was the promiscuous kissing of the ikons by rich and poor, clean and unclean alike, with no wiping of the pictures.' Behind the cathedral, the ice floes pushed on and on, glinting in the sun. I longed to hear them again but they were too far away.

Pavlodar is a place of industry not parade. There are no big sights. No flashy restaurants chasing tourist dollars. It was pleasant to witness a city so ordinarily going about its business, unbothered by you, with no tours to take, no attractions to tick off. No pressure to take away impressions, to make comparisons. A centre of the Virgin Lands campaign in the 1950s, once there was a secret chemical weapons plant here and today it is a city smoke-stacked still, home to tractor, oil and aluminium factories. Built by the Russian Empire, Pavlodar does look much like Siberia and there is only the slightest whiff of Central Asia about it. Yurt cafés look lost, a little out of place.

But the dislocation is more than scenery and geography. Faces are Slavic and Russian is spoken almost exclusively. There are old Soviet water pumps on street corners, still in use, for homes without running water, and Siberian izba-style log-houses painted green, blue and red with lace-like wooden window frames.

Since Russia annexed Crimea from Ukraine in 2014, Kazakhstan has increasingly worried about its northern region where ethnic Russians outnumber Kazakhs and Russian is the main language spoken. Pavlodar has not had its name Kazakhified, like many other regional cities, in efforts to de-Sovietise. I'd heard rumours that troublemaker politicians across the border have, at times, pressed Putin to seize it. Some believe that the capital was moved from Almaty to Astana (now renamed Nur-Sultan), further north, to be close, to watch and listen. To firmly put a stake in the ground. Pavlodar felt congenial but tensions bristle and this uneasiness spreads fear.

The redbrick Zimnyaya Vishnya ('Winter Cherry') on Lenin Street became my go-to café. A little window into how people live here. Next to the Chekhov Theatre, and surrounded by tsarist-era merchant's buildings, a hymn to simple Russian food played out. The service was all female and friendly and everyone ate solyanka soup, fried mashed potato balls – the kind of my 1980s childhood – and fish cutlets, a dusting of dill on everything. We drank virtuous things such as berry mors, and lemon crescents arrived on a saucer for cups of tea, in the Russian way, spiked with matchstick-size neon plastic swords. Two sticks of Orbit chewing gum arrived along with the bill in a black leather bill presenter. All that might sound a little dated and misery-making. It was not.

A PARADISE OF PAVLOVAS

The next day, I woke up on my prison-thin hotel mattress, spurred on and with a mind fully open to Pavlodar, a city that promised more but also, nothing at all. I left my hotel, named after the river, and walked down potholed Abay Street on a dirt pavement, past badly ventilated one-floor log-walled houses, their chimneys pumping out thin black plumes of smoke. Large unsettling billboards warned of intravenous drug use, suggesting this was a city with not a small-scale problem. Then, on a street corner, I spotted a throng of people gathering outside a smart modern building. I dodged the traffic to get a closer view. On its façade, a cheery mint-green logo read 'Krendel' (Russian for 'pretzel') and below that, a large video screen showed a woman in a puffy white chef's hat smiling as she carried a tray of biscuits across a kitchen. Open for business, a café appeared to be upstairs, but it was the ground floor into which people were eagerly filing.

Following two neatly dressed women smelling of lavender and talcum powder, I made my way in and found Krendel to be a cake shop and delicatessen as beautiful as I had ever seen. Frilly, plush and richly rococo, it reminded me a little of Magazin Kuptsov Yeliseyevykh in St Petersburg, with its froufrou art deco design and giant gilded pineapple centrepiece. Close to grimy garages, a football stadium and humdrum cafés, Krendel offered something else – an escape into softness and extravagance, a little absurdity, even. A foil to Pavlodar's tough industrialism. Less tractors, aluminium and chemicals, more truffles, amaretti biscuits and cupcakes.

Embarking on a pocket-size self-led tour, my nostrils led the way. Cakey scents pursued me, a wafting synthesis of vanilla and chocolate. Around the shop, hands moved over gingerbread, meringues and iced fairy cakes with utmost care. We customers were united, communally enchanted, willingly embracing a collective loss of control, appetites going giddily unchecked. I read the cake labels under my breath in Russian. A square neon-orange cake with little whipped cream islands on it was simply called 'novinka' ('new') while next to it was a 'mister twister apricot' large enough for ten or more. So many fancy cakes, so soft and so smooth in their metal trays. Arranged on counters: candied fruit, the Tatar favourite chak-chak, fruit jellies, nougat, little teddy bear biscuits, Turkish Delight, iced butterfly biscuits (12 to a pack), gingerbread, meringues, iced fairy cakes, éclairs, lemon bombs (yellow and round with little green sugar leaves on top) and cakes that looked like Bakewell tarts. A paradise of pavlovas dominated one corner. In a highly ornamental side room, wine racks of Georgian brandy and vodka. Down one aisle, a counter of pralines were made fresh to order, tended to with surgical precision by two women – a pair of maybe a dozen or so workers out on the shop floor – all dressed in branded turquoise blouses. By them, was an at-work chocolate fountain flowing like a mini-waterfall, and above that a bookshelf filled with ready-to-go boxed-up chocolates. Lunchtime queues for the tills snaked past rotating stands of lollipops. Celebration cakes took up an entire side room. Two, in the style of a basket of tulips, were going to Tatiana, for her 55th birthday, as stated on the docket. I asked one young woman queuing to collect her cake what she thought of Krendel.

'I lived in Germany and the bakeries were good, but the cakes were not as good as here. These are the very best.' Another woman joined in and simply said, 'Yes, I agree and I am from St Petersburg,' as though this was more than enough to certify Krendel's quality.

My questions brought forth the chief financial officer, Natalya Rudolph who, emerging from behind a sugar-fumed counter, produced impressive figures to feast on.

'We make one tonne of cake a day here. We keep 70 per cent of it, the rest goes to Semey and Nur-Sultan where we have concessions – northern cities only, Almaty is too far south. The cakes must be fresh, they can only travel so far.'

With so many different cakes, I asked whether there were any top sellers and without a moment's hesitation, Rudolph answered: 'The bestselling cake is made with white biscuit, Georgian walnuts and sweet milk.'

Next, a quick potted history. The owner is Zinaida Parkhomenko, who, born in Russia, learnt her bakery skills in Pavlodar. As elsewhere in the Soviet Union, there was a tradition of standardised cake shops, but Parkhomenko became a professional pastry cook, and in the years following the collapse of the Soviet Union in 1991, the opportunity came up to organise her own small business taking individual orders.

'You could say that the gamble to open a shop and café has paid off,' I said. Rudolph gave me a Russian-style 'of course' shrug.

I left Krendel marvelling. One of the best cake shops I'd ever been to – with heaps of atmosphere and optimism and business – all the way out here, in provincial far-north Kazakhstan. Do the people of Pavlodar have a particularly sweet tooth? I guessed they must. But it turned out I was wrong as once I started looking I found cake shops in smaller cities all over Kazakhstan, though none as good as this one. I had no idea Krendel was here but now that I did I couldn't stop thinking about it. A different portrait of Kazakhstan had presented itself in a most unforeseen corner of the country. Years ago I wouldn't have bothered to go into Krendel, but now that food pulls me in every direction, what an enticing picture it had painted.

Paper bag filled to capacity, I walked to Lenin Park to picnic, wondering as I went whether serendipity had sent me to Pavlodar. Babushkas waddled through the park trailing behind trolleys and a bushy-tailed stray dog skulked around a Chernobyl monument – a man throwing his arms up in horror in front of a spinning atom – a reminder that the disaster destroyed lives and families from all corners of the Soviet Union. I sat by a plastic-looking statue of a snow leopard, and one of those signposts that normally tell you how far you are from the major cities of the world, but in this case, only other Kazakh cities such as Shymkent and Karaganda (with no distances given). Lenin, cast in concrete, threw a long shadow across the park. It was surprising to see him, not smashed or relegated to the outskirts, as is usually the case.

Oily crows cawed from tree branches, eyeing the soft crumbs and slick white sour cream of the peach cake as I unwrapped it. The extravaganza of Krendel – a phantasmagorical patisserie, a show-off cake shop if there ever was one – resulted in great expectations. But I needn't have worried. The sour cream and peach cake was good. Soft and summery and full of sweet surprise – little peach bombs going off every other bite. But was it so very good? It was. Memorably good. I stared back at Lenin and chewed slowly. Later, I asked the waitress in Winter Cherry – it is important in new and disorientating cities to have your anchor, your café – if she knew Krendel. Her eyes shone with recognition, her face suddenly light as a fairy-cake. 'Yes. Yes, of course,' she purred. We nodded at one another knowingly.

After another night at the Irtysh Hotel, with its room service menu offering five different brands of cigarettes, it was time to go. I headed down several flights of stairs, past the nail salon and the saggy moss-green velvet sofas below bookshelves of Russian novels – and a sign that optimistically read 'library' – carrying my bags past two snoring men, slumped on chairs in the lobby bar at 9 a.m., flattened by a night of vodka drinking, their carafes, shot glasses and packets of cigarettes still in front of them, the staff too polite, too young, too subservient to tell them to leave. I paid, and then handed over my luggage for storage, carefully placing my Krendel bag, filled with tubes of mints for the journey, butterfly iced biscuits, a box of madeleines, and bottles of Georgian Borjomi water, on top of my duffel bag.

'You're so lucky to have it,' I said to the receptionist, pointing at the mint-green logo and she smiled in agreement. That cake shop is the key to the city, I said to myself.

My train to the capital, Nur-Sultan, wasn't until later so I had time for one final walk, past the city's square clock tower – reminiscent of English suburban civic centres – and the pretty, if undoubtedly uncomfortable, log-houses. I liked Pavlodar. I liked its honesty, its lack of fanfare, its strange parks, its remarkable river and its unforgettable, prom queen cake shop.

I walked on, down further still, to the naberezhnaya, past the thin pale birch trees and to the river's edge. It was warmer now, even by the chill water. Springtime was brightly marching northwards. There was no hint of the shifting ice floes. They'd gone now for another year.

Canned Peach and Sour Cream Cake

Of all the cakes I tried at Krendel the finest had a very simple name, translated from the Russian word for 'soft' or 'gentle'. It was a sponge cake with little nuggets of canned peach mixed through, topped with thin sour cream icing that also went between the two layers.

In northern Kazakhstan fresh peaches are rarities only dreamed of, so while this cake is airy and summery-tasting, it is best eaten in the depths of winter, when preserved fruit can be relied upon to brighten dark and dour days. One summer, at Lake Issyk-Kul in Kyrgyzstan, where Kazakhs, Russians and Kyrgyz go to sunbathe and swim, I met a woman from Siberia who was trying a fresh peach for the first time – I have never forgotten the expression of pleasure that spread across her face as she bit into it. I thought of her, too, when I ate this cake at the park in Pavlodar, straight out of the cardboard box, under Lenin's concrete coat tails.

MAKES 1 LARGE CAKE

FOR THE SPONGE

250g/1 cup plus 2 tbsp unsalted butter, softened, plus extra for greasing

250g/2 cups plain (all-purpose) flour, plus extra for dusting

2 tsp baking powder

¼ tsp fine salt

250g/1¼ cups caster (superfine) sugar

½ tsp vanilla extract

4 large eggs

60ml/4 tbsp milk

250g/1 cup canned peaches, drained: 150g/⅔ cup chopped into 1cm/½in chunks and 100g/⅓ cup sliced

FOR THE ICING

250g/2 cups icing (confectioner's) sugar

300ml/1¼ cups sour cream

Preheat the oven to 180°C/350°F/gas mark 4. Grease two 20cm/8in square cake tins then, using a sieve, dust a little flour into the tins before shaking out the excess.

In a large mixing bowl, sift the flour, baking powder and salt.

In another mixing bowl, cream the butter and sugar until light and fluffy. Beat in the vanilla extract and the eggs, one at a time, alternating with spoonfuls of the flour mixture. When all the eggs and flour have been incorporated, add the milk. Gently fold in the chopped peaches (not the slices) until combined. The mixture should fall from the spoon.

Divide the batter equally between the tins, smooth the tops and bake for around 25–30 minutes, until risen and springy but firm to the touch – a skewer inserted into the middle should come out clean. Remove from the oven and turn out onto a wire rack, allowing them to cool properly.

To make the icing, sift the icing sugar into a bowl. Add the sour cream, whisking the mixture together until smooth – you want it thick enough to pour on but not too dense, if it is too thin, add more icing sugar. Once the sponges are completely cool, use half the icing to sandwich them together and add the peach slices between the layers. Spread the other half of the icing on top.

SKYSCRAPER

Arriving to the seat of power

NUR-SULTAN, NORTH KAZAKHSTAN: Almost everything you've heard about the capital of Kazakhstan is true. Built from the architect's drawing board, it is a purse-proud and machine-made city, put up quickly. Mushrooming out of the extreme continental steppe, the city has a disembodied air, suiting its purpose. Relocated here in 1997, it is generally known that the shift northwards, around 650 miles from the former capital, Almaty, was strategic. Just as Canberra, the Australian capital, was partly chosen as it was further from the sea than Sydney or Melbourne – and therefore less likely to come under maritime attack – Almaty, a lovely city with history, culture, gardens and a mountain backdrop, was relegated because of its position on earthquake-ridden land and proximity to the Chinese and Kyrgyz borders. It is easier to protect the seat of power from uprisings and revolutions up here. You cannot simply 'walk in'. The airport, train stations and the city's radial of roads could be blocked if needed. And demographics matter, too. If you want to join one of Kazakhstan's largest employers, the government, then you move here, to Nur-Sultan, to the north, to heavily Slavic lands.

Split by the Ishim River, Nur-Sultan is a city of two parts, psychologically and geographically. While the left bank underwent a full-blown metamorphosis from nothingness to glitzy boomtown in the late 1990s, the right bank remains more settled, less vertical.

I checked into the oldest hotel in town, the four-storey Grand Park Esil, a colossal neoclassical mansion, with a columned facade, ruffled net curtains and too many saggy leather sofas. Its breakfast buffet, of instant coffee and weak porridge, was not up to much but, situated on the right bank, it had what most hotels in the capital lack: history and a sense of place. Marrow and bones. Things for the discombobulated visitor to grip onto. Outside, by local government buildings – clad in mirrored blue glass because blue is the colour of Kazakhstan – men went by in leather jockey-style caps that made their heads look like giant bulbs of black garlic. Down there, in the backstreets, are slices of the capital's earlier life as Tselinograd. In the 1950s Tselinograd attracted pioneering young migrants, called tselinniki, from all corners of the USSR. Encouraged by Soviet leader Nikita Khrushchev they came to colonise the 'virgin lands', the unploughed grasslands of Kazakhstan, united under the same Soviet banner, fully invested in the collective mythmaking of the Soviet Union that promoted being part of something bigger than themselves. Café Tselinnikov and the Astana Concert Hall, both of which I had plans to see, were within walking distance of the hotel. I felt the Grand Park Esil – with its endless wilting potted plants and hallways of swirling orange carpet – and I would get along just fine.

Originally called the Palace of Virgin Land Workers when it was designed by Lithuanian architects and built in 1963, Astana Concert Hall is a drab low-slung building, but when it was the largest concert hall in the region, it had a lush and bountiful indoor botanical garden in the foyer, with plants sourced from all around the USSR. Eclipsed today by the elitny Central Concert Hall on the left bank – which was designed to resemble a steppe flower but instead is called kapusta ('cabbage'), by locals – this reliable old venue is far more democratic, with fairly priced tickets and something scheduled most nights. It offers egalitarian entertainment and is popular with those who live on the right bank, many of whom settled here generations ago. I hoped it would remain.

Squeezing in past hundreds of middle-aged Kazakh women, I paid at the counter for a variety show for what a newspaper would cost back home. After an hour-long wait the show began, and on came one fabulous dress after the next, with much miming, some impressive (real) opera singing, strobe lights, K-pop synced dancing and eager teenagers with electric guitars. It was exhausting. During the interval, I felt a strong urge to leave, so ignoring the daggers shot from the coatroom attendant I sloped out to join the diners next door at Café Tselinnikov. It did not disappoint. Being inside the restaurant was like turning the pages of an old photo album. I handed in my coat to a beehive-haired attendant and threaded past tables surrounded by framed black-and-white photographs of old Tselinograd, showing tselinniki driving tractors, tending crops and dancing in fields. Once this was a cinema, attached to the theatre, and so dozens of Soviet-era movie posters hung above diners. In the far corner, bakers moved quickly, turning out flat Georgian-style shoti loaves, and on the bar were old-fashioned Georgian soda fountains. Relieved to be away from the mimed music, I adopted a fully Georgian state of mind and settled in to feast slowly. All around, couples, old and young, indulged in elaborate stagey greetings. Hands were thrown up and lingering hugs were given freely. The café was busy and filled with good feeling. It is hard to find such easy fellowship on the left bank, as if something of its bewildering steel and glass architecture – so out of reach and colossal – has marked the souls and faces of its residents and workers.

I took a seat, along with a visiting American journalist and his local fixer, by a revolving glass cabinet, artily filled with fresh cakes and little ceramic figurines of dancers and musicians. The menu – its cover decorated with a pencil sketch of a tselinniki couple posing with a ginormous tractor – was fully Georgian, offering spatchcocked chicken tabaka, khinkali (Georgian dumplings), Abkhazia-style meatballs and eight types of khachapuri, devilishly moreish boat-shaped, cheese-filled bread. Waiters served us lobio (beans), khinkali filled with rich mushrooms, kebabs and heavy red saperavi wine.

Hanging on the wall, among all the nostalgia, something modern looked out of place. It was a framed neon number counter, some sort of stopwatch, like you find in a sports stadium or a waiting room. Silently, it was clocking up digits. Kuralay, the journalist's fixer, identified it as a khinkali-zator, a device for counting the number of khinkali cooked in the kitchen. If your order happened to be the hundredth made, there's a free drink, if you're the devourer of the thousandth khinkali, your gift is a bottle of wine. A prize for eating dumplings. A very fine way to keep the khinkali coming. I immediately loved Café Tselinnikov, how could you not? It was not futuristic new wave dining inspired by Nur-Sultan's pioneering architecture, instead it offered something more organic, far more suited to the historical side of the city. The food, decor and vintage photographs on the wall revealing, and reminding us, of how Nur-Sultan once was.

I returned to the swirling orange carpet of my hotel, walking on Kenesary Street and passing a dome-roofed old merchant house with ornate corners and ironwork. Opened in 1905 by a trader named Kubrin, the merchant store was first called Kubrinsky, then during the Soviet era it was a grocery shop called Rainbow. Today it is named Astana, although perhaps soon it will be Nur-Sultan – the city's newest name. Shortly before I left home, in a television address in mid-March 2019, Nursultan Nazarbayev unexpectedly quit as president of Kazakhstan, sparking the first changeover of power in the country since independence from the Soviet Union. Kassym-Jomart Tokayev, a long-time loyal Nazarbayev official, was inaugurated shortly after as Kazakhstan's president, and immediately ordered the change of the city's name from Astana to Nur-Sultan, after Nursultan Nazarbayev. In parks, on buses and in cafés, Kazakhs spoke freely of the succession. For the younger generation, those under 30 who make up roughly half the population and who never knew life under the Soviets, Nazarbayev has been the only president they have known. They spoke of shock, excitement and a feeling that little, in reality, would change, at least for now.

I asked one older taxi driver, knitted navy skullcap on his head, what he made of the name change. 'Why rename the city? It will be expensive to make all the changes. In Great Britain, Thatcher and Churchill did not do it.'

Inside the Astana supermarket, Kazakhstan's food landscape was laid out: wheat, millet, oats, vats of sunflower oil, honey and cartons of dried fruit: pear, melon, apples. Bottles of kefir, camel milk and ayran in refrigerators. Packets of currants, bilberries, cranberries and raspberries. Whole freezers of horsemeat. I took my time browsing inside this rare building, one still serving its original purpose, selling goods to the public, one of the last of its tsarist-era sort in Nur-Sultan. A little history. A little seasoning. Food and trade once again bringing back to mind the past. A few doors down is another house once owned by the

Kubrin family – they were wealthy enough, I later read, to own one of only two cars in the city. The high-rise sparkle of the left bank simply cannot compete with these little morsels of culture and history.

EGGS, EGGS, EGGS

Planners could make the Ishim River a focal point of the city, like the Thames in London or the Chao Phraya in Bangkok, and balance the building boom between the banks, thereby better connecting the old city with the new. Failure to incorporate the past with the present risks Nur-Sultan going the way of novelist Gertrude Stein's Oakland. When she heard her childhood neighbourhood had been ripped down to make way for an industrial park, she famously wrote 'There is no there there,' meaning that her particular 'there' had disappeared for good, never to return. Of course much has already been lost in the building boom.

Nur-Sultan's crowning left bank spectacle is Bayterek Tower, a 105-metre tall construction, symbolising the legend of a golden egg atop the tree of life. An atomic rush merged with a surge of dizziness as I whizzed up in a glass lift, which opened into the glorious egg. Swaying, I peered out and down through shiny gold glass-shell windows. The tint made the view appear beige, as though all of Nur-Sultan, its dancing fountains and manicured gardens, were caught in a sandstorm. In the distance stood Norman Foster's Khan Shatyr, the world's largest tent, with indoor canals, fake beach and waterpark. When the climate outdoors fluctuates – from –35°C degrees in winter and 35°C and upwards in summer – Kazakhs know the temperature inside the tent will be warm and womb-like.

'Please give me your telephone and stand here,' a woman in a smart white trouser suit instructed. I gingerly stepped forward and, following her cue, placed my sweaty hand into former president Nazarbayev's palm print, impressed in a triangle of sparkling gold. 'Smile!' I grimaced, the photograph was taken and with my hand newly blessed with good fortune, I wobbled back to the window.

Youth likes to build, and so it does. From the gold-mirrored egg I counted dozens of cranes, steel skeletons, scattered pipes and hundreds of workers putting up buildings of dreadful height. Olympian and sky-scraping. Mountainous. The new concrete 'high tablelands' of Central Asia. For all the desire to deflate Soviet architectural history and start afresh, there is something decidedly Stalinist in these monster buildings designed to dominate, to make you feel, when simply walking on the pavement, suddenly intimidated. Dwarfed and blanked by sheer architectural scale. This can be said of the self-titled Triumph of Astana building, based on the Stalinist-style so-called Seven Sisters skyscrapers in Moscow. Gotham-like, it is one of the most elite places to live in the city, popular with those who want to live in a convenient 'city within a city' buffeted by extreme luxury against harsh winds, extreme heat and cold.

Back down below, under the energising sun, I stood in the shadow of the 210-metre tall Emerald Towers, which have splayed roofs like opened books, and spotted a welcome slice of nature. An egg van. Not golden architectural eggs, but real eggs. A deliveryman leapt out, opened the boot, and carried a full tray of them into a shopping mall. I stared and stared at the van, weirdly comforted by its presence. I counted the eggs on the advertising panel, soothed by their oblong whiteness, the green of the grass, the cross-hatching of the country basket they sat in. Because Nur-Sultan does that. It disorientates until you find yourself pathetically clinging on to strange but familiar things. Natural things. 'Strange' is what many visitors call the capital, and the architecture has gone a little mad, but more than that, it felt like a city of promise. A city enduring growing pains but a visionary phenomenon. And, I was also glad to see it now, to witness the old-fashioned right bank as it is, before developers inevitably begin converting it further to match the futuristic cityscape across the river.

Mushroom Khinkali

Georgian dumplings filled with peppery mushrooms, as eaten at the fabulous Café Tselinnikov in Nur-Sultan. I find the idea of making dumplings by hand a little terrifying but if I can do these, so can you. The version here does not have broth inside, as this makes them harder to prepare, but as they boil a little juice is released from the mushrooms and steam so they're not dry. If one goes wrong (if it bursts, is the wrong shape or your pleating and pinching of the dough veers off course), just move on, and keep the khinkali coming.

MAKES 12 KHINKALI

FOR THE DOUGH

290g/2⅓ cups plain (all-purpose) flour, plus extra for kneading and rolling

½ tsp fine sea salt

½ tsp freshly ground pepper

120ml/½ cup water

1 large egg, beaten

FOR THE FILLING

30g/2 tbsp butter

125g/4½oz chestnut mushrooms, finely diced

65ml/4 tbsp mushroom or vegetable stock

Sea salt and freshly ground pepper

Laza Hot Sauce (page 197) or garlic butter to serve

In a large mixing bowl, combine all the dough ingredients and mix to bring the dough together, then gently tip it out onto a lightly floured surface. Knead for 10–15 minutes until the dough is smooth, supple, and not so sticky. Shape into a rough ball and then place in a lightly oiled bowl. Cover the bowl with a clean tea towel and let it rest at room temperature for an hour.

To make the filling, add the butter to a frying pan and place over a medium heat. Fry the mushrooms for about 10-15 minutes, until golden brown and cooked through, seasoning generously as you go.

Next, add the stock to the pan; it will splutter so be careful. Let it reduce, then remove from the heat and allow to cool.

Once the dough has proved, dust your work surface with flour. Roll out the dough to about 40 x 40cm/16 x 16in and using an 8cm/3in glass or circular cookie cutter, cut out 12 discs. Fill each disc with 1½ teaspoons of the mushroom mixture (extracting as little of the cooking liquid as possible or they are more likely to burst). Pleat and pinch the dough at the top, creating a money bag shape. Ensure they are well pinched at the top to seal them.

Bring to a boil a large saucepan of salted water. Using a slotted spoon, gently lower in each dumpling and boil for 8–10 minutes. When ready they will float to the top.

Serve straight away with Laza Hot Sauce or garlic butter.

KARLAG

Remembering Stalin's victims

AKMOL, NORTH KAZAKHSTAN: Below the hand crank of a coffee grinder are the words 'when a man is tired of London he is tired of life', the famous Samuel Johnson quote, engraved in a style of old-school typography rarely used today. Square, and painted black and red, this mill once belonged to a woman called Naydis Yevgeniya Davidovna, and it is important to know this.

In a neighbouring cabinet stood other small items: two hand-carved spoons and an enamel cooking pot, decorated with poppies, cared for by Shafiga Nuralina, and a spool of cotton and geometric needlework that was created by Shakitay Tatimova. Everyday things. Domestic things. Personal things. Things once in the hands of women who were victims of Stalin's vast gulag labour camp system that swept up 18 million people, from the 1920s to his death in 1953. Kazakhstan's huge gulag chain, called Karlag (Karaganda Corrective Labour Camp) spread over thousands of miles and it included Alzhir, a camp 40 minutes' drive from the capital, Nur-Sultan. Alzhir was part of this giant system but it was grimly different. Alzhir, the Russian acronym for Akmola Camp for the Wives of Betrayers of the Homeland, was a women and children's internment camp for those guilty by association, the relatives of men labelled traitors during the Great Terror. And these personal items were the possessions of a handful of the thousands of women, of 62 different nationalities, who spent anything from five to eight years here between 1938 and 1953.

Today, Alzhir is a memorial museum, as chilling as it is brilliantly executed. I entered, as everyone does, past a mock guard tower and under the oblong-shaped Arch of Sorrow, designed to look like a towering traditional Kazakh headdress, and for the next two hours I lost myself in one harrowing personal tale after the next, appalled, engrossed and moved by the hundreds of stories. Alzhir housed many women with incredible minds, family histories and occupations – wives, mothers, sisters, writers, artists, actresses and translators – but under the gulag system identities were stripped away and the women were branded with one collective title only: 'enemy of the people'. The gulag was, at its core, forced reform through hard labour, an atrocious and bullying re-education system, a way to prevent the ideas of 'class enemies' from influencing the Soviet people. Many Alzhir women worked in factories, some producing uniforms for the Red Army, and on their backs, and sleeves, a string of numbers – targets, in case of escape. Elsewhere in the Karlag system, labourers were put to work in freezing fields on the many farms, or in copper mines, or were forced to build railways, while some worked at enterprises such as vegetable drying operations, creameries, sugar plants, meat-processing plants and butter factories.

In one photograph is Rachel Messerer-Plisetskaya, a Soviet silent-film actress. Her hair is neatly scooped back, her patterned blouse tied elegantly in a bow at her neck. Born in Vilnius to a famous Russian-Jewish theatrical family, she was the mother of Maya Plisetskaya who became prima ballerina at the Bolshoi Theatre. During the Soviet era and, with the KGB closely monitoring her, Plisetskaya was famously refused permission to appear at Covent Garden on the Bolshoi Ballet's western debut tour in 1956. But she went on to perform Swan Lake 800 times and on her New York debut in 1959, a critic reported that audiences 'moaned with delight'. She was one of the finest ballerinas the world has ever seen. A superstar.

And, there is Raisa Moiseevna Mamayeva, born in Ukraine in 1900, dressed carefully with round spectacles on her nose, bright lipstick and a silk handkerchief in her left breast-pocket. Wife of a military advisor, before her arrest she had worked as an English and Chinese interpreter.

Hair cropped short and boyish, Nina Vsesvyatskaya was born in St Petersburg in 1907, the wife of a well-known journalist of Korean descent and mother of the composer Yuliy Kim, one of Russia's most prolific songwriters, known for his cutting satire, whose work appears in at least 50 Soviet movies.

Back outside, I sucked in lungfuls of cool air and read across the giant memorial, a slab of black granite, into which thousands of names had been etched in rows. These enormous walls, painstakingly carved and powerful in scale, are what we tend to build to remember the war dead as a visual way to commemorate casualties and veterans, showing the scale of the disaster. At the end of the wall, poet Anna Akhmatova, one of the greatest voices of Russian literature, had the final word, a parting conundrum for visitors to take away:

'And wasting our youth
We were facing
Every blow
Of a fierce life.'

But it was the small domestic items, once in the hands of these women, so fine in their fragile material – glass, china, cotton – inside the museum, that impacted most, that force us to remember. Intensity and weight had been bestowed upon these everyday domestic items, loyal possessions full of memories, and the stories they told. A fragile teacup, a vintage wristwatch, an old-fashioned perfume bottle. All would have been valued and adored. Imagine how the heart would cling to such objects amongst those brutal circumstances. Lesley Blanch wrote about her 'unity with things' and in her book *Journey into the Mind's Eye*, she quoted the

Ukrainian diarist and artist Marie Bashkirtseff, 'One laughs at people who find memories, charm, in furniture and pictures, who say to them: Good morning, and good-bye; who look on pieces of wood and stuff as friends, which by being useful to you and constantly seen . . . become part of your life.'

Just beyond the museum railings, tall, bare, spindly trees held dozens of crows' nests. All around them a black plumage massed, wings beating. The birds appeared as shadow puppets, silhouetted black in the clear air. An eerie gothic scene.

To catch my train to Karaganda, 160 miles south, I took a taxi to Nur-Sultan's railway station. Famous for coal, copper and steel, Karaganda was close enough to warrant a look around and it had its own peculiar attractions, surrounded in spring by endless yellow Siberian peashrub, also called caragana, which gives the city its name. It is a city with strong links to cosmonauts, space history and dairy traditions.

The driver steered his car towards the railway station, the steppe golden and swampy with snowmelt. Horses grazed. A large cluster of graves and elaborate mausoleums lined the roadside, protected by a turquoise picket fence. In the capital we travelled down Nur-Sultan Avenue, went past Nazarbayev University, before arriving to Nur-Sultan railway station, all named after the former president. No longer in office, but everywhere all the same.

At the railway station, long-distance trains paused their journeys between Kazakhstan, Uzbekistan and Russia. Migrant workers filled the platforms, smoking and chatting before carrying on to Russia's cities to work, to send money home. I boarded my train in a rush, caught at the security barrier, bags fully searched, no time to buy water, let alone snacks. The sleeper carriages, where my 'seat' was, were decrepit. A broken samovar had illustrated detailed instructions of how to fix it but for that pliers were required. There was no dining car, no trolley and no food hawkers. No chance of what I call a 'steppe sandwich', or railway pirozhki, a pudgy bun filled with mashed potato or cabbage. But it was only a three-hour journey. The scenery was hypnotic and whatever the state of the train, it was an adventure. Trains are always a revealing world within a world.

We stopped periodically, sometimes at length which stoked fear that the old train had sighed its last, then we were off again, rolling through the landscape that had appealed so much to John Wardell, whose book, *In the Kirghiz Steppes*, I continued to carry with me. 'Nothing can be more perfect than a gallop over the steppe on a glorious summer day, with the horses' hoofs bruising the herbs so that the air is redolent with perfume . . .' he wrote.

The dozing woman opposite, with Fanta-coloured hair, woke at one stop and charitably handed me a plastic container of walnuts she'd bought in Tashkent. I took one gratefully and sucked it solemnly. The day had warmed up and the train was suddenly sweltering, the windows would not budge and I had several wool layers on. Living in Scotland does that to you, preparedness for the cold. I slumped back on thin cushions covered in blue and white Russian florals and a mattress with an Uzbek-style stripe, a dash of artistry and charm.

Rows of thin smokestacks and a muster of soldiers announced the outskirts of Karaganda and the penultimate stop. Just one passenger boarded here, a woman with white-blonde hair cut in a sharp bob. Thin, tall and with razor-sharp cheekbones and pale blue eyes she looked like one of the Russian models on Fashion TV, the channel of choice in Central Asia's cafés. From a crumpled Victoria's Secret carrier bag she showed passengers knock-off Italian socks she was selling for $5 a pair. She looked exhausted and bored and wore a sock on each hand. 'They're cashmere, it's cold outside', she said in perfect English with a weak smile. Guessing my nationality, she added, 'London! It is my dream!' I organised my luggage and the sock-seller left the carriage. I looked up and saw her walking down the aisle with her carrier bag, past the grimy windows that framed a row of tanks, before stepping off the train to wait for the next, to try to make a measly sale. I cursed myself for not buying the socks. How thoughtless, selfish and heartless I was. For a moment, I hated myself. Always buy the socks. Always.

At Karaganda's railway station, little kiosks sold apricot kompot, Korean salads, kefir and samsa and down by the tracks, women with buckets pulled back and forth blue pumps bringing up water. On the outskirts of town, mini-railway tracks for the coal trains criss-crossed the steppe, grass growing over their tracks. *Industrial Karaganda* is the name of the local newspaper, I learned. Until the late 1920s, when Soviet geologists, viewing the vast Kazakh plains as ripe for exploitation, began to develop the local coal basin remotely from their desks in Moscow, maps barely mentioned this place. Then, architects drew up a city plan, remotely from hundreds of miles away, and by 1934 Karaganda had a name. Then, problems began. Kazakh workers in the mines were going hungry and their housing was so poor that they erected yurts to sleep in, regularly returning to their auls ('villages') to rest and eat. Their absence meant the mines suffered which displeased those in Moscow. Around the same time, the arrival of the railway brought with it experienced miners from Ukraine as well as NKVD officers, the agency tasked with conducting police work and overseeing the country's prisons and labour camps. The officers set up a vast labour camp, Karlag (Karaganda Corrective Labour Camp), to the southwest of the new grid-like city. More camp workers – including many Chechens (current Chechen leader Ramzan Kadyrov's father was born in Karaganda) and ethnic Germans from Russia's Volga Region who Stalin feared as potential Nazi Germany collaborators – were brought in to till the land and to grow crops that would feed the miners. And that is how this city, rising out of the flat yellow plains, came to be in central Kazakhstan.

Grim as all this is, Karaganda's labour camps and heavy industry is not all there is to know about this remote city. 'Where? Where? In Karaganda!' the old Soviet joke went. John Wardell viewed this part of Kazakhstan with inquisitive eyes: 'Fresh from the English landscape, it took us some time to get used to the lack of trees . . . but when we did become accustomed to the steppes – and it is marvellous how soon this became a fascination – trees would have been out of place.'

And this is where cosmonauts, who blasted off from the world's earliest and largest space launch facility, Baikonur spaceport, 750 miles away in southern Kazakhstan, would often come back to earth. Newspapers reported that Kazakhs would wait out on the flatlands around Karaganda, then as the cosmonauts came parachuting down from their capsules onto the giant flat steppe surrounding Karaganda, they'd run forward with melons as gifts, cheering, 'Glory to the space heroes!' There is no fresh fruit or produce in space. Kazakhstan's golden steppe – enormous, bare and flat – became the Soviet Union's perfect landing site.

MILK FACTORY

Reimagining dairy lands

KARAGANDA, CENTRAL KAZAKHSTAN: Under a row of standard-issue Soviet glass bottles, I waited for the milkman of Kazakhstan. Outside, silver dairy tankers eased away from the parking lot, steered by some of the 60 or so truck drivers employed by the Natige dairy business. On factory floors below, caps were tightened onto bottles of kefir by workers in white coats. Ice cream was tested, tasted and went into tubs.

Yerlan Ashimov is someone you'd call a 'character' and his name is one that people in Karaganda know. A successful businessman, with a booming laugh and quick eyes, he provides central Kazakhstan – natural dairy lands where there is good grazing – with milk, kefir, yogurt, cheese and butter. After keeping me waiting half an hour, he swept into his office; arms stretched wide, roaring greetings, seemingly pleased to have a visitor. Wearing a perfectly pressed white shirt, he slowly sat down behind his large desk, shadowed by a floor-length traditional green velvet chapan robe, hanging from a coat hook and shining with gold embroidery. He was, I sensed, ready to perform.

'If you want to learn history, learn the food,' he said encouragingly, so we started at the beginning.

'Milk is sacred in Kazakhstan as sometimes it was all we ever had, all we ever needed. Nomads would take a sheep bladder, clean it, boil horse milk inside, when the milk thickened, they'd dry it and that would be their food. In the villages, kumis, fermented mare's milk, was made by churning the milk in leather bags using a wooden paddle, and that was our drink.'

Homer called the Scythians – who from around 900–200 BC extended their territory from Central Asia to the northern Black Sea – 'mare milkers', while fellow Greek Herodotus also noted that Scythian tribes lived on mare's milk. The Mongol Empire, during the 13th and 14th centuries, was successful partly because, like the Kazakhs, Mongols knew how to ride and eat without stopping or diverting their course over great distances. They survived partly on easily transportable kumis, to be drunk in draughts on the hoof, and qurut (dried milk curds). Kublai Khan had a love of horses and horse milk and had a herd of white mares for his own personal milk supply kept in a hunting park at his capital Xanadu. John Wardell wrote, 'Kazakh women claim to make about thirty kinds of milk foods from hard sheep's cheese to kumis.' Across the border in Kyrgyzstan, the capital, Bishkek, is named after the paddle traditionally used to churn fermenting milk.

Ashimov went on. 'When we'd go on a long journey, what could we eat that would last? Qurut. Our soldiers went to China or further and they had provisions, they had qurut. Christians and Russians often got caught out as they had no food. Not us.'

Qurut is a handy food for travelling warriors and it is the quintessential Kazakh snack to this day. Marco Polo knew of its benefits: 'They also have milk dried into a kind of paste to carry with them; and when they need food they put this in water, and beat it up until it dissolves, and then drink it . . . And when they go on an expedition, every man takes some ten pounds of this dried milk with him. And of a morning he will take a half-pound of it and put it in his leather bottle, with as much water as he pleases. So, as he rides along, the milk-paste and the water in the bottle get well churned together . . . and that makes his dinner.'

Behind me hung a framed caricature of Ashimov's face, his smile stretching from ear to ear. As we talked, his staff regularly knocked, entered, and then were quickly ushered away. Ashimov was holding court, and enjoying it.

Milking a horse is harder than milking a cow, he explained. 'When you milk a horse, you milk it every two hours over the course of the day and you get roughly one and a half litres. So when, in the 19th century, cows came here with the Russians, Kazakhs found it was very easy and comfortable to milk cows, from a simple movement came a lot of milk. Later, communists brought us all kinds of

ready products. And suddenly not only did we have the same haircuts as them, we had the same bottles of milk. Everything standard Soviet style.'

If the Soviet Union had not collapsed, Ashimov said he was sure he would have stayed in his home village, with a salary and with some livestock. But it did collapse, and that life was not enough for him.

'In 1991, I started to ask, "Who am I?" I began selling chewing gum and cigarettes; I had a corner in a shop to sell these things. Then I started a small bread baking business, baking and driving to sell the loaves. Then something happened, 20 years ago in February, it was –40°C degrees outside and a man, Alexi, arrived saying he wanted to talk about milk. "We don't need milk," I told him. But as a Kazakh I felt bad refusing him, so I invited him again. He was older, a Russian. He was a sales rep from a milk factory in the Kazakh city of Kostanay. He was frozen in the weather, going from place to place. It wasn't working out, people weren't paying. I didn't think about his products but I thought about him.'

Ashimov had clearly told this tale many times, but his eyes sparkled and his hands waved animatedly as he spoke.

'Alexi and I drank tea. He said he'd been cheated. We mended his car and he stayed with us. He was in a very hard situation. I wanted to help him and so in a few days we sold his milk to my network of shops. And then I thought, I can make a business with this man. We just celebrated our 20-year anniversary working together. This business came from one good deed.'

Cynicism crept in as I listened, it all sounded too straightforward to be true, but it was hard not to warm to Ashimov as he recalled the tale. Putting on his green velvet chapan, he led me next door where a huge spread of Natige products, all the goods, had been laid out. Like all the best products, they don't travel far, distributed close to production. His team had been trotted out to meet the foreign visitor, they all looked cheery enough, professional and smiling. The produce was very good. The cheddar, ice cream, yogurt and butter (salted and unsalted) was creamy, moreish and nourishing. The kefir, super-chilled and poured out of a glass bottle fresh off the production line was utterly sublime, the best I had ever tasted. But it was a cardboard milk carton that stood out, instantly reminding me of something. I picked it up.

LIFE-SAVING STONES

On the back of the green carton was a story, illustrated with a pencil sketch of a face I recognised. It was Gertrude Platays – a former prisoner of Alzhir, the women's camp near Nur-Sultan, whose photograph I had seen there, her young face tired but defiant, her hair in long plaits. It was clear her story was somehow linked to Kazakhstan's dairy traditions. But why, and how?

The tale was simple but incredible. On a freezing winter's morning, with a snowstorm whipping the air, female prisoners from Alzhir were outside building a barracks; cold, hungry, suffering and exhausted from the manual work that occupied them for at least 15 hours a day. Close by, in the free world, hidden by trees and thickets, local Kazakh villagers watched the women work. Then, on the order of village elders, local children began throwing stones at the women. They rained down, hard and fast onto the workers, launched over razor wire with force. The guards laughed. One of the prisoners, Gertrude Platays, was a young German, born in 1910, who before her arrest had worked at a print shop. She cried at the guard's cruel claims that not only in Moscow were the women hated, but out here, too. Hated so much that even children would throw rocks at them. For several days it continued and one day Platays's morale fell as low as could be. Completely broken, physically and spiritually, she collapsed on the ground, by the half-built barracks. And there she stayed, snow falling around her. As she lay there, stock-still, she recognised an unexpected but familiar smell, a milky scent. It was the small stones that had been thrown at her. Somehow, they smelled faintly of cheese. She put one into her tired mouth, and sucked slowly. Gradually, the stone softened and her mouth filled with the taste of cottage cheese. She pocketed as many of these strange magical rocks as she could smuggle and that night, back at the dormitory, shared them out. The Kazakh women prisoners knew immediately. The stones were not stones at all, they were qurut. The local villagers, watching the women toil in unbearable circumstances, had not thrown rocks to taunt them, they had flung vital sustenance that looked like pebbles, fooling the guards, and giving the women much-needed nutrients. The very food that for centuries Kazakhs had depended on, out on the remote steppe, food they knew could save lives. Food put into saddlebags, and carried long-distance over the ages.

The villagers, too, were survivors. Survivors of starvation, victims, directly or indirectly, of one of the world's greatest tragedies: Stalin's disastrous collective agricultural master plan of 1927. To Kazakhs this vast swathe of steppe was their nomadic home, the pastures criss-crossed with ancient cattle routes and ancestral burial grounds, but to the Soviets it was space to be conquered, calculated and exploited. In the late 1920s leaders in Moscow viewed the plains of Kazakhstan, rich in traditions of animal husbandry and with millions of heads of cattle, as a prime region for boosting livestock breeding. Nomadic pastoral Kazakhs were forced into sovkhoz ('state farms') or kolkhoz ('collective farms') and their animals – their source of food, clothes, companionship and identity – were requisitioned. Cattle were butchered for food to be sent to other parts of the

Soviet Union, or else were driven away to work at collective farms, with many dying in the chaos from lack of fodder or killed by their owners who refused to give them up. No animals meant no milk and no meat, and in this chaos a deadly famine – the Asharshylyk – was triggered, killing at least one and a half million Kazakhs between the years of 1930–33. Hundreds of thousands of Kazakhs fled to neighbouring countries, Kazakhstan lost most of its livestock and its people lost their traditional way of life for ever. Such collectivisation also triggered widespread starvation across Russia and Belarus, as well as the deadly famine in Ukraine known as the Holodomor where several million Ukrainians lost their lives. Numbers so terrible and huge as to be unfathomable.

GLORIOUS CABBAGES AND RED STEPPE COWS

The next morning, I headed to a small village called Dolinka, just outside Karaganda. There, the former administrative centre of the Karlag has been repurposed as a museum called the Dolinka Museum for the Commemoration of Victims of Political Repression. A young woman led me on a tour, pointing at maps, which showed the enormousness of the Karlag chain. She wore childish patent shoes, a neat plastic bow at the rounded-toes. Shoes that made no noise as she walked. I stopped in front of a black-and-white poster of a thin bearded man, his mouth agape, his hands thrown up in horror. 'Help me' was written at his bony bare feet and behind him was a sketch of a single broken wheat sheaf. A picture of famine terrifyingly memorable in its simplicity.

Panels in English and Russian showed how the system fed the workers in the local coal industry by growing mega-crops and unusual livestock. Monochrome photographs showed giant sunflowers and the harvest of a huge cabbage called slava ('glory'), an 'experimental field of corn' and a trio of Koreans – sent to Kazakhstan from Russia's Far East by Stalin – who as 'special settlers' harvested crops of onions. Test tubes of various grains stood in a wooden box. Other photographs showed urns of Karlag milk (cow not horse) being registered by camp members. Another poster announced the Karlag's cultural output: 1,954 lectures and a black and white photograph showing an unsmiling six-piece string band who gave performances. The guide slid along silently in her rubber-soled shoes, and I followed.

I asked the guide how she coped with talking about starvation, torture chambers and slave labour all day. She shuffled her silent feet, and then airily replied that she didn't feel a thing before chirpily running through the other exhibitions like we were going around a school art exhibition.

'But so many of your neighbours must have had grandparents who'd been victims of the Karlag,' I said, finding her apparent disconnect grating.

'They were. Mine were.' She said, blankly.

In 1991 journalist Adam Hochschild arrived at what was, by far, the biggest house in Dolinka. And there he met with former secret police colonel Mikhail Volkov, who was posted to Karaganda in 1949. Volkov explained to Hochschild that his job, seven years in the system, was mainly to ensure the quotas, such as grain harvests, were met. He spoke of 'following orders' – as guilty people tend to do – and talked of the camp in neutral terms, focusing on the agricultural economy, rather than what it was in reality: a terrifying spy-ridden prison camp.

'He sounded like a proud regional Party boss. "We had our own agricultural experiment station. Cattle breeding was also advanced. A special breed of cow, Red Steppe, was raised here . . . There were grain farms; we had poultry here. We sent food to the front during the war."' Hochschild wrote.

I left Dolinka, and the guide returned to her office, her cushioned shoes noiseless as she went, soft-stepping past pictures filled with horror. How far removed these mad agricultural experiments and quotas were compared with the lands of Ashimov's ancestors, where families roamed with their animals, following the seasons and old grazing routes, their knowledge of the land beyond compare. I recalled what Ashimov had said about the village where he grew up.

'If any milk went to waste, my grandmother would make sure a hole was dug in the ground. And then we would pour the milk there. We would carefully return it back to the earth. Nothing was more important, or more sacred to us, than milk.' As Ashimov had told me at the start of our meeting: 'If you want to learn history, learn the food.'

COSMODROME

Overnighting with space pioneers

KARAGANDA, CENTRAL KAZAKHSTAN: 'It is I, Seagull! I see the horizon. This is the Earth, how beautiful it is. Everything goes well.' And with these words, on the 16th June 1963, 26-year-old Valentina Tereshkova made history by becoming the first woman in space. Aboard Vostok 6, strapped to her ejection seat, Tereshkova blasted into space, her mission lasting two days and 22 hours. So secretive was her quest – the space race between Cold War rivals, the Soviet Union and the United States was on – that her mother, back home in the Soviet Union, only knew of her daughter's success when she saw the television news. Chaika, meaning 'seagull' in Russian, was her codename.

Tereshkova's photograph hangs above the reception desk of Hotel Chaika in Karaganda, its main building shaped like the spread wings of a gull, its design brilliantly retro. In the portrait she poses serenely, under perfectly coiffed auburn hair, her black jacket shining with dozens of medals. Next to her, a framed print of Yuri Gagarin – first human in space – in exactly the same pose, highly decorated with even more medals, and with an even wider grin. Soviet heroes, both. Men and women of the future. Unmissable at the front desk, too, is a diploma from 1987, proudly framed alongside the space superstars. From the Federation of Cosmonauts of the USSR it was awarded to the Hotel Chaika on the 25th anniversary of the first R&R stay of space travellers, acknowledging the hotel's role as part of the Soviet space programme. Quite fairly, the hotel continues to trade on its association with the cosmonauts.

Dozens of cosmonauts came here, to the city's first hotel – then simply called 'New Hotel' – to sleep and rest after landing by parachute relatively close by. They'd gone up from Baikonur Cosmodrome in the south of the country, a spaceport set in 4,200 square miles of semi-desert, from where Sputnik 1, the first artificial satellite, and Vostok 1, the first human spaceflight, were both launched. A little R&R before the universal fame that followed. These cosmonauts turned Karaganda into a space city of sorts. Streets are named after them, spaceship murals decorate the side of apartment blocks and in the centre of Karaganda, a huge shining, steel Yuri Gagarin statue is the centrepiece in a monumental Soviet-built square. In Hotel Chaika's restaurant, flavours and tastes are little changed since the time the cosmonauts were here. The menu lists forshmak, a pâté of herring and apple, Russian Olivier salad, stuffed pancakes, chicken julienne with mushrooms and Georgian-style chicken. To drink there are three choices: tea, juice or vodka.

As Yuri Gagarin was the first human in space, he ate the first meal in orbit, too, thrilling in its blandness: two servings of puréed meat and one of chocolate sauce, pastes he squeezed into his mouth from tubes. Project Gemini, during the 1960s, improved freeze-drying methods making possible shrimp cocktail, toast, chicken and vegetables with food coated with gelatine or oil to prevent crumbling. For space flights, Russians took fish such as sturgeon and cottage cheese-like tvorog. When China launched into orbit in 2003 for the first time, astronaut Yang Liwei brought herbal tonics and Chinese-made bite-size chicken and rice, coated in a thin edible film for ease of eating.

The caretaker of the hotel, Galim, led me to the adjoining mansion, which once stood alone as the original hotel. We crunched down a path over pine cones, to the place where the heroes of the Soviet Union once slept. Plaques commemorating the space men and women covered the exterior wall, while inside, by white ruffled net curtains, were dozens of mounted portraits. More museum than hotel. Cosmonaut Vladimir Shatalov, twice Hero of the Soviet Union, recipient of three Orders of Lenin, slept here on the 17th January 1969. At 7 a.m. that morning, when it was −30°C outside and the steppe was blanketed with 80cm of snow, Shatalov touched down Soyuz 4, a few dozen miles southwest of Karaganda. Five minutes after landing, he and his crew were on the recovery helicopter, then, at Hotel Chaika, they underwent a medical examination before giving a press conference.

EARTH – COSMOS – KARAGANDA

I didn't stay at the Chaika, overnighting instead at the Hotel Cosmonaut, a ten-minute drive away. Little of the original 1972 construction remains, but this hotel too was built specially for the return of cosmonauts.

I took a taxi downtown, to Moi Tbilisi, for a Georgian dinner. I opened the door, hopefully, onto a raucous party in full swing, everyone puffing on cigarettes in the doorway, couples ballroom dancing, the music spilling full-power from speakers. 'Full', I was told. Outside, glowing in the moonlight were more murals of Soviet workers and on the side of an apartment block Lenin's words, 'Art belongs to the people.' Three Bears, a Russian restaurant, had room, in fact they were empty. A waitress sat me at a table, turned all the lights off, and introduced two singers who took to a small stage. My heart sank as a candle was lit before me. I couldn't see what I was eating and had to simply hope it was what I ordered. But the crispy cabbage pierogi, forest mushroom soup and trout with potato croquettes were all good, even if the music wasn't.

Back at the Hotel Cosmonaut, the day's newspapers showed photographs of daredevil cleaners dressed in white overalls scaling Moscow's 70-metre-tall

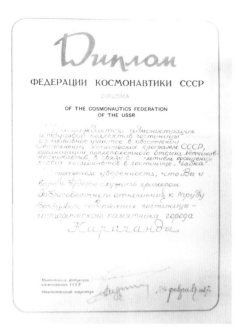

titanium Gagarin monument, weighing in at 12 tons, soaping, buffing and polishing him, ahead of Cosmonautics Day tomorrow. Upstairs, a gift from the management had been left by the bedroom's balcony door. A packet of 20 Parliament cigarettes, an ashtray and a box of branded Hotel Cosmonaut matches. Temptation. I stepped onto the balcony, into the cold clear night, and with the packet in my hand, looked up at the Milky Way, our galaxy, named after 'gala' the Greek word for milk, each star believed to be a drop of spilled breast milk from goddess Hera. I lit a cigarette and imagined the cosmonauts up there, then down here, landing somewhere on Kazakhstan's flat plains. Vast cosmic space and immense human achievements, mirroring the hopes, possibilities and loneliness of all life on earth.

Meatball, Lavash and Chickpea Soup

Rather than space explorers, the restaurant at the Hotel Cosmonaut nowadays serves geologists and experts who operate mines in the Karaganda region. But it still had an interesting menu. The best dish was a kyufta sorpa, a thin bouillon-like soup reduced down with chickpeas, lamb meatballs and shards of crispy lavash. Relying more on pantry basics than the seasons, it is a very simple, economical and handy recipe for a nutritious lunch. If you can't find lavash, pitta bread is a good alternative.

SERVES 4

2 tbsp olive oil

300ml/1¼ cups chicken stock

200ml/⅘ cup boiling water

½ tsp sea salt

1 x 400g/14oz can chickpeas (garbanzo beans), drained

150g/5oz lavash or pitta bread, toasted and broken into shards, to serve

½ bunch of dill fronds, roughly chopped, to garnish

½ bunch of flat-leaf parsley, roughly chopped, to garnish

FOR THE MEATBALLS

400g/14oz minced (ground) lamb

1 large egg

1 large garlic clove, crushed

60g/1 cup breadcrumbs

½ tsp sweet paprika

¾ tsp ground cumin

½ tsp fine sea salt

¼ tsp freshly ground pepper

In a large bowl, add all the ingredients for the meatballs and mix them together with your hands. Roll into 20 or so golf-ball-size balls.

Heat the oil in a large high-sided frying pan or saucepan over a medium-high heat. Fry the meatballs, for 5 or so minutes, working in 2 batches if easier, turning occasionally, until browned all over (they do not need to be cooked through at this stage, as they'll cook in the soup later). Transfer to a plate.

Add the chicken stock to the pan, along with the boiling water and sea salt. Bring to a boil, then simmer for 5 minutes. Add the meatballs and simmer for around 8–10 minutes until they are cooked through. Add the chickpeas to the pan, simmering for a minute to warm them through. Check the seasoning, then remove from the heat. Ladle the soup into bowls, scatter the lavash or pitta shards on top along with the herbs, and serve piping hot.

DAM

Watching fishermen on the Aral Sea

ARALSK, SOUTHWEST KAZAKHSTAN: In the waiting room of Aralsk's empty railway station, above heavy-duty Soviet-era radiators, a mural made up of tiny coloured tiles covers a wall. Thousands of small ceramic pieces depicting the physical features of the men and women who once fished in this small windblown town: men in rain hats and Breton tops drag nets next to strong-armed women while fishermen haul wooden tubs and sturdy barrows. From the far-right corner, Lenin watches, abstractly yet hungrily. In 1921 the Bolshevik leader summoned the people of Aralsk to provide wagonloads of fish to hungry people elsewhere in the burgeoning Soviet Union. Today, for the people of Aralsk, this mural is a reminder of what life once was.

It's not easy to get here, to the depleted Aral Sea, now so drained and reduced as to be split in two. It is not straightforward to reach the northern section of the sea, in Kazakhstan, nor the southern section across the border in Uzbekistan. First, I'd taken a flight from Nur-Sultan southwards. Flying over vast patchworks of rice paddies was a reminder of where once Koreans, exiled here by Stalin from the Far East of Russia where they had settled to escape Japanese colonial oppression, once farmed. Then, from where the aeroplane landed, in the southern provincial city of Kyzylorda, I'd taken a taxi for 280 miles to the old fishing port town of Aralsk. We'd followed the Syr Darya River before passing close to the Trans-Aral Railway, where the engineering of a steel path of tracks replaced the old camel caravan routes.

Halfway to Aralsk, an enormous alien structure rose out of the flat scrubland. Two huge discs forming the base for two giant skywards-pointing antennas: Baikonur Cosmodrome's Saturn tracking station. To see it, even from a distance, on Cosmonautics Day, was heart-skyrocketingly wonderful. To get any closer I needed paperwork and permission, neither of which I had. Its otherworldly sighting turned the taxi into a movie camera rolling on tracks, the car window, a huge lens. An imaginary sci-fi movie unfolded, a personal space opera, a constellation of ideas and images: the steppe, abstract in its grandeur, was as otherworldly as vast cosmic space and lunar soil. My mind swam with missions and machines, giant tripods and their steel-like romanticism, space pods and future-oriented motherships, sleek surfaces and speed. Future-orientated men and women. Heroic cosmonauts with nerves of steel and faith in science. Gagarin as propaganda, as Soviet cultural icon. Men and women who gave meaning to a world beyond the heavens. The space race, where ascendancy translated to scientific, technological, and therefore military, dominance on earth. Space, the ultimate escapism. An alternate fantasy world of glorious possibilities. The taxi driver stopped the car – he, too, seemed affected by my cosmic enthusiasm. Space, what better epitomises human wonder? Didn't we all once wish upon a star?

'When the rockets launch, the salt and dust from the steppe gets blasted hundreds of miles around, it's not very healthy,' said the driver bringing me back to reality. I had no idea whether this was true or not.

By the roadside, women wore woolly leggings, tracksuit tops and balaclavas, covering themselves from the blistering sun. Each waved a bottle of camel milk in one hand, and a splayed dried fish in the other, at cars that passed. Few people stopped to purchase these poverty-driven pit-stop offerings. Behind them, a herd of cows stood comically in the shade of a concrete bus stop, as if waiting for a lift.

MAROONED HARBOURS AND MAD MAX BIKERS

Given how large the Aral Sea's historical shadow looms in the mind I was surprised by how small Aralsk is. We drove in on a sandy road, past single-storey cottages. There were very few people around. Men moved from car to bottle shop to home. Nobody lingered on the street. Like Zhanaozen, the oil town in western Kazakhstan, outsiders are viewed with polite suspicion – with good cause as the only reason foreigners come here, where nothing grows, is to see the Aral Sea disaster, one of mankind's worst ecological calamities, firsthand. By the long-deserted harbour-loading docks old cranes tower over the hulls of abandoned Soviet shipwrecks.

The Aral Sea catastrophe is well documented but I wanted to come as I had read about a cautious return to fishing on the northern side here in Kazakhstan.

I wanted to see the fishermen I'd read about and I wanted to hear from people in Aralsk about whether they were optimistic or not. The facts are bleak: in the early 1960s the Soviet Union diverted the region's two major rivers – the Amu Darya and the Syr Darya – away from what was once the fourth-largest freshwater lake in the world in order to irrigate and boost cotton production. Cotton is an infamously thirsty crop. Freshwater fish stocks shrivelled due to increased salt in the water and the 'sea' is now a tenth of what it was and has split in two. The north Aral Sea is in Kazakhstan; the south Aral Sea, little more than a belt of water, is across the border in Uzbekistan. Before the ecological disaster, at its peak in the mid-1950s, almost 50,000 tons of fish were in the sea, by the 1980s all native species had gone; only introduced flounder, tolerant of the salinity, could survive.

Fruit trees once grew here, but they died with the desertification and increase of sand, dust, salt and chemicals from the dried-up seabed, which also brought TB and breathing problems to local people and severe weather quirks. Now nothing grows, all food is brought in. I felt guilty visiting.

Most foreigners who come here stay with Gulmira as her home offers a sliver of warmth and light in this hard place. She, along with her 72-year-old mother, Marjan, who was sporting an eye patch from cataract surgery ('you don't pay for the surgery here, just the bed') and a velour dressing gown, welcomed me in. The courtyard, which had a summer kitchen protected by a wooden picket fence, provided safety away from the roaming packs of bushy-tailed dogs that kicked up sand as they chased one another outside.

We sat at the dining table. On the mantelpiece, a framed photograph of her husband in his police uniform took centre place; he had died 20 years ago, she told me, a victim of the chronic health problems – cancers, respiratory diseases, anaemia, miscarriages – that have ravaged this unhealthy, man-made wasteland. Thousands of people left the Aral Sea, concerned for their health and livelihoods. Gulmira's children had also left home.

Exuding an air of resigned loneliness, Gulmira poured tea, a pretty floral enamel teapot in each hand, one with tea, one with water. A plate of fresh borsok, golden puffs of fried bread a little like doughnuts, and jam, were handed around. Marjan sat at the head of the table and reeled off the region's history with just a little prompting. She painted a picture of the past, one of multicultural optimism and plenty.

'When the sea was here, other nationalities were here, too. Ukrainians, Azerbaijanis, Russians. Big ships were in the harbour doing a lot of good business. Fishing boats were made here.'

As the sun set, we had an early supper of pike-perch from the Aral Sea, with potatoes and tomato ketchup. It was a little bony but as Lesley Blanch, that great travelling writer who ate so well in so many places around the world, asserted 'timidity and prejudice should have no place in the kitchen', and she was, of course, correct. I ate the fish gratefully and slept with the bedroom window open, the silent night broken only by the train whistle from the railroad which carried on until it was light. Cartoon-like toots. I thought of Aralsk's empty railway station, the giant mural and Lenin's hungry eyes, the wagons of fish leaving.

The following morning I met Serik Dyussenbayev, a local fixer and tour guide who has worked closely with Danish NGOs for many years to try to improve the state of the Aral Sea. As with everyone in Aralsk he has many personal connections to the disaster, not least that his mother worked in a fish canning factory for 26 years, as well as the fact that he grew up here, and raised his own children here.

In his Nissan Pathfinder we travelled to the Kok-Aral Dam, a piece of engineering hailed as a success story. The road we started on was good to begin with, then it worsened into spine-shaking sandy tracks that led past villages with camels tied up outside. I asked Serik about the taxi driver who'd said that the rocket blasts cause dangerous salty dust to be blown for hundreds of miles. 'Nonsense,' he sniffed, before adding that after a launch it can occasionally become stormy and that Baikonur's activity does have the power to shift local weather patterns.

Above us, a falcon soared. Men walked with their camels. In villages, animals were paired with their young – foals, lambs and calves. Along one straight road we didn't pass a living thing for an hour and then two tazy dogs appeared on the roadside with their owner. Hip-height and thin, their ears long and silky, looking not dissimilar to a saluki or gazelle hound, they are usually used for hunting rabbits on the steppe. Clocking 30 miles-per-hour is not a problem for them. Endangered today, once a rich Kazakh would be willing to trade dozens of horses for a top tazy. As we dodged a camel on the road, Serik told me, deadpan, their meat is 'pre-seasoned' as the ground they graze on is so salty. I laughed at this, but he remained long-faced. Serik makes a good living out of disaster tourism but it seemed to have crushed his soul. He did his job with a mixture of sadness, boredom and perhaps a dash of pride.

'Now it is spring and the babies are born, so animals return home to the villages but in the summer, camels can go a week without water so they stay out on the steppe, or go walking on the highways. They just stand, they don't run, you have to watch out for them at night.' Serik said, rolling up the sleeves of his camouflage shirt.

Soon, we were travelling on desert-like dirt, which was the former seabed. After three hours, as we got closer to the Kok-Aral Dam and its gushing spillways, a Mad Max scene unfurled. A motorbike and sidecar zoomed past, carrying two men, swimming goggles strapped tight against their faces, sand and dust whipping up around them. A motorbike behind them followed closely steered by a man wearing wellington boots, waders and a vest. Old Russian jeeps moved in convoy. Ladas somehow struggled along, coming down the hill behind us. The Nissan Pathfinder did a good job on the barely-there roads but it was headache-inducingly rough and we were thrown from side to side. Serik concentrated, his face fixed and steady on the tyre marks in front. We arrived at slung-up awnings and tents, lining the dam. Long reeds appeared like gilded walking canes in the narrow waters surrounding the dam. They are here because of the return of fresh water, Serik said. It wasn't quite what the artist Igor Savitsky (who we will meet later) described, but it wasn't impossible to imagine the scene he painted either: 'the desert borders the oasis and forests, where low-lying but very unusual mountains suddenly create a feeling of a fantastic and at the same time very real world, and where the fishing villages along the blue Aral Sea drown in the gold of reeds.'

There were elements of natural beauty but as soon as we stopped at the dam, the dull-tang smell of fish – sharp and metallic – entered the car and as I stepped out I was met by an intense, masculine energy. The atmosphere at the dam and

the rough improvised camp set up by the fishermen exuded a savage lustiness. The men were dirty, they hadn't washed in days, and they had a crazed living-on-vodka-and-dried-fish look about them. This was definitely not a place to linger.

COSMODROME COOKS AND DESERT FISHERMEN

While there were no other women whatsoever, nor children, nor any sort of facility, there was fish. Carp, roach and pike-perch, the sort of fish that Kazakhs like and want to buy and eat. I walked to the water, stepping over fish flapping on the sandy ground. Rods were cast overhead. Leisure fishermen cast off from the side of the dam, while professional fishermen were further out, working in wooden rowboats. Vans arrived to buy fish directly from these men. Robert, a Tatar fisherman in his twenties, hung on to his red rubber dingy and stopped to talk. Shirtless, he had wrapped a thick woollen jumper over his shoulders.

'We're here for three weeks in the spring, then we go back to Shymkent. In the summer we come for longer, August, September, October we stay here for all of those months. We sleep in the car.' The boat started drifting out, and Robert waded after it laughing. Shymkent is a ten-hour drive away at least. This was hard work for not very much return and the haul looked small today, but who knows what he caught yesterday, or last week.

The holidaying fishermen, next to the dam's spillway, were well-fed middle-aged ethnic Russians, on their weekend break from Baikonur Cosmodrome. They became cagey when I asked about the spaceport. 'We cannot talk about Baikonur,' they said immediately when I showed interest.

'Did you celebrate Cosmonautics Day though?' I asked one man, Anatoli, who was born in Karaganda.

'The whole of Russia celebrated but we worked. I was in the kitchen, as usual. At Baikonur it was just another working day. We're here for a long weekend. A nice place to be, to fish and relax, drink beer.' I pressed him on what he cooked at the spaceport.

'We're not allowed to talk about Baikonur.'

'I like to cook. You must be able to tell me what you ate? Where's the harm in that?' With the mention of cooking, a shared interest, he relaxed, and dramatically kissed my hand. A door had opened.

'Russian food. Kasha for breakfast, open sandwiches, salads, Russian borscht. For Cosmonautics Day I prepared French-style dishes. A lot of meat with sauce. A feast to celebrate.'

Eager to leave the dam before it got dark, we drove fast past more fishermen, their legs and rods dangling from small sandy cliffs. Then we were back on the car-battering roads again, past banks of reeds, past tents and makeshift shelters, past a steel gate in the middle of the dusty, sandy steppe, nothing either side, two jumping, scaly golden fish bookending it, and a blue anchor on top. Blonde Bactrian camels knelt in the steppe by lonely graves. The car rattled.

Three hours later, back in Aralsk in time for sunset, Serik parked the car at the railway station and lifted the bonnet to examine the damage. I went inside to see the mural again. The tragedy was all there, in those tiles. The pride in serving the young USSR, and then being obliterated a few decades later by poor engineering and environmental practices. Many of the roads Serik drove on years ago, along the seabed, are now sluiced with water once more. Slowly, progress is happening and the water is getting closer to Aralsk. At the peak of the disaster, Aralsk's harbour was marooned, the water 95 miles away; now it is 20 miles away. The dam has also decreased salinity levels allowing some freshwater fish to return. Back outside, in front of the mint-green tsarist-era railway station built in 1905, Serik continued to poke around the engine, his face gloomy. I asked him about the future, what he hoped for.

'One day, I'd like to open my curtains in the morning and see water again, at the harbour.'

'But do you feel optimistic?'

'Yes, yes, I do. I think one day, there will be water again at the port in Aralsk. It is coming.' And as he closed the bonnet, I saw, just for a second, what looked like a smile forming at the corners of his mouth.

Shashlik with Bottled Tarragon Vinegar

On the way to Aralsk from the southern Kazakh city of Kyzylorda, there is a giant wind monument rising out of the steppe. Korkyt-Ata is dedicated to Khorkhyt, a legendary musician and philosopher known for inventing the kobyz, an ancient musical instrument made of two strings of horsehair. Built to resemble the kobyz, this giant concrete tribute is made of four identical, eight-metre-high tubes, each with an opening at the top and each containing a sound box made of 40 metal tubes. The idea is that they face the winds in different directions, and sing a mournful tune to the lonely steppe. My guidebook asserted that the wind never fails to blow here. But when I stood in the shadow of the monument, waiting to hear the mystical mournful steppe music, it was utterly still. Therefore there was not a peep. No sound at all.

Sloping off for lunch, slightly disappointed, I was buoyed by a roadside shashlik canteen. On each table stood a quart bottle of vodka and inside the glass bottle not alcohol but a few sprigs of fresh tarragon, white wine vinegar, a single clove of garlic and a whole submerged chilli for a hint of piquancy. A hole had been roughly drilled into each bottle lid for ease of splashing onto salads and the simple, but delicious, shashlik.

Four skewers are required for this recipe – if using wooden ones soak them first in water for 30 minutes. For the vinegar, you'll need to make it a week ahead to give the flavours time to infuse (or see the cheat's version below to make it now). For a variation, dill works well in place of the tarragon.

SERVES 4

500g/1lb 2oz lamb leg, fat trimmed, cut into 4cm/1½in pieces

1 tbsp olive oil, plus a little more for rubbing the skewers

1 tsp fine sea salt

Freshly ground black pepper

Non Bread (page 120), to serve

Pink Pickled Onions (page 88) or raw onions, thinly sliced, to serve

FOR THE DRESSING

40ml/2½ tbsp white wine vinegar

55ml/3½ tbsp cider vinegar

1 small fresh red chilli, left whole

1 large sprig of tarragon

1 garlic clove, peeled

To make the dressing, add the vinegars, chilli, tarragon and garlic clove to a sterilised glass bottle or jar. Seal and pierce a small hole into the lid (a corkscrew does the job). Leave to infuse for at least a week.

To make a dressing which can be used right away, crush the garlic and roughly chop the chilli. Add them to a small saucepan along with the two vinegars. Place over a medium heat and bring to a boil. Once it starts bubbling, reduce the heat to low and add the tarragon, simmering for 5 minutes. Take the pan off the heat and once cool, pour into a glass bottle or jar.

Preheat the grill to a hot setting. Rub the lamb with the olive oil then season well with salt and pepper. As your hands are oily now, rub the kebab skewers with the residue and thread the meat onto them.

Cook the skewers under the grill for 15 minutes, turning occasionally. Remove from the grill and leave to rest for 2–3 minutes. You may need to work in 2 batches; if so, tent the first batch in tin foil to keep them warm.

When ready, serve the lamb on the skewers with fresh non bread and pickled or raw onion. Splash the vinegar dressing onto each chunk of meat as you go.

Pink Pickled Onions

These bright-pink pickled onion rings pair beautifully with shashlik, plov and traditional fruit-based Uzbek salads but they are also a nice thing to have in the fridge for livening up sandwiches. I use apple cider vinegar with honey here as it adds an extra level of sweetness but you can use regular apple cider vinegar or white wine vinegar. These pickled onions will keep in a sterilised jar for 6 months unopened, or 2–3 weeks in the fridge once opened.

MAKES 1 X 450ML JAR

250ml/1 cup raw apple cider vinegar with honey

2 tbsp caster sugar

1 tbsp sea salt flakes

10 black peppercorns

1 star anise

1 tsp dill seeds

1 fresh bay leaf

2 garlic cloves, peeled

½ tsp yellow mustard seeds

3 small red onions, thinly sliced into rings

Firstly, sterilise the jar. Preheat the oven to 140°C/275°F/gas mark 1. Wash the jar and its lid in warm, soapy water, rinse well and place it on a clean baking tray. Transfer to the oven for about 15 minutes, and then leave to cool.

When you're ready to make the pickle, place all the ingredients, apart from the onions, in a saucepan over a medium heat and simmer for 10 minutes. In the sink, place the onions in a sieve and pour boiling water over them, drain and then spoon them into the sterilised jar. Pour over the warm vinegar mixture and let it cool completely before sealing and putting it into the fridge to pickle. Remove from the fridge after a couple of hours then transfer to a cool dark place such as a cupboard. It can be eaten right away but is best after a couple of days when the flavours have developed.

DIVE BAR

Drinking Kazakh beer and Irish whiskey

SHYMKENT, SOUTH KAZAKHSTAN: Shymkent, a former caravanserai on the Silk Road, is southern Kazakhstan's major city with leafy parks, a plentiful bazaar, sizzling roadside shashlik stands and open-air karaoke booths where singers belt out songs. It could not have felt more different from industrial Karaganda or frigid Nur-Sultan. This was a city busy fostering its own identity, prospering its own attitudes and ideas. It felt warm, tolerant and louche. Being located at least 1,000 miles south from the capital was perhaps its winning ingredient.

Yes, there was something about Shymkent. As soon as I arrived, it quietly but confidently made me lose the will for any further locomotion. With luck, it is also the perfect exit-point from Kazakhstan and into Uzbekistan, with Tashkent, the Uzbek capital, a mere two-hour drive away. I decided to stay a couple of nights.

FRIDAY NIGHT

Not knowing a soul in Shymkent, I'd been put in touch with a group of young writers ahead of my arrival who'd invited me to go and listen to an evening of Russian poetry. I'd marvelled at their poise and dedication. Meeting several times a week, the women all dressed in smart skirts and blouses and some of the men wore three-piece suits. They knew long Russian verses by heart, and all they drank was coffee. Cigarettes seemed their only vice.

We sat in a semi-circle at The Cups café, the room giddy with possibility, filled with youthfulness. As a Russian-Kazakh poet called Ulugbek stepped up to the stage, a man put a book of Osip Mandelstam in my hands. Ulugbek began reciting his own heartfelt poems. The metal studs of his leather jacket caught the light and occasionally, a pianist would play compositions between stanzas, furniture music really, giving some of the young women in the audience a chance to catch their breath. Rarely had I seen an audience so enraptured. After an hour, Ulugbek pushed away the microphone stand, rubbed his fists into his wet eye sockets and threw off his jacket. Love poetry. The young Shymkent poets clapped. His reading was over, and five women queued to give him rose bouquets. Later I went to another café with the poets to talk about politics, the future and books. One poet considered her love life and the plate of food set down before her: 'A man can be an introvert, or not very talkative, but his food can communicate for him.' I noted this down.

But what I really wanted, needed in fact, lay in wait, saloon-style, down the road from my unusually nice hotel run by a gentle and charming man called Vladimir Lee. Yes, the Nash Bar looked perfect.

A particular mood had taken me and I was in for a drinking session. Several things need to be in your favour for a successful night of boozing: you should be in good health, not stressed, and certainly not argumentative or maudlin, you need plenty of time, a relatively anonymous setting, an outside smoking area (shipshape and swept), there must be no groups of drinkers dominating the space and the music must be good (just loud enough to mask the conversation of others). The drinks must be affordable, the staff helpful and alert but not over-familiar and the bar should be clean and dimly lit, and under it, there ought to be a foot rail or else coat hooks. Contrary to what amateur drinkers think, the drinks themselves are of little importance: one decent gin, whiskey or vodka plus one good beer on tap, is enough. The Nash Bar had most of those things. And it had the best beer in Kazakhstan, Shymkentskoe, on tap, at less than $1 a pint. Served in a dimpled glass tankard, it was fizzy, slightly citrusy and cold. I started with a couple of those. A four-piece band from up north in Petropavl came on stage and the room filled up with more drinkers. I sat on a spinny stool at the bar and watched. A group of ethnic Russians came in, dressed in sportswear and tracksuits, lines of bad luck knitted on their brows. They crowded around one table, ordering beer and vodka. Were they exuding an air of potential violence? Maybe. But for everyone else the booze sparked pleasure circuits. Generally, it was a nice scene with none of the soaked and dead-eyed men that Russians call 'partial suicides' hovering about.

Soon enough, everything began to fall loose and fast. Goth girls sipped spirits with Coke at tables, Kazakh women danced, their confidence newly jimmied open. The band did a decent ska-style version of 'Eye of the Tiger', and all eyes turned to the drummer, whose back, bowed like a whip over the kit, went for it. It was sweaty at the bar and lacking dinner, I ate twines of salty, smoky chechil cheese, the best beer snacks there are. Then, a tumbler of Irish whiskey, the warmth of it rising slowly upwards through my legs, towards my spine. First whiskey, second whiskey, then whiskey drinks the drinker, so they say, but we were just getting going with a cover of Gorky Park's 'Moscow Calling' from the early '90s, and this set off something in the prostitutes at the bar, all red leather jackets, gyrating denim and greasy slicks of red lipstick. They crowded me while winking at the men dressed in tracksuits. One, guessing I was foreign, asked for a selfie with liquor breath. I don't ever want to see that photograph. Men eventually bought them drinks and they left one by one. I worried about them in an abstract way that made me feel guilty and weak, which meant I surrendered to another whiskey, and maybe another, sipping tomorrow's hangover slowly but surely. Then I found the smoker's corner outside and joined in with a packet of Parliament Aqua Blue. First, a quick gasp from cold air sucked in, then a warm chest glow from the sweet smoke. I indulged the urge, the brief short-lived thrill of the cigarette that would

make the hangover so much worse. The night was merry, tomorrow would be deep and dire. Then, just as I wished the night could lollop along a little longer, two big small words ended it with the precision of a guillotine: 'closing time'.

The next morning, I sat soporific in front of a fish tank at breakfast while Vladimir Lee – his shirt pressed, his air organised – cheerily served sausages and bread in the hotel's café. A group of four men in their sixties were toasting some sort of deal with a carafe of vodka. It was no later than 9.30 a.m. I ate, and then walked through weak springtime rain, to the Metallurgists' Park. Unlike the Nash Bar, the park is full of rules. Don't stand on the sprinklers. Don't walk on the grass. No dogs. No littering. The acacia trees irritated my sinuses with their blooming while the whiskey sweated out. Inside the park, the old Palace of Culture rotted silently while a monumental gold-hued statue of Lenin stood glistening with rain. The air smelled of eggs, petrol and wet grass. A little later, the poets would meet again, by a statue of Al-Farabi, one of the great thinkers of the Islamic Golden Age. I wouldn't join them, as much as I liked them. I'd stay in Shymkent a few more days then travel overland to Tashkent. On long journeys such as this, it is important to let loose occasionally, to unwind and stop moving. To be at home in the world, wherever that might be.

Vladimir Lee's Kimchi

By the time I reached Vladimir Lee's excellent Orbita Boutique Hotel in Shymkent I'd not eaten anything spicy or chilli-laden for weeks. Lee's fried kimchi, served on plain white rice, was as welcome as it was warm, sour and hot. I ate it for both lunch and dinner over two days.

I had a few trials with cabbage and salt while testing kimchi. My tips are: ensure your cabbage is as fresh as possible, I found that old cabbage leaves do not soak up salt very well, resulting in a brine that is way too salty. The second important tip relates to the type of salt used; I once tried making a batch with regular table salt, and again, it was far too salty for my taste (and was binned). I found that crushed sea salt flakes give just the right saltiness. When mixing the kimchi, food-safe gloves to protect hands and eyes from the gochugaru chilli powder are a good idea.

MAKES 1 X 1-LITRE JAR

1 Chinese (Napa) cabbage, fresh as possible, quartered lengthwise through the stem (removing the tough core at the base) and cut into bite-size pieces

3 tbsp sea salt flakes, crushed with a pestle and mortar

1 small carrot, julienned

1 red or yellow (bell) pepper, thinly sliced

3 spring onions (scallions), thinly sliced lengthways

FOR THE PASTE

4cm/1½in piece of ginger, peeled and grated

2 garlic cloves, peeled and crushed

2 tbsp gochugaru

2 tbsp rice vinegar

1 tbsp tamari

1 tbsp fish sauce

Basmati rice, to serve

To ferment safely, you'll need to spoon your kimchi into a sterilised jar. Preheat the oven to 140°C/275°F/gas mark 1. Wash the jar in warm, soapy water, rinse well and place it on a clean baking tray. Transfer to the oven for about 15 minutes, and then leave to cool. To sterilise the lid or rubber seal, boil them in a large saucepan for 5 minutes then drain and leave them to air dry on a rack.

Put the cabbage into a large bowl and rub the salt through it, scrunching it with your hands to make sure it's applied evenly. Let it sit for 1½ hours.

Combine the ingredients for the paste in a mixing bowl. Add the cabbage (including the brine that's been created by salting it) and the other vegetables, and use your hands to work the paste thoroughly through the mixture.

Decant it into a large sterilised jar. Push the kimchi down, packing it tightly into the jar. This should cause brine to come up over the level of the vegetables. If not, take another smaller sterilised jar filled with cold water and place it on top of the vegetables to weigh them down. You want to make sure that the kimchi stays under the brine – and therefore, vitally, avoids contact with oxygen – while it ferments. If using a clip-top jar, remove the rubber ring – that way gases are allowed to escape.

Leave to ferment at room temperature, out of direct sunlight, for five or so days. Check on the kimchi daily and press the vegetables down if necessary, making sure they stay submerged below the brine.

Five days is usually about right, but the best way to know if your kimchi is ready is by tasting it. Once it's fermented to the level you're happy with, put the jar in the fridge, where it will keep happily for weeks, if not months.

You can eat it on its own or, to serve it as Vladimir Lee did, simply fry it in a little sesame or vegetable oil and serve it with basmati rice.

WRITER'S HOSTEL
Reflecting upon poets and painters

TASHKENT, NORTHEAST UZBEKISTAN: Rows of buttermilk-coloured apartment blocks line Tashkent's Mirzo Ulugbek Avenue. Drag race-straight, the busy street is bookended roughly by Botkin Cemetery, the city's oldest Christian graveyard, and a children's TB sanatorium. In the middle is the Great Silk Road metro station. An asteroid and moon crater are also named after Ulugbek, 15th-century astronomer, husband to 13 wives and grandson of nomadic warlord and emperor of Samarkand, Tamerlane.

I'd rented an apartment for a couple of weeks, just off the main street where nobody bothers you and nobody stares. A solid Soviet-built apartment scenario, safe and quiet. Only the clattering myna birds dominated with their croaks, squawks, chirps, clicks, whistles and growls. The lanes between the blocks were green, fruitful, leafy and productive, and windowed balconies provided shelter for laundry and caged birds. Inside the dusty shared stairwells, similar to Scotland's tenements, laminated calendars, depicting labradors and Japanese snow monkeys, covered the worst wall cracks. Some mornings, I'd go to the shop under my apartment to buy breakfast: a large golden non bread, bulbous sugary-pink tomatoes and bottles of thick, ice-cold kefir. Maybe cherries. None of it imported. Here, a seller will tell you his walnuts are from Samarkand, his apricots are from Fergana. Often, I'd buy a potato samsa and eat it messily as I went back up the stairwell.

In the afternoon, drivers positioned their cars in the thin tree-shaded lanes that snake through the apartment blocks, popping open their boots to show off their produce: snowy-white cauliflowers and buckets of strawberries, the heart-shaped berries of spring, not summer, in Uzbekistan. A freestanding weighing scale would be set out on the concrete and the seller would sit back and wait for buyers. I watched as one sold-out vendor packed his weighing scale back up and, reversing out of the block, licked the fingers of his right hand and counted the banknotes straight onto his ballooned belly. At night, cats roamed for bones, and small dogs dressed in padded coats were led along by women who would smile and say good evening in Russian. Windows at the foot of the bed were always left wide open to let in the night, and the dark unreachable sky. I'd open the curtains in the morning to look for swallows, wagtails and swifts.

Taxi drivers do not know this address. They know it only as the 'artists' quarter' in Russian. Housed here during the Soviet period, the artists have long gone but their ghosts hang on because Tashkent is a city of artists, and of writers and poets. But more than that, it is a city of bread. Symbolising nurture and plenty, bread became an emblem of this city and its ability to shelter the needy.

South from Moscow, and with relatively mild winters, Tashkent had a reputation for generosity and reliable local harvests during times of hunger. Away from the frontlines, in June 1941 when Hitler's armies invaded the USSR, it became a magnet for evacuated Russian writers. The European-style section of the city, built in the late 19th century by Russian colonisers, looked familiar to Leningraders and Muscovites with its Russian-style houses and gardens. The officers who'd advanced southwards, crossing the Kazakh steppe in the 1860s, had found no backwater in Tashkent, but rather a garden city, an artisanal city with a healthy economy, set in a fertile valley fed by the Chirchik River. Many mahallas ('neighbourhoods') shared giant allotments on the outskirts of the city, looked after by cooperatives. The city's main bazaar had over 2,000 shops. Long a stop on the Silk Road, from Tashkent camel caravans went north to Moscow while others went south to trade with Afghanistan. Luxury fruits, winter melons and golden peaches went to Chinese and Mughal emperors. Oasis merchants, travelling east-to-west and vice-versa, carried plums, Chinese cut tobacco, pears, pomegranates, pistachios, cinnamon, star anise, gold brocade. Walrus tusks went to Bukhara where artisans would carve them into abacuses and dagger handles.

Tashkent was never irrelevant but, until recently, it was ignored. Sealed off and repressive during the late Uzbek president Islam Karimov's long autocratic reign from 1989 to 2016. And now his time is over.

7 KARL MARX STREET, CITY OF BREAD

At Efendi, a failsafe Turkish restaurant at which I ate lunch every other day, I discussed these things with local historian Boris Golender. I found him, dressed in a heavy tan leather jacket and a thick woollen sweater, sitting under a poster advertising a Turkish beach resort. It was April but Tashkent was dressed for November. Outside, rain hammered clusters of pink roses, scattering their petals. We'd talk first, and then eat, we agreed. For now, we asked the waiter to keep the tea coming. You cannot get a drink here.

'Where you are staying is one of three quarters built for artists in Tashkent during Soviet times. Many artists lived in those blocks,' Golender said, counting off Russian and Uzbek avant-garde artists working in the 1920s and '30s, on his hands. Alexander Volkov ('close to Picasso in his brilliance'), Alexei Isupov ('when not in Rome, he was here') and Nikolay Karakhan. His moustache twitched and his thick glasses bobbed on his nose as he spoke, but otherwise Golender sat still as a statue. By the time the great Russian poet, Anna Akhmatova, arrived in Tashkent in October 1941, she had witnessed many different Russias: from her Black Sea youth to the horrors of Stalinism. In 1921 her ex-husband, Nikolay Gumilyov, was shot. In 1925 her poetry, considered anti-revolutionary, was banned in the Soviet Union until 1940. By the mid-

1930s her police file ran to hundreds of pages. Her son had been arrested and rearrested.

Fleeing under-siege Leningrad, Akhmatova travelled first to Chistopol in Tatarstan, and then on to Tashkent. She stayed in Tashkent for three years, finding inspiration in a city many evacuees considered luminous and exotic even during a time of hardship for the entire Soviet Union. Inspired by the sunbeams, almond and apricot trees, Uzbekistan's fabled fruit began to drop into Akhmatova's lyrics: the moon as a slice of melon, the pomegranate bush as a 'royal dwarf'.

'Tashkent, city of bread' is a phrase still heard today. The city's reputation to feed and house the hungry was on the minds of those, like Akhmatova, who arrived. Golender and I talked about Shukhrat Abbasov, father of Uzbek cinema, who used bread as an emblem for Tashkent's ability to shelter the needy in his popular film *Tashkent – City of Bread* from 1968. Based on the book by Alexander Neverov, the film follows a young boy's journey during the 1921 famine from the Volga region to the Uzbek capital where he manages to buy grain for his starving family. Abbasov's film cemented the city's reputation as a place of relative abundance in a region often tormented by rationing, war and famine.

Today in Tashkent, tandoor ovens are still used to produce golden non bread, dense roundels with thick, crusty bottoms and soft, chewy tops, just as they have done for centuries. Bread is central to Uzbek culture: a soldier going away will be given bread to take, and a loaf will be hung in his absence until he safely returns. The anxious may place bready scraps under bedtime pillows, in the hope that birds will fly away with crumbs at night, taking demons with them. The bread baking process is a basic but time-honoured practice and it is famously hard to imitate. The Soviets tried in vain, mechanising bread production in the 1970s, but Uzbeks were unimpressed, spurning the state-made bread and returning to the tandoor.

The after-work crowd piled into Efendi. Plates clattered and were cleared around us. Canteen-like in its scale and efficiency, serving everyone from students to ambassadors; if Efendi is open, it is never empty. The waiters moved at speed across the tiles, ferrying plate upon plate of puff lavash bread – round as balloons – saj kebab and sticky baklava to tables already loaded with nigella-scented bread, soup and salads. We kept talking but caved in – the smell of grilled meat and fresh bread was too much. We asked for the menu. Boris ordered Iskander kebab, I asked for lentil soup. Both are Efendi's forte. Bread arrived first in a wicker basket, warm and pudgy and flecked with black onion seeds. Golender tore it up, handing pieces to me in the Uzbek way.

When Akhmatova arrived in Tashkent, some say she had in her hand three movements of Shostakovich's Seventh Symphony, a monumental work of 78 minutes, incorporating eight horns, six trombones, three drums and two harps. Powerful war music. Composed during the summer of 1941, it is one of Shostakovich's greatest works, known as the *Leningrad Symphony*.

'Arriving on Stalin's order was a little weird, of course, as he did not like her, but instead of executing her, he sent her away. So we could say Stalin saved her life. And it was here, in Tashkent, that Anna had her second major artistic inspiration,' said Golender, sipping his Turkish tea, red as blood in its tulip-shaped glass.

Akhmatova took a room at the 'Hostel for Moscow Writers', 7 Karl Marx Street. The writers called this residential area Noah's Ark, because of all the sheltering families, Golender explained. The hostel had previously been the consul of Afghanistan, and Akhmatova found herself bedding down in a room that was once the cashier's office.

'The room was eight metres square, not meant for sleeping in. It had a hatch where previously passports and money were passed through. Anna was the poorest poet of all in Tashkent because she did not write for the power in charge. And, she was very poor because she'd not been published in so long. Others laughed that she slept there. The irony of staying in the cashier's office.'

She then moved to 54 Zhukovskaya Street, a clay-built Russian house with a balakhan-style balcony, a tiny mezzanine that hangs over the street. Sometimes, she shared her living quarters with Osip Mandelstam's wife, Nadezhda – a trusted friend who memorised her poems – and it was there she stayed up late drinking with the comedian Faina Ranevskaya, who would bring bags of peaches and firewood for the stove, and who'd tickle Anna's feet. They'd walk in Tashkent's markets together and drink tea with vodka. In her Central Asian poem cycle, *The Moon at Zenith*, Akhmatova wrote:

'My Asian house is sound,
And I can be tranquil . . .'

The composer Alexey Fedorovich Koslovsky visited. Elena Bulgakova circulated banned scripts of her late husband's book, *The Master and Margarita*. Jóseph Czapski, the Polish artist who belonged to the Cézanne-centric Kapist movement, listened to Akhmatova chanting her poems. Nikolai Punin, best remembered as hero of the Russian avant-garde and Commissar of the Hermitage and Russian Museums, lived a while in Samarkand, and had a relationship with

Akhmatova. Despite the potential for evacuation loneliness, Tashkent did not feel foreign to Akhmatova. Together, all were penniless under a warm Uzbek sun.

Such ease came, perhaps, from her roots. Akhmatova's real name was Gorenko. When her father objected to her signing her family name under her poems she took the name Akhmatova. Some historians trace the name Gorenko back to a relative of Genghis Khan, Achmat Khan, who belonged to the 13th century khanate, the Golden Horde.

BREAD ROLLS, BREAD RIOTS

Akhmatova got typhoid twice in Tashkent and recovered just 40 metres away from Efendi. Often dreamy, sometimes feverish, her mind swam with dark visions of her beloved Leningrad: crows circling, bells ringing, dark cathedrals, bodies in the street, in the shadow of Orthodox churches, the beautiful gilt of their cupolas destroyed. It was here that she wrote the nationalistic poem, 'Courage' ('The bravest hour strikes our clocks: may courage not abandon us!'). Back in Russia, she wrote that in Uzbekistan she had 'learned the meaning of human kindness.'

Her cycle *The Moon at Zenith*, written in Tashkent, contains some of her finest works and by 1944, local bread had slipped into her lyrics:

'I will remember the roof of stars,
in the radiance of eternal glory,
and the small rolls of bread
in the young hands
of dark-haired mothers'

'The poets felt a need to perform here in Tashkent, so they'd have salons but they'd also read in hospitals.' Golender said, wiping his hands. Belarusian poet Edi Ognetsvet, a friend of Akhmatova, captured the generosity, and the beauty of Tashkent's bread, in her evocative poem 'Uzbek Sky'.

'You've saved me, you've given me shelter —
you've given me sunshine and bread.
As long as I live, I'll remember
Tashkent's golden sky overhead.'

'A woman I knew, told me that for years she thought Anna was dead, there had been no news of her for years in Tashkent. Then one day she was looking out of her window and Anna simply walked slowly past. She said it was a miracle. Like seeing a ghost.' Today, you cannot find Akhmatova in bricks and mortar, and there are no plaques commemorating where she spent time in Tashkent. But there is value in searching for her spirit, of being present and of walking the streets that she once walked.

Boris ate his baklava and the bill arrived. I asked him about the winter of 1992, when *The New York Times* reported that thousands of Tashkent students, already enraged by soaring prices due to free-market changes, only really set about rioting once deliveries of bread failed. Golender does not remember this event. Could the reporter have been wrong, I asked?

'I don't remember it, if it happened at all,' he replied, releasing a weak sigh. Golender finds none of this particularly remarkable. Not the bread riots, not the city as bread analogy, nor the fact that Akhmatova's work is entwined with the city. Why should he? He knows it all so well. But Tashkent as the 'city of bread' sums up part of the appeal of this busy capital. Generosity and community are as basic and vital here as bread itself. Food again, proving a useful passport to the past and a means of revealing an alternative portrait of place.

As I stood to leave he stopped me. I knew what he was going to say before he said it. 'You asked me, is Tashkent still the most important city in Central Asia? This is my answer. There are five capitals in Central Asia, but none can compete with Tashkent. The others are small cities. From here you can go east to China, north to Russia, west to Europe and south to Afghanistan. Tashkent, you see, is not just the capital of Central Asia, it is, in many ways, the capital of the world.'

A Bread Pudding for Anna Akhmatova

With the culinary powers of Tashkent's legendary bread bakers in mind, this is a popular pudding combined with a few classic Silk Road bazaar flavours. It is inspired by that old question: Which six people, living or dead, would you invite to dinner? Anna Akhmatova would be top of my list and I'd serve this pudding for dessert, in the hope she'd like it. The cardamom and dried pear halves really make this dish.

SERVES 6

35g/2 tbsp salted butter, softened, plus extra for greasing

6 slices white bread, crusts cut off

2 cardamom pods, seeds removed

170g/1 cup dried fruit (I use a mix of raisins, apricots, cranberries and pear halves), larger fruits cut into bite-size pieces

½ tsp ground cinnamon

350ml/1½ cups milk

50ml/3 tbsp double (heavy) cream

2 eggs

1 tbsp cornflour (cornstarch)

3 tbsp granulated sugar

½ tsp ground nutmeg

Single cream, to serve (optional)

Grease a deep-sided 1-litre/2-pint baking dish.

Butter each slice of bread on one side and cut each slice into 4 triangles. Place the cardamom seeds in a frying pan and dry-fry over a medium heat for 2–3 minutes, tossing occasionally. Remove from the frying pan and crush them lightly using a pestle and mortar. In a bowl, mix together the dried fruit, cinnamon and cardamom.

Arrange a layer of bread triangles on the bottom of the dish, buttered side up. Sprinkle over some of the dried fruit and spice mixture, and then top with another layer of bread triangles. Repeat until you've used up the bread and fruit, making sure the top layer is bread.

Next, in a small saucepan, gently warm the milk and cream, bringing it to just below boiling point (taking care not to let it boil). Then, in a bowl, whisk together the eggs, cornflour and 2 tablespoons of the sugar until pale and a little frothy. Slowly pour the milk and cream into the egg mixture, whisking as you go until smooth and well combined. Pour this evenly over the bread, and sprinkle over the remaining tablespoon of sugar and the nutmeg. Leave to rest for 30 minutes and preheat the oven to 170°C/325°F/gas mark 3.

Bake for 30–40 minutes until the creamy custard has set and the top is golden. Serve warm with a jug of very cold cream.

STOLOVAYA

Witnessing Easter in the capital

TASHKENT, NORTHEAST UZBEKISTAN: Springtime thunderclaps echoed around the Tashkent neighbourhood I was staying in, sending children hollering. By midnight, the storm had tapered off but my duvet, under which I sweated and rattled, had become a malevolent and heavy cloud. I cursed the fever that made rooms and beds feel wicked; the everyday and ordinary, sinister. Flushed delirium had, I remembered, interrupted another journey in Uzbekistan, a couple of years ago in Bukhara, also in April, when the weather is wildly changeable: rain, sun, cold, hot. Back then, the distemper had completely cleared within 24 hours. No explanation, no lingering symptoms. A peculiar spring fever.

Clattering myna birds, combined with the sun's warm fingers stretching in through slatted blinds, forced me up the next morning. Remedying myself with sugary-pink tomatoes and a glass of cold kefir I went out, feeling a little better. It was Sunday and therefore quiet, and the air above the acacia-lined pavements was thick with pollen and the uniquely musky, melon-y smell of Central Asia. Within a few minutes I was at U Babushki, my morning café. A reliable stalwart.

The café is a spruced-up pastiche, or parody, of a stolovaya, the utilitarian cafeterias of Soviet Russia, with everything served canteen-style. Traditional, predictable tastes of the past dominate the counters: white bread, milk, porridge, fried turnovers, cutlets and stews. All are cooked well. And when convalescing, isn't food reminiscent of childhood what you want, even if it is not exactly the food of your own upbringing? U Babushki, where the menu rarely changes, felt like a place of improvement. A place where you carry a tray to a clean table and sit down to eat unfussy food, in peace. There are no unwanted surprises here, which is good as surprises are a menace in restaurants, and especially so at breakfast.

Of course it isn't perfect. The lively fairytale decor – all Russian florals, horses and babushkas in bonnets – is comforting in its simplicity but also kitsch and distracting. Plus, sleeplessness had left me particularly alert to the smell of fish being fried ahead of the lunchtime service and the sound of servers slopping out kasha from steel ladles. The floor was constantly swept and sloshed with water, with little regard for tray-carrying diners.

I moved carefully down the slippery lane, pushing my tray along the line with one hand, while using tongs to pick up a trio of small pancakes stuffed with snow-white tvorog. Towards the drinks counter, I took a pot of blueberry jam, some sour cream and added a glass of quince mors to the tray. As I queued, next to a row of shiny samovars garlanded with ropes of bagel-like baranki, I procured a tea bag and filled a mug with hot water from a shared kettle. I paid and sat down. I'd become used to the system and how it worked, having eaten here a few times. There was also a certain place I liked to sit. Slowly, I'd started to make U Babushki mine. The familiarity settled and comforted my fever, as I knew it would.

Once, many traditional versions of this canteen space existed in Tashkent, but newer cafés have replaced them. Isn't it strange to have this reproduction stolovaya when so many authentic ones have gone? From the book *Basics of Culinary Technique*, published in Moscow in 1930, comes this viewpoint, very much of its time, on stolovaya dining: 'Thanks to the Great October Revolution, other goals stand before contemporary cuisine: not to slake the capricious tastes of the perverted bourgeoisie and not to dote upon French cuisine with its incomprehensible terminology, but rather to provide a mass, healthy, and nourishing dinner to a new customer, the worker, who comes to the cafeteria not to gorge, but rather to dine healthily, deliciously, and nourishingly – to receive new calories.'

Orthodox Easter celebrations had just begun in Tashkent. Waitresses in frilly aprons marched past me, bringing out baskets of painted eggs and individually baked Russian Easter breads called kulich, a cross between Italian panettone and hot cross buns but denser than both. Each one had been topped in the traditional way with snow-white icing and hundreds and thousands in their rainbow colours. They displayed the eggs and bread with care around the café. Feeling stronger, I left U Babushki to seek out Tashkent's Easter celebrations.

SCOTCH REELS AND EASTER CAKES

Barriers for crowd control were still up following last night's midnight celebrations at the blue-painted and gold-domed Holy Assumption Cathedral. I squeezed past the barricades, pulling a scarf over my head, as I went. In front of the porch, a dozen tables had been set up displaying kulich for sale, each one iced with the letters X and B meaning, Христосъ Воскресе, 'Christ is Risen'. Others sold jam. There was just a whiff of the farmers' market about it all. Trays, baskets, buckets and carrier bags were all filled with painted eggs, thin candles and wrapped sweets. Some babushki had decorated their kulichi with marzipan chicks and strawberries. One seller had set up an entire shed of kulich, with stacked wooden trays spilling over with them. The church grounds had transformed into a kulich world, just like the popular artwork by the Russian illustrator Ivan Bilibin, prominent in the 20th century, that includes these words:

'Kulich-city is standing, glorifying itself;
Lauding itself over other cities;
There is no other place better than me!;
For I am all dough!'

And, isn't that the point of glorious festival food? Made by many hands and extolling age-old traditions, it must be bountiful, rich and dazzling, produced for a particular time of year, and that time of year only.

A pair of large fabric ornamental eggs flanked the entrance where crowds jostled, waiting for the priest. Slowly, he came out into the sun, a long plait of blonde hair down his back, flanked by his clergy, all of them glowing in red, orange and gold liturgical robes. The priest walked slowly, flicking holy water over the heads and holy kulichi of the congregation. Inside the cathedral, dust motes flickered in the hushed air as sunshine poured in through the stained glass windows. Together, carrying their baskets of cakes and bread, women lit hundreds of candles and paid their respects to the icons.

It was an Easter scene similar to the one witnessed by Isabella 'Ella' Robertson Christie, the pioneering Scottish traveller, author and gardener, widely believed to be the first British woman ever to visit Khiva. In a chapter entitled 'A Russian Easter' from her book *Through Khiva to Golden Samarkand*, she stays with a Swiss-French couple, the Müllers, in Tashkent, where she enjoys a 'deliciously light' Easter cake, made with 85 eggs. She attended the Russian church, and marvelled at the gowns. Tashkent was a very 'dressy' place, she wrote, noting that the holy city of Bukhara was, by contrast, a 'sheepy' place because first you eat them and then you wear them as hats or coats. Here, she noted the 'elaborate cakes' and 'the blessing of bread' and because it was a busy scene, she feared gauze hats could be set alight by procession-goers carrying wax tapers. Over a supper of veal, apple tart and local red wine, served by her hosts on 'Easter Day', she wrote: 'We had music after feasting: Caucasian airs, which must resemble Scotch reels, and the picture of the sword dance seemed quite familiar.'

Ella Christie was as formidable as she was sharp-eyed. A few years ago, I had lunch with her great-nephew, Robert Christie Stewart, at his home in Clackmannanshire, Scotland. At the dining table, we flicked through boxes of her black-and-white photographs, most no bigger than a playing card. The pictures showed what had changed in Uzbekistan, and what had stayed the same. Robert remembered his great-aunt Ella as a generous woman. But she hated social chitchat. A man on the platform at the nearby railway station in Dollar once asked if she was going to Edinburgh for the day. 'No,' she shot back. 'I am going to Samarkand!'

In Uzbek mahallas she noted how in spring the roofs of houses, made with plastered mud and straw that carried seeds from the meadows, had magnificently blossomed with 'masses of poppies and other field flowers'. It was to Tashkent's mahallas I was headed next to see how they had changed as the capital tentatively opens up to the world.

Kulich - Russian Easter Bread

Taste and texture-wise, these cakes, cooked in cans, are a cross between a panettone and a hot cross bun, with added drama from the height and the icing. You'll need four empty 400g/14oz cans (the sort you find chopped tomatoes or baked beans in). Soak off the label and clean them thoroughly before use.

MAKES 4 SMALL BREADS

50g/3½ tbsp unsalted butter, cubed, plus a little extra for greasing

350g/2¾ cups strong white bread flour

1 tsp ground mixed spice

½ tsp fine sea salt

85g/⅔ cup caster (superfine) sugar

2 x 7g/2¼ tsp sachets fast-action yeast

150ml/⅔ cup tepid milk

1 egg, beaten

½ tsp vanilla extract

½ tsp almond extract

A pinch of saffron threads, steeped in 1 tbsp of boiling water

40g/¼ cup raisins

40g/¼ cup unsulphured dried apricots, cut into pea-size chunks

1 tbsp lemon zest

FOR THE ICING

120g/1¼ cups icing (confectioner's) sugar

Juice of ½ lemon

¼ tsp almond extract

Hundreds and thousands, to decorate

Firstly, prepare your cans. Lightly grease the inside of each can with butter, then cut out rectangles of non-stick baking parchment, roughly 30 x 14cm (12 x 6in) – these line the insides of the cans as well as extending over the top (helping to remove the loaves once cooked) – and cut out a circle for the base of each can.

Sift the flour into a large mixing bowl along with the mixed spice, and then rub in the butter until you have a breadcrumb consistency. Form a well in the middle of the flour, adding the salt and sugar to one side, and the yeast to the other. Into the well, pour all of the milk, egg, vanilla and almond extracts, and strain in the saffron water using a sieve (you don't want the strands). Using a wooden spoon, mix until you have a dough.

Turn out onto a lightly floured surface and knead. It will be gluey, but persevere and keep kneading for 10–12 minutes (a dough scraper is helpful here) until most of the stickiness has gone, then knead in the raisins, apricots and lemon zest. Grease the bottom of the mixing bowl and add the dough back in. Cover the bowl with a clean, wet tea towel (this stops it from drying out) and place it in a warm spot for an hour. The dough will rise a little during this stage but not a lot.

Place the dough on a flour-dusted surface, and knock out the air by folding the dough in on itself a few times. Shape into a ball, put it back in the mixing bowl covered by a tea towel and leave to prove for 30 minutes, again in a warm place.

Preheat the oven to 200°C/400°F/gas mark 6. Divide the dough into 4 equal balls (each weighing around 210g/7½oz), then shape into oblongs and place in the lined cans. Leave them for 30 minutes in a warm place to rise a little.

Bake for around 30 minutes until golden, checking on them about halfway through and tenting them with tin foil if the tops are catching at all.

When baked, remove the bread from the tins carefully; a little shake should do it – don't pull them out by the domed crowns or you'll rip the dough. Tap the bottom of the buns – they should sound hollow. Leave to cool on a wire rack.

Sift the icing sugar into a bowl, gradually add the lemon juice and almond extract until you have a thick icing that will still run lazily down the sides of the kulich, as is traditional. If it's too thick add a few drops of water.

Once the breads are cool, pour over the icing and scatter hundreds and thousands on the top of each one. Serve with a pot of breakfast tea.

Tashkent Fever

What sort of refreshing cocktail can sharpen the brain and cool the tail-end of a springtime fever? One with a lot of ice, some vodka, some pomegranate juice (so beloved by Central Asians) a dash of lime and the aroma of the sort of small-ish not-too-sweet strawberries that fill Tashkent's markets. The strawberry split upon the glass offers a glorious scent as you sip.

MAKES 1 COCKTAIL

FOR THE SIMPLE SUGAR SYRUP

15ml/1 tbsp water

15g/1 tbsp granulated sugar

(If you like you can make more than this recipe requires but keep to the 1:1 ratio of sugar and water)

2 ice cubes

40ml/2 ½ tbsp vodka

50ml/3 tbsp pure pomegranate juice (not sweetened or from concentrate)

Juice of ½ lime

1 strawberry, sliced lengthways up to the stalk, to decorate

To make the syrup, combine the sugar and water in a small saucepan and slowly bring to a boil, stirring all the time until the sugar dissolves. Remove from the heat and allow to cool.

Add the ice to a tumbler and pour over the vodka. Top with pomegranate juice, simple syrup and lime juice. Stir a couple of times. Decorate the glass with the split strawberry.

Ella's Carrot and Honey 'Jam'

Just before Ella Christie crossed into Uzbekistan in 1912, travelling by steamer on the Oxus River from Turkmenistan, she noted a curious preserve, 'a special kind of marmalade made of finely chopped carrots in honey'. I love the idea of this and have created a version here, it is not very jammy, but with a beguiling hint of cinnamon it is good on hot heavily buttered toast.

MAKES ENOUGH TO FILL 4 X 200G/7OZ JARS

600g/1lb 4oz carrots, coarsely grated

2 lemons, zested and juiced

1 small orange, zested and juiced

450g/2¼ cups granulated sugar

2 tbsp runny honey

2 cinnamon sticks

1 tsp fine salt

¼ tsp vanilla extract

400ml/1⅔ cups water

Add all of the ingredients, apart from the water, to a medium-size saucepan. Gently stir and then let the mixture rest in the pan overnight, covered, to soak up the flavours.

Once the carrot mixture has steeped for about 12 hours, add the water to the saucepan. Bring to a boil and maintain a rolling boil for 40 minutes.

While the jam is cooking, sterilise the jars. Preheat the oven to 140°C/275°F/gas mark 1. Wash the jars in warm, soapy water, rinse well and place them on a clean baking tray. Transfer to the oven for about 15 minutes. To sterilise lids or rubber seals, boil them in a large saucepan for 5 minutes, then drain and leave them to air dry on a rack. Leave the jars in the warm oven until the jam is ready to be potted up.

After 40 minutes of boiling, the foamy bubbles should have gone and the jam ought to look glossy and thick. This is not a particularly jammy jam and while it is sticky, it will not 'set' as such.

Leave the mixture to settle for 10 minutes and then scoop the jam into the hot jars – a ladle and a jam funnel are very helpful here – and seal. You can keep the cinnamon sticks in if you like.

You can eat it right away but once the jar has been opened, refrigerate. It'll keep for around three months.

MAHALLA

Exploring the Old City

TASHKENT, NORTHEAST UZBEKISTAN: If cities and districts are like people with their own distinct personalities, souls and quirks, as indeed they often are, then Old Tashkent is the capital at its warmest and most enticing. With ancient fruit trees entangled with kites, tiny fruit shops and narrow canals, this is where lives are more or less played out as they have been for centuries, the atmosphere retaining the air of a small provincial Uzbek town where elders have the last say.

Deep in the walled mahallas of Old Tashkent, much life is hidden from view but the occasional open door offers glimpses of courtyards filled with families, laundry, caged birds, laughter and food. On corners are quiet vine-shrouded chaikhanas ('teahouses'), built for contemplation, next to old bakeries with tiny windows and serving hatches. Bicycles go silently through dusty disorientating alleys and lanes of mud brick housing fronted by giant steel gates.

It is a deep shame that, in the name of progress and modernisation, some mahallas in Tashkent have been flattened, with others under threat, echoing their destruction elsewhere in the country. During former president Islam Karimov's controversial 27-year rule his restrictive, Soviet-style economic policies made foreign investors wary, and during those hard, paranoid years, the city's development was sluggish, almost suspended in time. Now Karimov has gone and economic reform has come, investors are moving in along with the wrecking ball. Prestige projects are going up and central Tashkent has become a playground for developers, a petri-dish for experimental luxury and corporate gloss: designer shops in chilled malls, restaurants with globe-spanning menus, city sanctuaries with sleek furniture and soft furnishings, all designed for a tiny number of big spenders. Built to impress, rather than to serve. All of it way out of reach for the vast majority. Olmazor, home to a centuries-old mahalla, was bulldozed to make way for the Tashkent City development. Year on year Tashkent is becoming louder, faster and more mechanised. With all this in mind, I went to Old Tashkent to meet a friend, to spend an afternoon in her mahalla.

WE SHALL SING OF THEM IN OUR SONGS

Heavy rain, a beating force, bounced off the little lanes of Chuvalachi mahalla turning them into gushing streams. This neighbourhood is a ten-minute walk from Tashkent's main tourist draw, the Khast-Imam complex where the Moyie Mubarak Library Museum claims to house the oldest Qur'an in the world, made of deerskin and brought initially to Samarkand by Tamerlane. Across from the

library is the Barak Khan Madrassah and Hazrat Imam Mosque with its elegant minarets. Traditional mahallas, full of life and large families, used to directly surround this complex but now they have gone, making way for a new mega-museum that will celebrate the Islamic arts. Amidst the vast construction site are scattered reminders of what was once there in the form of an old post-box, a door, the facade of a house. The rubble brings to mind the 1966 earthquake when Tashkent was flattened and hundreds of thousands of people were left homeless. Children were sent to school in other Soviet republics and from those republics came builders, ready to work and repair. Attic walls still bear inscriptions where these workers left their signatures and the names of their countries of origin.

Chuvalachi mahalla survived the earthquake in part and it continues to display the national virtues of Uzbekistan: politeness, hospitality and tradition. My friend, Shokhinakhon Bakhromova, in her twenties, exceptionally bright and with a head of bouncy brown curls, led the way, the pavements now burbling streams of rainwater. We turned through the tight maze-like corners and lanes where her mother's family have lived for several generations, before stopping in front of an obelisk war memorial. Sheltering under a giant white mulberry tree, Shokhinakhon read the inscription:

'We won't forget the good memory of our fathers and grandfathers who fought for us in foreign countries during the Great War. We shall sing of them in our songs, we shall read them in our poems. We have no right to forget.'

The Great War was the Soviet name for their fight against Nazi Germany in 1941–45.

BLOUSY ROSES, BONE MARROW SAMSA

Rain thundered clusters of white mulberries off branches, scattering them down, laying a mushy carpet at our feet. The names of Shokhinakhon's grandfather, grandmother and uncles are all inscribed at the top of the obelisk. Told, made known and remembered.

Next to the obelisk, a shrine the size of a small kiosk. A very different form of memorial, dedicated to a local figure known as the 'father with the blue coat', this is where mahalla dwellers come when relatives are sick, looking to divine powers for help. When the blue-cloaked mystic died he was buried here, and it remains one of the holiest places in the mahalla. Cosy under the giant mulberry tree, set on a thin canal, people come here to sit and pray and to read the Qur'an.

In the mahalla, everyone stops to talk. Everyone greets you. As we darted in the rain, men yelled, 'Tell her this!', 'Tell her that!', calling out nuggets of random advice for Shokhinakhon to pass on to me, the outsider. At the obelisk, one man offered some unsolicited health advice: 'If you have heart problems, or circulation problems of any kind, try dried apricots steeped in water.' I made a note.

Sheltering from the relentless rain at Shokhinakhon's family home, it struck me just how very far from the capital the mahalla felt. We poured one another tea, while her sister-in-law, Nazima, served us freshly baked samsa. Among the grand furniture from Nazima's dowry were family heirlooms. Portraits of bearded grandfathers and a two-stringed dutar hung on the wall, old photograph albums and postcards of Tashkent were laid on the table. The dining room where we sat – eating the warm samsa, shaped like sausage rolls, cooked with bone marrow and served to us on gold-rimmed plates – sits above a cellar filled from floor to ceiling with vintage Uzbek teapots, plates and glassware. Nazima gave us non bread that had come all the way from the Fergana Valley and I told her in truth that her samsa was the best I had ever eaten. Their elderly grandmother, bed-ridden in the sitting room, wept as Shokhinakhon knelt and kissed her goodbye. 'She's just pleased to see me,' Shokhinakhon said, smiling and shaking her head of curls. Several generations live in the rooms surrounding the courtyard of this beautiful old single-storey house.

We ran back outside, through tiny twisting lanes and the pouring torrents of rain, loosely following thin waterways. Tashkent, set in the Chirchiq River Valley, is intercrossed by a series of canals. Turning a corner, a baker, surprised to see us, pulled a scorching hot non bread out of the tandoor, cooled it briefly by running a quick hose of canal water over it, then frisbeed it into my hands as a gift. 'Don't worry, it's the cleanest water in Tashkent,' Shokhinakhon said, laughing.

Ponds, watercourses and trees are key ingredients for chaikhanas, shade and water being essential for relaxation. What is more welcoming than the sound and sight of cool gurgling water during the torpor of a hot Tashkent summer?

We took shelter from the rain by one chaikhana. The men – teahouse customers in traditional neighbourhoods such as this one are exclusively male – had moved inside to pass the time by playing chess and drinking tea, their shadows just visible through dusty net curtains. Old-fashioned pink roses, huge and blousy, the sort of English gardens, grew in tangles all around the chaikhana's exterior walls. And it was here that Shokhinakhon told me this mahalla, too, is under threat of the citywide blow-down. A notice had been served. Her family home may be gone within five years. When I saw her again, a few months later, she said they'd been granted more time, but that the future was uncertain. The price for progress was being paid and the city's most alluring and interesting quarters were disappearing, and fast, before our eyes.

Old Tashkent Non Bread with Raisins and Walnuts

I first tried this fruity, nutty non bread under the shade of a wooden pagoda at the Chigatay Cemetery in Old Tashkent. I'd brought it with me as part of a picnic lunch I'd put together at the nearby Chigatay Bazaar. The market was thick with the smell of chickpea and lamb stew, a local speciality called nokhat shurak. I'd also bought Turkish-style gözleme, flatbread with pumpkin and spinach, and a kilo of Uzbek cherries. The cemetery is fascinating. One grave had been carefully planted with alternate green and purple basil plants and you can see the burial place of Turson Akhunova, Hero of Socialist Labour and the first woman to drive a cotton-picking machine.

A chekich, a traditional Uzbek bread stamp, can be bought online and works well for this recipe, but you can also use the tines of a fork. Less easy to source is a traditional parak, an old-school bread-stamping tool made of 50 or so sharp-tipped rooster feathers.

I've given instructions for hand-kneading the dough but if you have a food mixer with a dough hook you may want to use that instead.

MAKES 1 LARGE ROUND NON BREAD

250g/2 cups plain (all-purpose) flour

1 ½ tsp fast-action yeast

½ tsp fine sea salt

½ tsp caster (superfine) sugar

180ml/¾ cup tepid water

2 tbsp sunflower oil, plus extra for greasing

Handful of raisins

Handful of walnuts, shelled and quartered

Ice cubes

1 tsp black or white sesame seeds

Put the flour into a large mixing bowl, then add the yeast to one side and the salt and sugar to the other, keeping them separate. Form a well in the middle of the flour and slowly pour in the water, mixing it all together with a wooden spoon.

Lightly oil a work surface, turn out the dough and begin to knead. It will be very wet and sticky at this stage but persevere – it will come together. For best results, use a dough scraper to work the dough, moving it around as best you can until it has firmed up and is silky to the touch. The slap and fold kneading method is very helpful here.

After about 10 minutes, once the dough is firmer, smoother and less sticky, shape it into a ball. Clean the mixing bowl, grease it with a few drops of sunflower oil and set the dough back inside. Cover the bowl with a clean and damp tea towel and place it in the warmest spot of the kitchen. Leave it to rise for 2 hours, or until it has doubled in size.

Gently knock the air out by folding the dough in on itself a few times, and reshape it into a domed round. Cover a chopping board with parchment paper and dust with flour, placing the dough on top. Re-cover it with the tea towel and leave to rise again for 45 minutes; it should eventually puff up to a little dome about 17cm/7in in width.

Preheat the oven to 240°C/475°F/gas mark 9 or to its highest temperature. Place a greased baking sheet or a pizza stone inside to heat up.

Once the dough has proved for a second time, make a depression, roughly 8cm/3in, in the middle using the heel of your hand. Brush the depression with sunflower oil, then using the tines of a fork, or a chekich bread stamp, stamp holes in it (the idea is that it won't rise). Then using a sharp knife, with the blade dipped in a little oil to stop it sticking, make 10 slashes in the fat ring around the depression and stuff, as deeply as possible without cutting all the way through, one raisin followed by one walnut, alternately. Get them buried or they will burn. Add 5–10 ice cubes to another baking tray – this tray will be going into the oven at the same time as the non, on the shelf underneath it, to create steam.

Liberally brush the whole non with the remaining sunflower oil then decorate with little clusters of sesame seeds. Slide it onto its warmed baking sheet or pizza stone and carefully whip away the parchment. Transfer to the oven along with the tray of ice placed on the shelf underneath. Bake for around 20 minutes until golden and the bottom is crusty. Eat on the same day or to bring back to life, simply spritz with some water and place under the grill for a few minutes.

Steamed Pumpkin Khunon

At Tashkent's eccentric but wonderful Pumpkin Museum, located in a private home dating back 300 years, I was served a pumpkin-centric lunch. There was a whole pumpkin stuffed with nutty buckwheat groats, a plate of pumpkin samsa and best of all, a dish I'd wanted to try for a while, pumpkin khunon, which is like a roulade-style open dumpling. A dough scraper and a small, thin rolling pin (cheap and available from Asian supermarkets) are useful here but not essential.

MAKES 16 SMALL KHUNON

FOR THE DOUGH

250g/2 cups plain (all-purpose) flour, plus extra for dusting

½ tsp fine salt

100ml/⅖ cup water

FOR THE FILLING

1 large carrot, roughly chopped

100g/3½oz pumpkin or butternut squash, peeled, deseeded and roughly chopped

½ red or yellow pepper, roughly chopped

2 spring onions (scallions), finely chopped

2 garlic cloves, peeled and crushed

1 tbsp dill fronds, finely chopped

½ tsp sea salt flakes

1 tsp freshly ground pepper

Pinch of chilli powder

½ tsp dill seeds (optional)

1 tbsp sunflower oil

Sour cream, to serve

Laza Hot Sauce (page 197), to serve

Freshly ground pepper, to garnish

Dill fronds, to garnish (optional)

Make the dough first – combine the flour, salt and water in a bowl and mix with a spoon until a shaggy dough forms. Transfer to a lightly floured work surface and knead for 10 minutes until the stickiness has gone and it becomes smooth. A dough scraper helps here. Shape into a ball and transfer it to a lightly floured bowl. Cover the bowl with a clean damp tea towel and leave to rest for an hour.

Meanwhile, make the filling. Put the carrot and pumpkin or squash into a food processor and pulse a few times, then add the pepper. Pulse it all together until you have a very finely chopped mix. If you don't have a food processor, just grate the vegetables as finely as possible. In a large bowl, combine the finely chopped vegetables with the rest of the filling ingredients, and mix it all together well.

Prepare a steamer with the water boiling, so that it's ready to go. Lightly flour a work surface and flatten out the dough before dividing it into 16 pieces. Cover any dough you're not yet working with a clean damp tea towel, to prevent it drying out. One by one, using a rolling pin, roll out each piece to roughly 15 x 5cm/ 6 x 2in – the dough should be paper-thin. Spoon in 1½–2 tablespoons of the filling, spreading it in an even layer down the middle of the rectangle, making sure you leave a border all the way around.

Roll the rectangle starting at one of the shorter ends. As you roll, tuck the dough of one of the long edges in towards the middle – this will seal in the filling and form the base of your dumpling. Stand up the dumpling on its newly formed base – it should look like a slightly open rose. Repeat with the remaining dough and filling, placing each dumpling on a piece of non-stick parchment paper. Gently transfer the dumplings to the steamer – depending on the size of your steamer, you may need to cook them in batches. Make sure the dumplings are well spaced to prevent them sticking to their neighbours. Steam for 10 minutes; the dough should look almost translucent when it's done.

Carefully remove the khunon using a spoon. Serve with sour cream and Laza Hot Sauce on the side, sprinkle over black pepper and a little extra dill, if you like.

Sweet Turnip and Mung Bean Pilaf

This is a take on the classic Uzbek recipe mosh palov, included in *Uzbek Cuisine* written by master of plov cookery, Karim Mahmudov. His recipe includes 300g/10½oz lamb, which you could happily add here, but I like the idea of a vegetarian version bulked up by sweet little turnips.

SERVES 4

50g/3½ tbsp butter

2 onions, thinly sliced

200g/7oz baby turnips, halved, or regular turnips, peeled and roughly diced

2 tsp sea salt

1 tsp ground cumin

½ tsp cayenne pepper

100g/3½oz dried mung beans

200ml/⅘ cup water

300g/1½ cups basmati rice, rinsed

5 garlic cloves, peeled

Handful of flat-leaf parsley, finely chopped

Flaky sea salt, to serve

1 lemon, cut into wedges

Melt the butter in a large saucepan, over a medium heat. Add the onions, turnips and 1 teaspoon of salt, and fry until they've taken on colour and softened. Stir in the spices and cook for a minute or so longer. Add the mung beans to the pan in an even layer, then pour over the water. Put the lid on, bring to a boil and simmer for 10 minutes.

When the mung beans have cooked for 10 minutes, add the rice in an even layer on top of the beans and pour over enough water so that it just covers the level of the rice. Season with 1 teaspoon of salt, bring to a boil, reduce the heat and simmer with the lid on for 12 minutes.

Remove from the heat, poke 5 holes in the rice with the handle of a wooden spoon, place the garlic cloves in the holes, and let the pilaf steam for at least 25–30 minutes. If it is not cooked by then, splash over a little more water and return to the heat until cooked.

Scatter over the parsley and flaky sea salt, and serve with lemon wedges. Uzbeks tend to mash the softened garlic through the rice as they eat.

GALLERY

Paying homage to the avant-garde

TASHKENT, NORTHEAST UZBEKISTAN: In a Tashkent café I sipped black coffee, slowly digesting a conversation I'd just had with Uzbekistan's preeminent art curator. I had wanted to meet Marinika Babanazarova, long-time director of the Savitsky Museum, for years. The museum, located between the Kyzylkum ('red sand') and Karakum ('black sand') deserts in Karakalpakstan, western Uzbekistan, holds a huge range of prized and highly valuable Uzbek and Russian avant-garde artworks.

In an outlandishly remote region hard hit by the Aral Sea disaster, the museum is Karakalpakstan's gem, attracting tourists, art fans and journalists. When collectors arrive, it is Babanazarova that they call. Nobody knows more about the collection and nobody, other than its artist-collector founder Igor Savitsky, long dead, has been closer to it.

During a recent visit to the museum, I noticed a recurring motif. And once I'd noticed it, I saw it everywhere. Food. Depicted in all its multi-coloured, glossy and tempting diversity, captured in watercolour, pastel and oil. Kitchens and laid tables. Feasts and fruit sellers. Collective farms and couples dining. Harvests and cafés. Dozens of still-life paintings of fish, fruit, bread, bottles and samovars. Come here hungry, and it is enough to turn the brain.

Paintings of chaikhanas are everywhere in the gallery. There is Aleksei Isupov's *The Oriental Café*, tempera and gilt on plywood, a painting of visual poetry, showing a tea boy in fine clothes and skullcap presenting his rose-emblem teapots and decorated trays to the viewer. Then there is Nikolay Karakhan's *Teahouse Near the Pond Under Elms*, bringing to mind Persian miniatures with its turbaned men, niches and bright primary colours.

Many artists who came to Uzbekistan from Russia in the 1920s and '30s, arrived with ideals and practices garnered from avant-garde artists such as Chagall and Kandinsky. On arrival, they mixed those styles with what they found in the east – desert light, bazaars, old city walls and food. So often, food.

On one wall is an eye-catching trio of huge still-life paintings. One shows a kitchen table and on it, a rolling pin, a cluster of pelmeni dumplings on a wooden board, a pot of bubbling water atop a miniature stove, a bowl of cut-open tomatoes and cucumbers, a vase of flowers and two bowls of half-eaten dumplings. The table, laid but with no guests, shows where the pelmeni are both prepared and eaten – the marriage of practicality and enjoyment in a kitchen.

To the right of this painting, another still-life shows pattern, colour and form via an arrangement of cakes, tea and citrus fruit. The third depicts a row of skewered shashlik, rigid and stiff, in contrast to a leathery pomegranate ready to spill its wet seeds. These are Mikhail Kurzin's paintings from the 1950s. Tremendously talented, Kurzin was a 'forbidden artist' whose work was considered bourgeois and banned by Soviet officials. He was treated horrendously by the regime and was set to work on the Kolyma Highway, the infamous 'road of bones', with a pickaxe. His still-lifes of food were painted just before he died in 1957.

Until perestroika in 1985, when political and economic reforms were put in place to boost the idle 1980s economy, only Socialist Realism – usually in the form of pictures of victorious youth and happy farm-workers – was permitted. Many of Kurzin's paintings were confiscated by the NKVD but some were saved, squirreled away by Savitsky in Karakalpakstan, then a secretive province of the Soviet Union, host to the Red Army's Chemical Research Institute, a testing site for the Novichok nerve agent. This corner of Uzbekistan, between the deserts, became home to one of the world's largest collections of avant-garde art. A safe hiding place for the work of banned artists.

Savitsky was a man as fascinating as his acquisitions. Born in Kiev to a wealthy family, he enrolled in Moscow's Surikov Art Institute in 1941, then, in 1942 was evacuated along with the school to Samarkand. There, he had his first taste of Central Asia, experiencing the 'sound' of colour in the desert. After visiting Karakalpakstan in the 1950s, as an artist accompanying an archaeological expedition, he left his smart apartment on the Arbat in Moscow and settled in Karakalpakstan a place he 'loved with all his soul'. He quickly became a champion for local Karakalpak craftsmanship, showing textiles, jewellery and crafts in Tashkent and Moscow. For him, the Karakalpaks were a 'people, until recently lost among the sands and waterways of the Amu Darya . . . the owners of magnificent art . . .'

Putting down his own brushes, Savitsky opened the museum in 1966. At first it was purely a Karakalpak folk art collection with pile rugs and appliqué work but no paintings, and as an artist, he longed for canvases. He knew that many dissident artists who'd once worked freely in Uzbekistan before Stalin's 'Reconstruction of the Literary and Artistic Organisations' crackdown in the early 1930s, were now either dead, locked up, in gulags, or toeing the Socialist Realism line. Unless he saved their paintings now, they risked being lost for ever.

Travelling frantically in his search for lost and hidden artworks, he found many widows of artists had buried canvases away under beds or in sheds, or had even burned the frames as winter fuel, rolling the paintings up, cracking and damaging them. Savitsky went to Moscow overland, convincing the heirs of these paintings to part with them, then – sometimes filling two train compartments – carried them back to his remote desert outpost. These journeys put him at great personal risk, but he completed 20 such trips in order to save the paintings. As the artist Alexander Volkov said, 'Igor Savitsky lived two lives – as an artist and a collector. If he had been only an artist, this would have been enough.' Savitsky kept these artists' stories alive by making his museum their storyteller and by somehow managing to gather local communist leaders around him, bringing them on side, persuading them to help fund his collection. Few had only a vague idea of what he was doing with their cash.

Just before Savitsky died in 1984, Babanazarova was instructed by him to be his successor as director. Babanazarova's story made international news in 2015 when she was ousted from this position by the government, on allegations of forgery and theft. Her supporters have suggested that these charges were invented by the authorities who would prefer to move the museum to Tashkent, or who were jealous of the museum attracting international media attention to Karakalpakstan. A joint letter was signed by museum staff showing their support for Babanazarova after her removal, and calling for their director to be reappointed, an act not common, or without significant personal risk, under President Karimov's regime at the time. I hoped to learn more about Savitsky, the avant-garde artists and their fascination with the colour, form and precariousness of food, by meeting Babanazarova.

TEA WITH MARINIKA BABANAZAROVA

In central Tashkent, Taras Shevchenko Street slices through the nicest part of town where cafés and museums are shaded by tall, leafy trees. The Ukrainian poet Taras Shevchenko has a statue and a mural dedicated to him here and below the plinth, admirers lay fresh red carnations at his feet. Nearby is a French-style patisserie called Bon!, a branch of a small chain serving omelettes, florentines and macaroons. It was at Bon! that I met Marinika Babanazarova, who arrived right on time, dressed smartly in a scarf and blazer, her auburn hair short and styled. The interview took place mid-afternoon, over a tray of tea. Nina Simone played softly in the background.

CE: Was Savitsky particularly interested in food?

MB: Yes, he was. You couldn't say this in his last years when he was exhausted in his fight for the museum and he was ill but as my mum remembers him, he was always nostalgic about his early childhood, how the celebrations were arranged, what kind of food there was.

Savitsky was born in Kiev, to a family of professors who were members of academies. They travelled to Europe. They had a French governess. He was very open with Mum because they both had parents repressed by the regime, and both had 'good roots' as we say. My parents would visit his apartment on the Arbat in Moscow, and he would treat them to fantastic dishes, such delicacies, foods my mother had never before tried. The chicken was stuffed, like a 'stocking', she said, and made by his own hands. He always liked celebrations. When inspectors or art experts came from Moscow or Tashkent, he would arrange the table himself and the staff members would cook. This, he loved.

When it was my first year at the museum, I baked petit fours for his birthday. It's not like now when you just go to the café, in the Soviet past when everything was deficit, we had to do everything with our own hands. I made them with cream custard and I brought them to the museum to treat just him, because he was alone.

CE: Can this love of food, and of celebrations, be seen within the collection?

MB: Yes, and in many ways. Savitsky used food to charm people, to get the paintings. He would arrive to an artist's widow with a cake, or a bouquet. Or oranges, as those were so rare in the Soviet Union. Oranges were imported from Morocco. Georgian citrus was not as good as Moroccan. We waited for this season, winter, when they would come. A real luxury. In Moscow you could find them but not in Central Asia, and he would bring such fine things from Moscow back to us as well.

There were always ways of getting things. There was a community of Ural Cossacks who were living in the southern part of the Aral Sea, exiled there at the end of the 19th century. They ran a fishing business, mainly sturgeon from the Aral Sea, and sold caviar in big jars, at affordable prices. And we would eat it, one-litre jars of it, of course it was more expensive than just bread and butter, but it was a bit better than that. The Ural Cossacks would smoke the sturgeon and eat it with potatoes, but the Kazakhs and Karakalpaks would make beshbarmak with it, or a fish porridge. It's long in the past but I remember these things.

At the museum, for the captions and descriptions, Savitsky would never tell us to just write 'still-life with grapes', it would be 'lilac rose blue yellow grapes'. He would be so lyrical with colour, it would make our lives much harder in typing up the information. Savitsky appreciated food for its beauty, not just its taste.

CE: If you think about food in the collection, which artists in particular come to mind?

MB: Mikhail Kurzin, certainly. When he was released he was suffering from malnutrition, because political prisoners were not allowed to work. He had no job and he was ill. He was almost dying but he created fantastic feasts in his mind, in his work, in the still-lifes of shish kebab, pilaf and pelmeni. What we don't know is if the art was his true spirit or if food was simply a safe subject, so he could be free and not be pursued.

Also, Ural Tansykbayev, the best colourist of the Uzbek School of Art in the 1920s and '30s. He was most sensitive at perceiving colour in the shade and in sun. Ethnically Kazakh, Tansykbayev lived in Tashkent and studied in Russia and in 1929 visited Moscow's Pushkin Art Museum, which showed French Impressionists, and you feel it in the art. When you paint en plein air, in the mountains, you see the clouds change and the sun change. Many others became artists in Samarkand where everything changes so quickly depending on the sunlight. [Tansykbayev's work at the gallery shows collective farms, melon fields, wheat fields, fishermen on the Aral Sea at different times of the day, from bright morning, to golden afternoon and dusk. His eerily lit *Teahouse at Night*, is strangely reminiscent of Edward Hopper's *Nighthawks*.]

CE: What were Savitsky's final years like?

MB: It was a very tough environment in Nukus – remote, hot, hard. In the end, it was terrible, but his spirit was so strong, and his obsession kept him going for so many years. Maybe another person would have died much younger, but he survived until 69. [Preserving art eventually killed Savitsky, his lungs destroyed by breathing in formalin that he used to clean old bronzes.]

His body was brought back from Moscow and he was buried there in Nukus. He must be close to the museum and his grave is now a symbol, in the middle of the desert. It is in the Russian cemetery with the salty dust everywhere. His grave monument has a statue of a muse playing the flute. Very different to the others in the graveyard, another sign that even in the next world he is different to others. As we say in Russian, he was a white crow.

Mikhail Kurzin's Meat Dumplings Brought to Life

If you go to the Savitsky Museum in Karakalpakstan, make sure you take time to stand back and revel in Mikhail Kurzin's giant homage to pelmeni, unaffectedly entitled 'Meat Dumplings'. The photograph overleaf – showing the rolling pin, bulbous tomatoes and bowls of pelmeni – was shot and styled in a London studio but the idea was that it reflects Kurzin's table and captures something of the essence depicted in the painting. This recipe, for gently spiced beef pelmeni, is good as a main for two, or as a starter or side dish for four.

MAKES AROUND 35–40 PELMENI

FOR THE DOUGH

220g/1⅔ cups plain (all-purpose) flour, plus extra for dusting

1 medium egg, beaten

1 tsp sunflower oil

1 tsp fine sea salt

75ml/⅓ cup warm water

FOR THE FILLING

220g/8oz minced (ground) beef

1 small onion, diced

½ tsp cayenne pepper

½ tsp ground cumin

½ tsp caraway seeds, toasted and crushed

1 tsp fine sea salt

½ tsp ground black pepper

1 tbsp very cold water

TO SERVE

50g/3½ tbsp butter

2 large onions, thinly sliced

Sea salt flakes and freshly ground black pepper, to season

Sour cream

First, make the dough. In a mixing bowl, sift in the flour and make a well in the middle. Into the well pour the egg, sunflower oil, salt and warm water. Start off by mixing it with a wooden spoon to combine the ingredients, then knead on a lightly floured surface until you have a smooth dough. Return to the bowl and cover with a clean damp tea towel for 30 minutes.

Put the beef, onion, spices and seasoning into a clean bowl, then add a tablespoon of very cold water and mix well.

Lightly dust 2 baking trays with flour (these will need to fit inside your freezer).

On a lightly floured surface, roll out a quarter of the dough at a time – you are aiming for as paper-thin as possible – and using a cookie cutter, cut out 8cm/3in circles. Keep the rest of the dough covered with a clean damp tea towel so that it doesn't dry out. Place ½ teaspoon of filling on one side of the circle, then fold the dough over and seal the edges using your fingers, to form a crescent. Then take each end and pinch them together (as a friend put it, 'almost like you're crossing the arms of the pelmeni across its stomach'). Repeat the process with all the remaining dough and filling, placing them on the baking trays as you go. When they're all assembled, put the trays into the freezer for an hour – this important step helps them from sticking and exploding in the boiling water.

Half an hour before you take the pelmeni out of the freezer to boil them, fry the sliced onions. Melt the butter in a frying pan over a low heat and fry for about 30 minutes to caramelise. You want them to be tender and golden-brown in colour; stop before they get crispy.

Bring a large saucepan of salted water to a boil and cook the pelmeni in batches so as not to overcrowd the pan, for 3–5 minutes, or until they float to the surface. Stir them gently very occasionally as they boil. Test one to make sure the filling is fully cooked (i.e. the meat is no longer pink), and if so, remove the rest with a slotted spoon.

Serve the pelmeni with the fried onions spooned on top, along with a sprinkling of sea salt and black pepper. Place a small bowl of sour cream for each person on the side.

STUPA

Bridging centuries and religions

TERMEZ, SOUTH UZBEKISTAN: Termez is the southernmost city of
Uzbekistan, with Afghanistan a mere ten-minute drive away. If visitors come
here, and very few do, they come for the ancient Buddhist sites on the outskirts
of town. They were the reason I had come, too. Sort of. It is an hour's flight from
Tashkent to get here, but in many ways feels like a different hemisphere.

Everyone stays at the Hotel Asson, from airline staff to soldiers and wedding
parties. Faces I recognised from the Tashkent flight: a man with one leg
amputated at the hip, a bride who'd rushed through the airport terminal in
a meringue dress, soldiers in fatigues, a po-faced Russian tourist, an alsatian
dog. In front of the whitewashed hotel, taxi drivers waited for fares, dozing on
shaded benches, while around them the garden blossomed with springtime roses,
fragrant and pink. Inside, arrow-straight corridors stretched on and on, barrack-
style, decorated with framed artworks of peachy-bottomed nudes, galloping
horses and needleworks of Arcadian meadows. Threadbare carpet was hoovered
dawn till dusk by cleaners morosely resigned to their task. At the front desk, guests
grumbled. They grumbled about the rock-hard beds and they grumbled about the
lack of hot water. It was the heat. Over the four days I stayed here, the temperature
rose a degree a day, a golden-like heat steadily rising like bread until, demonically,
the mercury hits 50°C in mid-summer.

The hotel's draw card is its position on the main drag, Al-Termezi. This is where
the city's soundtrack plays out: shashlik grills sizzling on pavements, love songs
floating out of café speakers and ice cream vendors teasing children. The daytime
clatter of chaikhanas and waiters ferrying out pots of tea to lounging men on sun-
bleached thin mattresses was a constant whir and strum. But nowhere, not in the
chaikhanas or restaurants, could I find any hint of Afghan food, as I'd hoped.

I got to Fayoz-Tepe, a Buddhist monastery complex, by taxi, paying the guard
at the entrance gate a small fee to let the car pass. The site was eerily quiet. Tiny
yellow and purple pansies pushed through the sandy scrubland. I carefully stepped
over them, towards the ancient remains, sweat dripping from my forehead.
Breaking hectares of flat nothingness, a platform made of brick rose from the
dirt. Slung long and low, connected to wide buff-coloured steps and foundation
walls, on the top was a sand-coloured dome, the size and shape of an igloo.
Surrounding the platform lay fragmented foundations of former meditation
halls, kitchens, sleeping cells, and ancient water pipes that once brought in water
from the nearby Amu Darya River. Silently baking in the heat, the complex
looked like a *Star Wars* film set, or a religious epic brought to life.

In the centre of the dome on top of the platform was a tiny door. The guard came over, unlocked it, and walked off again. I peered in. There sat the original ancient crumbling stupa, a symbol of the Buddha's burial mound, built in the 3rd century. So vulnerable, yet so magnificent. Unearthly. Its simplicity, fusing with the absolute stillness of the landscape, rendered me mute. The only sound I could hear was my own breathing, and the clicks and whirrs of my bones and nervous system. Fayoz-Tepe, the stuff historians dream of, was left alone for centuries until archaeologists arrived in 1968.

Under the heat of a hundred suns, I read my guidebook. The liberal Kushan Empire spanned the 1st– 3rd centuries AD, stretching from northern India to Afghanistan and parts of Central Asia; it promoted trade not only of goods but, in classic Silk Road style, also ideas, craftsmanship, religious renaissance and cultural exchange. Termez became an important commercial centre under the Kushans, with Buddhist monks and missionaries following merchant routes to Xinjiang and elsewhere in China. By the time of the dynasty's great leader King Kanishka all manner of luxuries came flooding through this region: Greek bronzes, Indian ivories and wine, imported in clay jars.

The giant 6th century sandstone Buddha statues at Bamiyan in Afghanistan – which stood 58 and 38 metres tall – were reminders of this same religious passage. To the world's horror, they were blown up in 2001 by dynamite, over several weeks, at the order of Mullah Omar, Afghan commander of the Taliban.

THROUGH LANDS OF FANS AND FURS

Some say the name Termez comes from the Greek word 'thermos' and I believed this as the sun glowered down on the stupa. Persians called Central Asia the 'land of fans and furs' because you always need one or the other. In an untitled poem dated 1945, Anna Akhmatova wrote:

'And oppressive, and as difficult to bear
As the noonday heat of Termez.'

I read how, at the site of Kampyr-Tepe, a short drive away, Soviet archaeologists had excavated pits and a sunken palace on the Amu Darya and had discovered chess pieces that some consider the oldest on earth. They dug in the winter of 1979 which was when Soviet tanks rolled into Afghanistan, and the nine-year Soviet–Afghan War began.

Kara-Tepe, walkable from Fayoz-Tepe, although the taxi driver insisted on taking me there, has been at times both a royal temple and a necropolis where the dead were buried with coins in their mouths (payment for the ferryman carrying souls across the river separating the living from the dead in the ancient Greek tradition), as well as a Buddhist monastery. Excavations here revealed Sanskrit manuscripts written on birch bark. Built on a hillside, it was not closed to visitors as my guidebook warned, but it is located in a 'military zone' with the site facing the Afghan border and watchtowers. The atmosphere was peaceful and calm but distinctly hinterland and frontier. I didn't take many photographs. I wandered over a labyrinth of what remained of caves and monk cells dating back to the 2nd century, subterranean refuge from the relentless heat and cold of the plain. Being at the sites was immersive. A bit like being lost in a good book.

The sun relentlessly pummelled down, eventually driving me out. I wanted cool shade and trees, the sort of garden Babur, founder of the Mughal Empire, great-great-great grandson of Tamerlane and nicknamed 'the gardener king', appreciated. The taxi driver, who'd given up on trying to get the air-conditioning to work, knew where to go: the mausoleum of Al-Hakim al-Termizi.

AN AFGHAN INVITATION

Perfectly balancing form and nature, the burial place of the 9th century Sufi saint, Al-Hakim al-Termizi, nicknamed 'the sage of Termez', is perfection in garden form with cool running water, clean air, fruit trees, roses and birdsong. Shaded wooden pavilions, each elaborately carved, were filled with long-distance visitors from Dushanbe and Kabul. By the mausoleum, pilgrims tied ribbons to mulberry and pine trees, in the traditional Sufi way. Inside the burial chamber, gold stucco and elaborate plasterwork shone over new and immaculate thick carpets. In short, it was the ideal place to escape the heat, the ultimate hot weather sojourn. Many people had come for the whole day. Behind the wall, the muddy Amu Darya pushed on, dividing us from Afghanistan.

By a mulberry tree, I took off my shoes and sat in the cool shade of a wooden pavilion. Three Afghans named Safar, Mr Waiz and Muhibullah (whose name, he told me, means 'friend of God') immediately struck up conversation. They were holidaying friends from Kabul, a banker, an NGO worker and a businessman, respectively. With good English, they exuded enviable nonchalance, suavity and charm. They had a worldly ease, different from the people of Termez whose lives, it seemed, didn't tend to travel far. I asked how things are nowadays across the border.

'Business is good, security remains the problem. Not many outside people will invest there.' I mentioned my desire to visit Mazar-i-Sharif, only an hour away, but unreachable as a last-minute trip without connections or paperwork, or the right clothes. In reality, Afghanistan felt a whole world away.

'When you walk in Mazar you will see people from other countries, just your embassy tells you not to go. Mazar is safe. If you drive from Kabul, you will see rivers from the mountains, the most beautiful rivers in the world. Isn't that right, Mr Waiz?' Mr Waiz nodded and told me he has plenty of family in the EU, especially the UK.

'You should come to Mazar,' Mr Waiz said.

I asked whether they'd come across the romantic-sounding 'lamb smoked in pine needles' dish that I'd heard about, and mentioned that I'd given up looking for Afghan restaurants in Termez.

'No, there are none. I heard that Mansour, a famous restaurant in Mazar, will open here. But it is not open yet. For that, you need to go to Mazar itself. We wish it was here, for it is a most famous and wonderful restaurant. A truly wonderful place. Tonight we will go to Dubai restaurant, for drinking, for dancing. That's the best place in Termez. Last night the president was here, in Termez, so there were a lot of soldiers, but anyway we went out and danced.' That explained the military overnighting at the Hotel Asson. During the Soviet invasion of Afghanistan, there was a heavy military presence in Termez but nowadays it's mainly border guards. Al-Hakim's shrine marked one of the furthest-southern points of what was the USSR.

'Now we are friends, now we know each other, let me ask you again – why don't you visit Mazar if you say you want to see it? Next time, go. You must go. Go to the Mansour restaurant.' I nodded and promised that one day I would, and wished them safe travels.

GONZO PEACHES AND SINGING DUST STORMS

Back in Termez, tightrope walkers had strung up a wire the height of a single-storey building, by the bazaar. Hundreds of locals crowded around, watching as the men in their silk shirts and black leather boots strolled slowly and perilously, holding a pole at their waists for balance. One bobbed up and down in the middle of the tightrope, squatting and springing back up, before gingerly walking to the end. The crowd cheered and whooped.

Encircling a decrepit courtyard, the bazaar, an old and crumbling relic from the Soviet era, was where most life happened. Wheelbarrows of apples and wagons of counterfeit branded underwear went whizzing underneath carpets hanging over balconies. Fountains were full, not with cool gushing water, but rubble and pigeons. Inside, lit by shards of sunlight, the main thing for sale was sweets. Every Central Asian biscuit and cake imaginable was available. I bit into a shaftoli, named after a peach, but it had nothing of the 'golden peaches of Samarkand' about it. It was a gonzo peach. A round plum-size ball made of chocolate sponge, injected with a pleasingly thick and milky filling, wrapped in a sugary synthetic shell dyed with food colouring, fuzzy-looking and pink as a peach. I bought six.

At the local museum, right next to the hotel (another plus point), displays showed how once Termez was a Silk Road city. Alongside coins from Ulugbek's reign there were Timurid copper coins, Bukharan coins from the 14th century, and a charming bowl from the same century made specifically for raisins. An assistant opened a heavy door and led me into a vault holding lapis and turquoise jewels and postage stamps from 1950s China. Spotlights throughout the museum are branded 'Beijing 2008', from the Summer Olympics. How they ended up here is anyone's guess.

Every evening, a routine unfolded. As the sun set, hoses were hauled out from shops and cafés by the hotel, for spraying down courtyards in an effort to battle an unwinnable war against dust. Rainbow arcs hovered and momentarily the air cooled blissfully. Once the watering had finished, I'd slosh along the terrace of cracked tiles at the Hotel Asson, taking up a regular spot at the only table in the garden – lime-green, Formica, wet and wobbly. The waiter would bring out a plate of Uzbek pistachios, cheaper, smaller and saltier than Iranian ones, and a crystal glass filled to the brim with cold Sarbast lager. Then, I'd watch and wait for the sunset murmurations of myna birds. Rising from the trees, as one collective flapping mass, they'd soar into the sky, to perform their twilight dance. Paying no attention to international borders. Flocking freely to and from Afghanistan.

Staying in rickety hotels reinforces an important life lesson: take pleasure, as much as you can, from simple, everyday things, for those will make you glad. Sadly, Termez did not charm the English travel writer Rosita Forbes who was here in the 1930s. As the afternoon sun sank she sat upon the ground, ate a hard-boiled egg and concluded, 'Termez is one of those scrag-ends of earth and building material that are left lying about in the hot lands without apparent purpose.'

Sunset was the time in the day, also, when the wind picked up a little. Termez is regularly afflicted with singing dust storms said to be just as blinding as a Russian blizzard. Hot, fine, sharp dust forms a whirling, hurling, howling screen of sand where you cannot see further than three paces. Blowing in from the Hindu Kush, these fast-moving winds can snuff out harvests, covering crops and fields for days. Like all significant winds, it has a name: Afghanets.

The next day, I sat in a taxi, to the east of the city, to watch trains sluggishly heading off, having crossed from Afghanistan over the half-mile-long bridge that

straddles the Amu Darya. Originally built to transport cargo to the Soviet Army in Afghanistan, now freight trains cross carrying all manner of goods. I could see a sliver of the bridge, but the driver was nervous and refused to take me closer to the border. It is an important bridge, known somewhat outrageously as the 'Friendship Bridge'. Buddhist sites aside, I'd really come to see this.

On 15th February 1989 Red Army soldiers rolled across here and out of Afghanistan, throwing bars of Russian chocolate to Afghan children before going home via Termez, then part of the Soviet Union. On the Soviet side, Uzbek dancers in silk ikat robes twirled. Soldiers signed autographs. Bread and grapes were handed out by locals. Boris Gromov, the Soviet Union's last military commander in Afghanistan, was the last Soviet soldier to return home, personally steering the last armoured personnel carrier across before walking the last few yards into Soviet territory with his son, who carried a bouquet of flowers. Moscow's invasion of Afghanistan in the 1980s had ended where it had begun in 1979, in Termez. The war left 15,000 Soviet soldiers and officers dead, killed two million Afghan civilians and sent up to five million Afghans into refugee camps in neighbouring Pakistan and Iran.

Later, in 1997, frontier troops were put on high alert and the bridge was completely sealed off by the Uzbek government as the Taliban clashed with opposition forces in northern Afghanistan, and fears that violence could spread across the border rose. Today, if peace could hold in Afghanistan, goods could, in theory, travel all the way from here to the Indian Ocean, and onwards, and Termez could find itself an important trading centre once again, just as it was as a stop on the Silk Road when it was famous for the pungent spice, asafoetida. For now, this town of 140,000 people, surrounded by lemon orchards, feels somewhat tucked away and concealed. As unfamiliar and unknown to the outsider as the Afghanets wind.

Dimlama – An Uzbek Harvest Stew with Quince

Here's a chunky harvest dimlama ('stew') with added quince, a variation on the traditional recipe. Popular throughout Uzbekistan and bordering countries, according to the Malika Gold restaurant in Termez, it is especially loved down south. This is a hearty, pleasingly sweet one-pot stew, ideal for autumn.

SERVES 4 GENEROUSLY

4 tbsp olive oil

500g/1lb 2oz lamb leg steak, cut into matchbox-size chunks

Salt and freshly ground black pepper

1 tsp ground cumin

½ tsp cayenne pepper

1 large onion, roughly chopped

1 quince, peeled, cored and cut into bite-size pieces

2 medium-size potatoes, peeled and cut into bite-size pieces

4 large carrots, sliced into coins

1 red, orange or yellow (bell) pepper, sliced into wide strips

3 garlic cloves, peeled and thinly sliced

500ml/2 cups beef stock

1 large tomato, sliced into wedges

½ savoy cabbage, core removed and leaves cut into thumb-size strips

2 tbsp fresh dill fronds, chopped, to garnish

In a large casserole or saucepan with a lid, heat 2 tablespoons of olive oil and fry the lamb over a medium heat for 10 minutes. Transfer to a plate when almost cooked through, season with salt and pepper, and cover with foil to keep it juicy.

Add another tablespoon of olive oil to the same pan and over a medium heat, warm the cumin and cayenne pepper for a minute to release their scent and flavour. Add the onion, quince, potatoes, carrots and pepper, and coat with the spice mix. Season generously, add the last tablespoon of olive oil, and cook for 10 minutes, stirring from time to time, until the vegetables start to soften.

Add the garlic and cook for another minute, then add a splash of the stock and the tomato wedges, cooking for 5 minutes before adding the remaining stock. Stir everything to combine and bring to the boil.

Carefully place the cabbage in a layer on top of the stock and vegetables (without stirring it through), then lower the heat to a simmer, put the lid on and cook for 20 minutes.

Remove the lid and cook over a low-medium heat for another 10 minutes to reduce the stock. Check the seasoning again, then spoon the lamb and its resting juices on top of the cabbage to warm through for 2–3 minutes. Serve in large bowls with the dill scattered over.

A Bygone Uzbek Salad

Before New World ingredients such as chillies and tomatoes arrived in Uzbekistan, fruit was used to provide sweet or sour flavours. Quince was paired with lamb while black and pink radishes went with cherries and blackberries for salads to serve with plov and shashlik, which benefit from acidity. Interestingly, there is no generic word for 'salad' in Uzbek.

SERVES 2

150g/5oz black radish, sliced into wafer-thin coins

100g/3½oz Pink Pickled Onions (page 88)

Handful of pistachios, shelled

1 tbsp of olive oil

Flaky sea salt and freshly ground black pepper, to season

There is no detailed method here, as the flavours happily do their own thing. Simply arrange the radishes, pickled onions and pistachios on a plain white plate to let the colours sing. Drizzle over a little oil and add a pinch of salt and pepper.

FORT

Re-entering the Red Sand Desert

NURATA, CENTRAL UZBEKISTAN: After springtime rain the Kyzylkum Desert becomes a garden. Stretching from southern Kazakhstan, across the border to Uzbekistan, red poppies blaze for hundreds of miles in every direction. Natalia Trotsky, wife of Leon, wrote of them in 1927 when the couple lived in Almaty, Kazakhstan's former capital: 'the spring . . . yielded to red poppies. Such a lot of them - like gigantic carpets.' Travelling from Termez in southern Uzbekistan, I'd arrived in the centre of the country to meet Ruslan, a guide who runs a guesthouse in the town of Nurata, on the edge of the desert. From the moving car, the blindingly bright poppies had blurred into one livid mass in the heat and families periodically pulled over, leapt out, and posed for photographs among the flowers. This is the same 180,000 square mile desert that the Swiss adventurer and writer Ella Maillart travelled through in winter, where she found 'nothing but grey sky and grey ice . . . grandiose in its desolation.' In January, it is −25°C, and in summer temperatures compete with the Sahara. The Afghanets wind blows and fog comes in, too. There is a lot of weather here.

I dropped my bag at Ruslan's and we headed into the Kyzylkum for an afternoon walk. The desert light was clear and clean and there was no cloud cover at all, promising sunburn and wide views. We snaked slowly along, driving through sandy loam and clusters of bluegrass and camel thorn, the aromatic spicy, woody bitter smell of silvery-green sage brush wafting in through open windows. Gnarly saxaul, the desert bush burnt for fuel, which needs not a drop of water to grow, dominated other desert life, groping the sand with its thin branches. We stopped at a village known as Old Circle, settled by Kazakhs. Once nomads dwelling in yurts, they now live in lonely single-storey houses, whitewashed against the sun. Glittery cappuccino-coloured sand packed tightly against the pale walls of their homes, nudging window frames and doorposts. We got out and walked. In a busy, increasingly connected world, strolling in the desert certainly has its joys. Ruslan led the way through drifts and depressions and we padded along, passing sun-bleached skulls of long-dead goats, their brown horns curved and pleated. Old Circle, behind us, was deserted except for a single bubblegum-pink Lada and a woman pulling up water from a well. We went over one dune, then another, and another, before the stifling heat sent us back to the car.

DESERT AMBROSIA

We drove on further into the undulating desert scrub. The track was poor, bumpy and deserted. Thorny bushes and strange black lilies tangled together at the roadside. Distances were measureless, but we didn't pass another soul or car for

an hour or so, then, just off the way, among the poppies and the saxaul, a large wooden wagon appeared. We stopped, reversed and zigzagged across dirt towards it. By the trailer stood a couple of other wooden caravans behind, as well as dozens of old milk churns, and a string of sky-blue wooden boxes, all numbered and lodged in a sandy thicket. A man appeared, dressed in gloves and a veil. As he lifted the mesh of nylon covering his face, to talk, a bee wedged itself angrily in my hair. Introducing himself as Olim, he told us that here, in the middle of the Kyzylkum Desert, he produces three tons of honey a year. The milk churns have all been emptied and have been filled with honey, he said.

'The bees mean I have to live like a nomad, moving every month. Now it's the desert season and there are lots of flowers here but when they go, I move. Other months I am where the flowers are, where the bees are, often in the cotton fields. I have to be a botanist and beekeeper.' Closer to the trailer and boxes, the air was alive with roving bees.

'Would you like to try some cotton honey?' Olim handed me a spoon. The colour of cloudy wheat, with a trace of dark gold, the honey was swoony, waxy and tasted of sun. Notes of peach, caramel and a little vanilla. Cotton flowers open in June and July, when it is hot. A single cotton flower opens at daybreak, shrinks in the afternoon and closes in on itself by sunset. 'Cotton honey is my best seller by far. I export it to Turkey, Korea, China and Dubai.'

It looked lonely but Olim assured me that he was happy: the bees' ambrosia and the desert quiet, more than enough. 'It is so interesting, living in nature, in the desert. I love this job. I've been doing it for ten years.' The seasons and the flower-fed bees dictate his life. From March to September, he stays with his hundred hives and minds his 3,000 or so bees. In winter, he repairs boxes and makes his sales. Meeting Olim was a surprise, but desert lore says that no meeting is ever by chance, or luck.

The soft muffled peace of the desert, offering space to reflect, reminded me that this was the halfway point of my journey. So far, collisions between food, people and places had been plentiful. But what had I learned? That Tashkent was changing at a rate far quicker than I had realised, and that some of the most valuable parts of the city – filled with tiny bakeries, old mud-walled houses and a million stories – were being systematically reduced to rubble, and were set to scale down further still. Later in the journey, this blow-down theme would continue apace in Samarkand, the Fergana Valley, and in Dushanbe. Paired with rapid development, tourism, striding ever quicker on the old Silk Road, may eventually destroy the very things that it set out to see.

Histories I'd not paid attention to before had been revealed and demanded attention: how hungry and repressed avant-garde artists of Uzbekistan and Russia had painted the food they longed to eat; how small domestic items belonging to women held in gulags were not inanimate objects but precious beacons of hope and memory; how milk was not only the food of nomads but a symbol central to Kazakhstan's identity. And, I found that the newspapers were right: fishing is slowly returning to the northern section of the Aral Sea.

Then, there was the sheer glee of food, often pressed generously into my hands as gifts and welcomes, that told its own stories: I couldn't have hoped for a more alluring konditorei than Krendel in Pavlodar, nor a better dinner on the Caspian Sea in Aktau, or a more restorative breakfast spot in Tashkent – edible treasures, all, experiences that could have been easily passed over by someone in a rush, but that with time paint a different, more flavourful, picture of this often misunderstood region. Food, as the anthropologist, Claude Lévi-Strauss, said, is 'good to think with'.

LUCKY PARTRIDGES AND SACRED SPRINGS

More quiet relaxation waited back at Ruslan's guesthouse where life was mainly lived outdoors, centred around a sunny courtyard where a ladder extended through a large mulberry tree laden with white berries. Below the tree, surrounded by blousy springtime roses, a chukar partridge the size of a hen, gurgled and called from its wicker basket. I longed to let it out. They are a comfort, a lucky charm, a distraction and are popular pets in Central Asia. Extolled yet enslaved. I wondered whether Ruslan felt the common contradicting urges of wanting to own another living creature and the desire to set it free.

I sat in the shade and was served green tea and fresh bread. It arrived on classic Uzbek navy and white cotton-pattern china used for each meal, trimmed with gold edge. This crockery is an active reminder – every time you drink your tea from your handle-less piala cup, or eat your tomato salad and plov – of Uzbekistan's cotton industry, the backbone of its economy. The toil in the fields, the exploitation, the reason for the Aral Sea disaster. So light to touch, and so hard to fulfil your Soviet-era cotton collective quota of two dozen or so kilos a day. Completely back-breaking work.

As well as cooking and collecting mulberries, Ruslan's mother and wife worked on suzani embroideries, simple in pattern and technique but captivating and distinctive. They stitched onto aprons and cushion covers for the trickle of tourists who come here. For mealtimes, they worked in a little summer kitchen just off the courtyard, preparing food made from the realities and habits of family life. In the morning, always homemade quince jam with fresh bread, a little plate of young walnuts and freshly baked lamb samsa dotted with onion seeds. For lunch, mastava, a Tajik soup of mung beans, chickpeas and rice; for dinner salads, plov or golubtsi and potatoes. In Uzbekistan, everything revolves around food: you can ask whether someone is from the same family by enquiring whether they are from the 'same cooking pot'. But best of all were the plates and plates of plump white mulberries served at every opportunity. To eat these juicy white mulberries, picked from drooping branches off the tree right in front of you, at precisely the right moment in the season, is nothing short of eating ecstasy. And, that's before considering its crucial role in the production of silk, so vital to historical trade here, made by a flightless, blind moth that lays its eggs in the leaves of white mulberry trees.

At dusk, I walked into town and up the hill to the mud-walled fortifications that once made up a grand fortress built by Alexander the Great, who named this town Nur over 2,000 years ago. Beyond the trees of the city, the desert stretched out, not so much 'red sand', more a collage of brown, beige and ochre. Foundations of the old centre-of-town mahallas are still visible but the families were rehoused years ago. In their place is the same style of town square – with manicured gardens and benches too hot for the sun – that has been built in many Uzbek towns. A little soulless, a lot underused. Despite asking, it wasn't made clear to me whether the families of Nurata who once lived there had ever been fairly compensated.

The setting sun picked out the sacred springs nearby, crowded with women and children, their clothes sparkling with velvet, sequins and silk. The next morning, I packed up, and sat in the early morning sun, ample time for one last alfresco breakfast: a vast spread of quince jam, lamb samsa and omelettes. Bread arrived in a constant stream, fresh from the tandoor. And, in the centre of the courtyard, by the gurgling partridge, arms stretched upwards once again to collect more white mulberries. The tree, bountiful, plentiful and ever-giving.

Blushing Quince Jam

Nubbly, buttercup-yellow and apple-like, then once cooked, highly perfumed and rosy-pink, quince has an undoubtedly fairytale quality to it. A quintessential Uzbek ingredient, here it goes into plov, jellies and jam. At the guesthouse in Nurata, Ruslan's wife and mother always put deliciously fragrant quince jam on the table for breakfast and in the sun it would glow gem-like. Typically, it would accompany freshly baked, still-warm crusty non bread or pancakes. The quinces for this recipe should be 'just' ripe.

MAKES 2 X 450ML/16FL OZ JARS

650ml/2¾ cups water

500g/1lb 2oz quince, peeled, cored and cubed

350g/1¾ cups granulated sugar

10g/⅔ tbsp butter

Juice of ½ lemon

Place a small plate in the freezer before you start cooking. In a large uncovered saucepan, bring the water to a boil, add the fruit, then simmer for around 20–30 minutes until the quince is tender – the timing will vary slightly depending on the ripeness of the fruit.

While the jam is cooking, sterilise the jars. Preheat the oven to 140°C/275°F/gas mark 1. Wash the jars in warm, soapy water, rinse well and place them on a clean baking tray. Transfer to the oven for about 15 minutes. To sterilise lids or rubber seals, boil them in a large saucepan for 5 minutes then drain and leave them to air dry on a rack. Leave the jars in the warm oven until the jam is ready to be potted up – hot jam has to go into hot jars.

Stir in the sugar, add the butter (to give the jam sheen and help stop scum forming) and the lemon juice, and keep stirring gently to dissolve the sugar. Bring the jam to a hard rolling boil, then reduce the heat to a simmer for about 45 minutes – stirring gently and very occasionally so that it doesn't stick – by which time the jam should be breaking down and looking rosy-coloured. Check for a set, when the bubbles are rolling lazily and the jam looks glossy. Drop ½ teaspoon of jam on the plate you've had in the freezer, wait for it to cool then nudge it with a fingertip; if it wrinkles when it's pushed, setting point has been achieved. Remove from the heat and leave to rest for 10 minutes, then scoop into hot jars and seal.

Sealed and kept in a cool, dark place, the jam will last a year. Once the jar has been opened, refrigerate and eat within a couple of months.

MOSQUE

Breaking the fast

ALMATY, SOUTHEAST KAZAKHSTAN: I left Uzbekistan, travelling by
aeroplane to Almaty, the former capital of Kazakhstan, to take my return flight
home for the summer. Heaven-scraping mountains loomed over the city.
Reaching the height of the Alps, the granite stacks are a finger of the Tian Shan,
capped year-round with sugar-white snow. Forming a natural compass, wall maps
in metro stations illustrate where the exits are in relation to the peaks, helping
passengers to navigate above ground. The mountains are south and from there,
the city slopes down and northwards. For a few days, I rented an apartment
on the 14th floor of a high-rise, by the Alatau metro stop. It came with a small
balcony, and from there I'd sit and gaze up at the range, when morning broke,
when storms thundered and at twilight gloom. The solid crags exuded a constant
steadiness but, depending on the time of the day, the bands of mountain rock
morphed from one colour to the next, pinkish to golden to dove grey. A sublime
backdrop.

Nature is never far away here. Fountains are fed by mountain snowmelt that
flows through irrigation systems, called aryks, some so wide that people once
bathed in them. Nearby valleys, rivers, gorges and lakes all call out for picnics and
hikes in the warmer months. The snack here is qurut, traditional trail food for
out on the steppe.

But it is furthest away from the mountains, in the lower northern part of the
city, where some of the most fascinating corners exist, in the micro-districts,
places that best reflect Kazakhstan's great multicultural mix, where Tatar,
Ukrainian, Russian and Korean minorities live.

TO TOUCH THE MOUTH

Take Sultan Kurgan, a Uyghur neighbourhood, out past Almaty I railway station,
past restaurants run by Meskhetian Turks, Georgians and Azerbaijanis and just
beyond a diner called 'Jesus Café'. Sultan Kurgan, home to a Uyghur restaurant
called Anjur, recognisable by its yellow facade and Moorish arches. And it was
there, sat at the dastarkhan, I took the traveller's earnest, often ignored, vow: to eat
and drink all that is set before you. Uyghur chai was easy enough – black tea, milk,
kaymak (thick cream), with a little dash of salty butter pooling on top – only tricky
in its generosity, coming as it did in a soup bowl. Pale opke hessip, a boiled sheep's
lung dish, was memorable. But real satisfaction was found in a plate of chopped and
braised tofu, distinct with its fried bitter green peppers and complex sauce.

And it was in Sultan Kurgan, on a busy intersection, where a matriarch and her daughter-in-law emerged from a grand mansion into the midday sun, light streaming onto their cardigan-covered backs. They came out as I was accidentally trespassing on their property. With a local friend, Mark, I was admiring the upturned Chinese-temple style eaves of their house, high above the rough coated weather-repellent pebbledash known poetically here as shuba (literally, 'fur coat'). They welcomed us in. The Akhun family were proud to be living in the handsomest Uyghur house in Almaty. Built by their relatives in the 1970s, the woodwork in the courtyard was carved by master Uzbek craftsmen. Flowers, leaves and climbing vines decorated wooden window frames, the sort that adorns elm and walnut pillars at Central Asian madrassas. A woodworked canopy, elaborate with carved roses, fans, vines and cross-hatching – months upon months of work by multiple hands – stood above a tapchan topped in the usual style with a thin cotton-stuffed floral mattress. According to the historian Antony Wynn 'Uyghur' comes from the Turkic 'oy qur', literally 'house builder', as in a settled person, not a nomad.

Neither woman was fasting for Ramadan. The mother-in-law was unwell and her daughter-in-law was expecting a baby. This led us to the subject of food and their Uyghur diet that includes laghman noodles and manti, which in the summer months are filled with local herbs. The daughter-in-law then disappeared, returning with a disc of non bread. In Kazakhstan, Mark told me, it is not possible to leave someone's home empty-handed. If you have someone to visit, expected or not, you must give them something to eat, something 'to touch the mouth'. Made with enriched milk dough, the non bread was as wide, flat and round as a bicycle wheel and the dozens of indentations on the surface, to stop the bread rising in the middle, had been made by fingers. Gratefully, I slid it under my arm.

But mostly, if I think of Sultan Kurgan, which I often do, I remember the Ali Mukhamed Mosque, tucked away in its own complex with tended-to gardens full of flowers and bird song. Of the 2,000 to 3,000 people who attend Friday prayers there, at least 80 per cent are Uyghur.

WALNUTS FROM XINJIANG

Standing by the gate to the mosque was Alim. His bushy beard matched his head-to-toe grey sportswear and like the Akhun family, he would not let a stranger pass without a welcome. A halal butcher by trade, Alim is here most weeks, his brown Lada parked up and operating as a small shop. On its roof stood five bucket-sized tubs of golden honey, from the Altai region, straddling Russia, Mongolia, China and Kazakhstan, and in the popped-open boot, boxes of walnuts, herbal

chewing sticks called miswak, little vials of perfume, halva and nabat, a kind of crystallised sugar, all presented neatly next to a spare wheel. A movable market. All of the nuts and fruits had been brought in from China's Xinjiang region, bordering Kazakhstan and Kyrgyzstan, beyond the Tian Shan Mountains. A staggeringly beautiful swathe of northwest China, this is where economic development has been paired with large-scale immigration of Han Chinese and persecution against Turkic-speaking Muslim Uyghurs who have been accused of harbouring extremists and separatist forces within their territory. The crackdown has been severe and brutal and this officially 'autonomous' region is now occupied by an enormous military and police presence. Families have been separated. Ancestral graveyards have been destroyed. Mosques and shrines torn down. There is widespread surveillance, human rights abuses, forced labour and a network of re-education camps, places of complete physical and mental control. Kazakhstan has one of the largest diaspora of Uyghur people outside of Xinjiang.

'This is Uyghurstan,' Alim said placing small walnuts into my hand as he pointed towards the mosque. 'And, these are not ordinary walnuts, they are from Hotan in Xinjiang, famous for their flavour.' Woody, aromatic and smoky, the walnuts cracked open with just a slight tightening of the fist. In the boot were also dozens of boxes of dates, from Iran, especially popular now for Ramadan, used for breaking the fast when blood sugar is low. Alim's family left Kulja, in Xinjiang, during the Cultural Revolution, and came to Almaty, he told me.

'According to Islam, as you are not local, it is my obligation to look after you, I have a responsibility before God to take care of you. Let me give you this gift.' Alim handed me a little box of perfume that smelled of rose water and some zingy green raisins from Turpan in central Xinjiang where the famous long grapes known as 'mare's nipples' grow, with festivals held in their honour.

'Do you have family in China now?' I asked.

'Yes, but I can't go. I can't get a visa. They think I'm a terrorist when they see this beard.'

Then, another man arrived at the Lada. Short, and with a kind face soft as marshmallow, he wore a cream woven skullcap matching his trousers and shoes. Introducing himself as Ilham, he joined in with the conversation. He said he left China as a baby and has not been able to return since 1997.

'My parents are there but I can't call them because it is too dangerous. If I try, the line gets cut off. Now, I don't know who is alive and who isn't. We can only ask God for help. It must be a test from God. Peace and friendship, that's all we want.'

'A photo?' Alim asked. Visitors are a rarity here and so we all stood together, a polite distance between us, smiling for the mobile phone camera held by a Uyghur truck driver, about to set off to Germany.

Together, we walked towards the mosque, through blossoming trees, pink and red roses and peonies filling the borders. Alim's generous gift of walnuts, green raisins and the little bottle of perfume swung by my knees in a bag. Men lounged on shady benches in pairs, talking. Sylvan beauty such as this isn't hard to find in Almaty. Founded by the Russian Empire as Fort Verny in 1854 as a border fortress and Cossack village, it was christened Alma-Ata in 1921. When Russian botanist Nikolai Vavilov arrived in Almaty from Moscow on horseback in the 1920s, he wrote: 'All around the city one could see a vast expanse of wild apples covering the foothills which formed forests.' Dachas on the outskirts of the city still maintain apple orchards and nearby groves are filled with Malus sieversii, the likely ancestors of almost all apples eaten today. One traveller in the 1930s looked upon Almaty's apples and, based on their shape, declared them 'sheep-nose apples'.

The gold dome of Ali Mukhamed, and its four minarets glittered. It may be the oldest mosque in the city, but it is not old at all. All existing mosques in pre-Soviet times were destroyed and this was simply the first to be built after the collapse of the Soviet Union in 1991. Through the thick scent of roses in full bloom came the unmistakable waft of mutton. Somewhere, someone was cooking.

I followed Ilham to the back of the mosque where a kitchen, used only for Ramadan in the warmer months and therefore covered only by a corrugated iron roof with no walls, was busy with cooks preparing food. Ehmet, the chef, was a man of numbers and while stirring two giant kazans ('cauldrons') of mutton he told us that in six hours, at 8.17 p.m., 500 men will arrive. To feed the men will cost $700. The plov alone needs 50 kilos of rice, 45 kilos of mutton and two packets of salt. On the last day of Ramadan they will feed 1,400 men, which means 12 kazans to cook the rice dish. Ten trestle tables, lined with 20 long benches either side, had been set up close to the kitchen. In the background, two women, Ehmet's helpers, chopped a pyramid of carrots and onions into matchsticks, later they would serve the men food, as the only women present.

'Will you come to iftar, as our guests?' Ilham asked. I was honoured, and intrigued. It would be my first iftar. But I was worried I'd cause offence. Women don't attend. Mark reassured me that the offer was genuine. We agreed to return.

AT THE TOP TAPCHAN

The next night, Mark and I came back to the mosque kitchen, a little ahead of time. Ehmet had been joined by three men and four women in headscarves who flew about preparing hundreds of bowls for soup. The long tables had been laid. On shiny plastic pink and purple tablecloths were dates to break the fast, sugar cubes, bowls of apricots from Uzbekistan, apples from Almaty, cherries, yellow plums, borsok (fried puffy bread), tomato salad with dill, and non bread in baskets. Pineapple and cherry juice in cartons. Pepsi and Fanta. The kitchen whirred, operating like a busy restaurant. Familiar faces from yesterday began arriving.

Alim told us that as guests we would be seated with him and Ilham at the one tapchan present, a raised wooden platform close to the kitchen, not on the benches with everyone else. He instructed us to sit. Despite heavily protesting this generosity ('we are not even fasting'), I got nowhere. The hungry arrived at exactly 8.17 p.m. and with them seated, we sat down too. Checking my headscarf, I crossed my legs under the square tapchan. Enamel teapots made their way to each table, one at each end. Young men, wearing T-shirts, chinos, and everyday clothes began taking their seats. Then, with a full house and freed from the day's fast, I saw Ehmet down almost a litre of water in one long gulp.

Over my shoulder, I watched as cooks heaved heavy tin pails of steaming chicken broth into hundreds of lined-up china bowls, identical with their floral motif, already filled with noodles and vegetables. At the tapchan, we were joined by the imam's helper, an elegant man named Mehmut who wore a maroon velvet dopi hat with gold stitching and a perfectly pressed shirt. A well-fed muezzin, sat down, too. No one paid me any mind. Our table was served first by the anonymous hands of the female helpers. John Wardell, the English copper miner who arrived in Kazakhstan in 1914, also witnessed iftar feasting: 'During the whole of this month they neither ate nor drank from sunrise to sunset. At night, however, they made up for the day's privations by feasting and singing for hours to the accompaniment of two-stringed guitars and howling dogs.'

It was humid under the corrugated iron and Ehmet, who looked absolutely drained, absolutely flattened, was once again engrossed in his task. This time, finishing the plov. I later found out he had suffered a heart attack and had undergone heart surgery only a few months before. He would have been up since dawn for first prayers.

We started on the chicken noodle soup, and then moved on to the plov, mutton and rice with yellow and orange carrots. We were always served first and I felt my cheeks flush with shame. We'd eaten two meals already that day and had drunk as much water as we'd liked. The plov was good and we shared it and Ilham encouraged me onto second helpings. Leaning over from the crossed-leg position meant some rice got lost on the way, raining down onto the cloth. Chattering

across the hub-bub we didn't want for elbow room at the top tapchan but on the long tables men were crammed in close together, feasting quickly on the chicken noodle soup, salads and plov. Everyone ate loudly. Smacking lips, champing jaws. There was some muffled but indulgent belching.

'This food is a gift. It is God's mercy,' said Ilham.

How rare it is to see such a gathering, such a community in these numbers. Every night, for a month. And what discipline it takes to fast. My great-grandfather, convinced of its health benefits did it once a week, every Sunday, and lived well into his 90s in a southeast London terraced house without heating and a coal bunker at the bottom of the garden where the trains went past.

I asked Mark what the wives, mothers and sisters of the men here tonight might be doing and an elder at the table chipped in explaining that they go to one another's houses, taking turns through Ramadan. Female communities are tight here, Mark added, often operating an informal loan system where women will help each other out with money. A large poster attached to the corrugated iron wall read: 'Do not fast to lose weight, only fast in gratitude to Allah.' More and more people in Kazakhstan, I heard later, are interested in fasting for vanity, using Ramadan as an excuse to slim down. As it says in the Qur'an: 'Woe to those who pray, but are unmindful of their prayer, or who pray only to be seen by people.'

A microphone was passed down to Mehmut, the imam's helper who was sitting next to me, who began reciting a prayer. From sitting crossed-legged I realised I had lost all feeling in my ankles and knees and feared I may not be able to get up again. Sitting like this for any length of time is humiliatingly impossible for most westerners. No one else seemed bothered by it. Mehmut then introduced the muezzin, a portly man who, sat opposite me, looked like he could be from the North Caucasus, and handed him the microphone. Likely to have trained in Egypt or Turkey, I had spotted him cramming scripture on his mobile phone before. He began to sing in Arabic to the otherwise silent gathering. A pure, beautiful voice, liquid notes filling the room, soft, powerful and determined. I felt the sting of tears, and quickly fought them back. His head moved ever so slightly, languishing movements with the melody. Eventually, tears fell, hidden behind my hand. I cried at the beauty of devotion and I cried because of the contrast across the border in China where Uyghurs have been labelled as extremists simply for practising their religion.

The men at the table chatted. 'The most important thing in Islam is not to do bad to anybody, and to respect your elders. It is a religion of brothers. Don't drink, don't smoke. Live a good life,' one man said. 'And if you grow your beard,

it's not only good for you and your face but also your vision, and your teeth.'
Everyone laughed at this comment except the man who'd uttered it. Then, far
away, somebody dropped a bowl, and on hearing it smash, everyone cheered. A
bit like in a pub when a glass slips and shatters. The women began the mammoth
task of clearing up; they'd stay, they told me, until about 2 a.m.

We headed outside. The night was fresh and cool, and the scent of roses
lingered on. The caretaker followed me out and gave me five Almaty apples as a
parting gift to put in my pockets. Then the caretaker's wife appeared, and having
never met me before, put a bunch of wrapped roses and peonies into my hands.
In a high-pitched voice, she reeled off generous blessings, promises and a little
personal history. 'He is the guard, I am the gardener. Together we make a good
team. We have been married for 45 years. Come next month when the garden is
ready I'll give you a whole bouquet.'

To make a donation, I stepped inside a small office and put some banknotes
into a wooden box sealed by a huge padlock, and was handed an official receipt.
'May we accept your donation. This will go towards the needy, and in your name
we'll say a prayer that you'll have good luck and good health,' Ilham said, softly.

I thanked Ilham again for the hospitality, the food, the unfussy natural
welcome, the opportunity to share such an extraordinary and unforgettable meal.
'Don't even think about the food. But please remember us and our conversations.'

'How could I ever forget?' I replied.

I returned towards the mountains in a taxi. I couldn't see the peaks in the dark
but I could feel their presence and the power of nature. Mountains are places
of spiritual renewal. For Chinese Taoist priests, embarking on a sacred ritual is
to 'enter the mountain'. The mountain Muztagh-Ata, located in Xinjiang, its
name Uyghur for 'father of ice mountains', was believed by locals to hide a garden
of Eden under the snow and to be inhabited by camels of ghostly whiteness.
Godlike, divine in their making, their remoteness and power is an antidote to
the cruelties of man. I'd keep Ilham and Alim, and the Uyghur iftar feast, at the
front of my mind long, long after my plane had taken off, long after the celestial
mountains were far out of sight.

*Names and other identifying details in this piece have been changed to protect the
people mentioned.*

Sultan Kurgan Tofu

A punchy and lively dish, this is a version of the memorably good spicy tofu eaten at Anjur, in Sultan Kurgan, the heart of northern Almaty's Uyghur community. Fried green peppers (usually harvested before they fully ripen, which gives them a slight acerbic quality) have a pleasing bitterness, so do use these rather than yellow, red or orange ones. Chilli-wise, add more or less according to taste.

SERVES 2

FOR THE BRAISING STOCK
150ml/5fl oz vegetable stock

2 tbsp soy sauce

1 tsp ground or crushed Sichuan pepper

1 tsp Chinkiang black rice vinegar

1 tsp Shaoxing rice wine (optional)

1 star anise

½ tsp chilli flakes

2 cloves

10–15 whole peppercorns, crushed

2 tsp granulated sugar

FOR THE TOFU
Vegetable oil for frying

400g/14oz firm tofu, cut into 3cm/1in cubes

1 green (bell) pepper, sliced into thin strips

Pinch of sea salt

1 tbsp tomato purée (paste)

1 tbsp of water

Basmati rice, to serve

2 green or red chillies, sliced and deseeded, to garnish

To make the braising stock combine the stock ingredients in a jug and stir until the sugar dissolves.

To prepare the tofu, you need to make it as dry as possible. Place it between two clean tea towels, then lay it on a plate and put weight on top of it (I use a few heavy cookbooks). Leave for 20 minutes to let the water drain out into the towels.

Pour enough oil into a high-sided frying pan or a wok so that it comes up 1cm/½in and place over a high heat. The oil needs to be really hot otherwise the tofu will absorb it rather than fry. Add the tofu in batches, using tongs to avoid splashing hot oil. Turn until each side has a golden crust and releases easily (if it sticks it's because the crust hasn't yet formed). Remove and set on paper towels.

Carefully remove most of the oil from the pan, leaving just enough to fry the pepper, add a pinch of salt and fry for around 5 minutes until soft and lightly coloured. Remove and wipe out the pan, add a splash of oil and cook the tomato purée over a medium heat for a few minutes. Add the braising stock, plus a tablespoon of water, then add the tofu and the pepper, just to heat them up.

Remove the cloves and the star anise before serving it all up on a bed of rice with some sliced chillies scattered over the top.

Sour Cherry Borscht

Kazakhstan has long absorbed cuisines from other cultures. Of course there are restaurants serving the national dish, beshbarmak (boiled noodles with horsemeat), but equally it is very 'Almaty' to order Dungan noodles or Georgian khinkali. In the former capital, there is a Russian restaurant called Gosti ('guest'), housed in a salmon-pink merchant's house. Inside, it has lacy freestanding lampshades, rows of samovars lined up on bookshelves, velvet armchairs and sepia-tinted photographs of the trading family who used to own the house. Of course it's a little kitsch, that's the point, but it's romantic, too, and the food is excellent. It was here that I ate borscht named after Sverdlovsk, the old name for the city of Yekaterinburg (although I never did understand why). I hope you'll like it for its cherry-sweet-sour flavour.

SERVES 4

1.5 litres/6 cups beef stock (or vegetable stock if you prefer, though it will lose a little depth)

500g/1lb 2oz beetroot (beets), peeled and halved

2 medium-size floury potatoes, peeled and cubed

1 large carrot, grated

1 onion, thinly sliced

200g/7oz cabbage, shredded into strips

1 fresh bay leaf

½ tsp ground black pepper

1 tsp sugar

1 tsp salt

Dash of cayenne pepper

2 tbsp cider vinegar

250g/9oz frozen or dried sour cherries

Sour cream and fresh dill fronds, finely chopped, to serve

Garlic bread and gherkins, to serve (optional)

In a large casserole or saucepan, bring the stock to a boil then add the beetroot and boil for 10 minutes to soften them slightly and to begin infusing the broth with their deep-ruby colour.

Carefully remove the beetroot using a slotted spoon and when cool enough to handle, grate them (you may want to wear gloves if you do this by hand).

Return the grated beetroot to the stock with the potatoes, carrot, onion and cabbage, and cook for 10–15 minutes, or until the vegetables are tender.

Add all of the other ingredients except for the cherries, sour cream and dill. Stir, return to the boil and simmer for 15 minutes.

Finally, add the cherries and warm through – if using frozen they can go in straight from the freezer, just cook them through for a couple of minutes.

Serve topped with sour cream and a sprinkling of dill, perhaps with some garlic bread and a little plate of gherkins on the side.

Chingiz's Apple Vanilla Vodka

In Almaty there is a bar called Frau Irma. The staff are friendly and one barkeeper in particular, Chingiz, often treated me to a couple of free shots of his homemade vanilla apple vodka which he'd pour from a large flask.

You'll need a 1-litre/2 pint jar or decanter with a lid for this and the trick is to tightly pack in the apples. It is quite eye-catching with the fruit suspended in the pitcher. What to do with the apples once you've drunk the vodka? You could make a granita or chop them through a fruit salad.

MAKES 1 LITRE/4 CUPS

5 small apples such as Fiesta, peeled, cored and kept whole

2 dried pear halves

1 litre/4 cups vodka

2 small drops (and no more) vanilla extract

Pack the apples into a tall glass jar (I use a Kilner). Drop in the pear halves and pour over just shy of 1 litre of vodka and finally add the vanilla extract. Seal and let it sit for at least a week, in a cool, dark place, where it will take on the flavour of the fruit.

To serve (ideally at a party), pour 40–50ml/3 tbsp of the vodka into a chilled glass. Remove the infused pear halves from the jar, slice them into long strips to sit astride the top of the glass.

PART TWO

AUTUMN

REGISTAN

Celebrating a wedding

SAMARKAND, CENTRAL UZBEKISTAN: With the cold wind yet to come and the summer breeze trailing, I returned to Uzbekistan. A friend's niece was getting married, and I had a wedding invitation in hand, so I travelled to Samarkand by train from Tashkent. From the station platform, appetite drove me first into the lunchtime belly of a busy unnamed restaurant on Lev Tolstoy Street.

There was no menu so the rosy-cheeked men I shared my table with took charge, gently hastening the waitress ('she's come from Scotland!'), ordering for me what they were having themselves. Gold-rimmed teapots arrived, brimming with green tea, followed by baskets of non bread and side plates of refreshing tomato and purple basil salad, all partners for the platter of plov which came piled high as a sandcastle. The same meal for all. An edible expression of the community and the people who cook it best, Tajiks and Uzbeks. A little greasy, but nonetheless demanding second helpings. There is something mystical about plov that elevates it above taste and presentation. It is a shared obsession, generally served for lunch, representing hospitality, community and identity. People pride themselves on their skill in preparing it. The most talented chefs, called oshpaz, can serve plov for up to 1,000 people from a single kazan ('cauldron') at weddings and festivals. Plov is identity here and it has become a symbol of the country, to be marketed to foreigners. 'All you need is plov' (a riff on the Beatles song 'All You Need is Love'), is printed on T-shirts. Plov is sold, as a meaty souvenir, in cans with ring-pulls at airports.

Arminius Vámbéry, in his 1863 book *Travels in Central Asia*, witnessed plov being prepared in Samarkand: 'The princely pilow [plov] . . . consisted of a sack of rice, three sheep chopped to pieces, a large pan of sheep's fat (enough to make five pounds of candles) and a small sack of carrots . . .' Out here, it is easy to take this legend of lunchtime for granted, but we shouldn't. Elsewhere in the world, plov, the real thing, prepared slowly, rich with lamb tail fat, onions and carrots, is a rarity. You'll only find dedicated cafés selling it in pockets of New York City and Moscow and a few cities of the former Soviet Union, where Uzbeks live, their kitchens and cafés a continuity of homeland and family. 'If you're rich, eat plov; if you're poor, eat plov', as the Uzbek saying goes.

It felt good to be back in Samarkand. To be among golden pears, quinces and monuments made of desert-coloured brickwork built on the order of 14th century emperor Tamerlane, in the same city where his astronomer grandson Ulugbek demanded every resident to 'strive for knowledge'. But then, a sobering sight. Another victim of Uzbekistan's nationwide beautification project, this time

the old 11-storey Intourist hotel. Imperially positioned, right by Tamerlane's mausoleum, the Gur-e-Amir, this long-neglected hotel had blended brutalist hulk with a little Oriental flair, displaying Samarkand's city seal, a legendary winged snow leopard known as Aq Bars, on its facade. Deemed worthy of postage stamp fame only 50 years ago, now it has been reduced to dust. Another gem gone for ever. Throughout Uzbekistan, officials have tended to restore, or demolish, often using improper and irreversible restoration materials, where they might have preserved more holistically. In nearby Shahrisabz, 50 miles south of Samarkand, UNESCO monitors reported concerns that the 'authenticity and integrity' of the city's historic centre had been 'compromised'. As in Tashkent and Nurata, whole traditional mahallas ('neighbourhoods') have been flattened. In Samarkand, tilting minarets, crumbling ribbed domes and collapsing mosques have been straightened, reconstructed and polished to the point where gazing upon them is to swim in a sea of gleaming tile work, as turquoise as a Caribbean atoll. Beautiful but a little too flawless. At odds with the original brickwork made of mortar mixed with camel's milk and egg yolk. I wondered whether the robe-wearing merchants, as seen in vintage photographs – sat in crumbling bazaars both magnificent and filthy – would, given the chance, even begin to recognise this sanitised version of their city.

Samarkand does, despite all this, stand high. Despite the earthquakes and conquerors that have rocked and flattened it over the ages, despite the looting treasure-seekers and despite overzealous restoration. Cities evolve and change, it is their nature, and old buildings must be preserved lest we lose them for ever. Ella Christie wrote of Tamerlane's final resting place, the Gur-e-Amir, 'I can never forget the sight of that fluted blue dome rising far above the delicate spring green' and it is impossible not to stare, however many times you may have seen it. It is lustrous and sublime. Beware nostalgia.

BRAVE DRINKERS, GOLDEN GOBLETS

The Samarkand wedding, as you'd expect, was elaborate. My friend, Abdu, steered me through a thronging restaurant, the size of a small stadium, where friends and family members had gathered. Nervous-looking relatives rearranged roses, and chatted at round tables covered with plates of food. A band took to the stage and an electric guitar started up, then a keyboard, and so began a series of mournful-sounding songs. The singer nodded to the tune, a row of banknotes tucked into his hat bobbing by his ears. The music was stirring, and fantastically loud. Unable to speak, we silently ate Tajik and Uzbek dishes. Manpar, a meatball noodle soup with chickpeas, yogurty chaka, and naturally, plov. Uzbek weddings are big business and they had recently made the newspapers. President Shavkat Mirziyoyev had criticised the cost of celebrations, singling out 'shameless' spending on wedding feasts and the number of guests, which almost always run into several hundred. Mirziyoyev, who came to power in September 2016 following the death of Islam Karimov, is following a tradition of state authorities in Central Asia trying to steer and control civil morals. In Tajikistan, across the border where many Samarkand families have roots and relatives, Tajik President Emomali Rahmon referred to extravagant wedding receptions as 'unnecessary and unaffordable gatherings'. For now, in Samarkand, things continued as usual with enormous amounts of food, symbols of plenty, hope and generosity for the newlywed couple.

Abdu's sister took me by the hand to see the symbolic 'taking out the bride' ceremony. Crossing a busy street, with dozens of other guests, we edged past the wedding car, a hired Rolls Royce, and a band of musicians who, dressed in gold and black velvet robes pointed their karnays – long, thin trumpets – skywards, blessing the wedding with their songs. Upstairs, on the top floor of the house, glittering bridal outfits for the coming week hung on mannequins, all featuring the most work-intensive designs possible: gold embroidery, silk ikat, feathers and lace. The bride, standing under a glittery wedding canopy, elegantly bowed up and down showing her respect to her future in-laws. Once joined by her new husband, a woman in a gold headscarf stepped forward, handing the pair a small bowl of honey to dip a finger in, and sliding two non bread loaves under his arm for the couple to eat together as man and wife. Auspicious food gestures for a happy life together.

Samarkand, byword for exoticism, has long been the setting for the very grandest of weddings. In her book, *Through Khiva to Golden Samarkand*, Ella Christie quotes from Edward Gibbon's *Decline and Fall of the Roman Empire* who wrote of Tamerlane: 'The marriage of six of the Emperor's grandsons was esteemed an act of religion as well as of paternal tenderness . . . Whole forests were cut down to supply fuel for the kitchens; the plain was spread with pyramids of meat and vases of every liquor, to which thousands of guests were courteously invited . . . After the marriage contracts had been ratified by the cadhis, the bridegrooms and their brides retired to the nuptial chambers; nine times, according to the Asiatic fashion, they were dressed and undressed; at each change of apparel pearls and rubies were showered on their heads.'

Tamerlane was a fabulous eater and host. Ruy González de Clavijo, nobleman of Madrid, arrived in Samarkand in the autumn of 1404. Attending a feast with other envoys, nobles and grandees, he wrote of gigantic round leather serving platters with strong handles, piled high with mutton and horsemeat. Whenever Tamerlane called for a particular stew or meat, his attendants would grab the handles, and drag the smooth-bottomed dishes along the ground to him. They

were too heavy to lift. Carvers, dressed in aprons and leather sleeves, would then kneel before him and cut the meat, which was then placed in 'trencherlike basins . . . some of gold, some of silver'. Servers would then pour over a broth, 'as a sauce for the meat' and fill golden goblets with sugared mare's milk. There was enough food to last a whole year. Gifts were paraded in front of the emperor, although he'd accept no present 'that had not been lying awaiting his pleasure three days under inspection', Clavijo noted. At these feasts, the term 'bahadur' was reserved for the very greediest of imbibers, it meant 'brave drinker'.

I slipped out of the wedding, taking a taxi to the Jewish cemetery, close to the Shah-i-Zinda, an avenue of mausoleums and an ocean of blue tile work dating back to the 14th and 15th centuries, filled with the tombs of Tamerlane's relatives, and the mausoleum of Kusam ibn-Abbas, a cousin of the Prophet Muhammed. At the cemetery, portraits and illustrations on gravestones, inscribed with Hebrew and Cyrillic, hinted at the lives of those buried here: tailors, hairdressers and fabric dyers. Many Samarkand Jews were musical, absorbing Islamic traditions and playing at courts of the emirs. At Bukhara's famous synagogue I was once sold two CDs by a caretaker.

The number of Jews in Uzbekistan has shrunk significantly. Many fled because of anti-Semitism under the Soviet Union, although it was grim long before as well. In the 1800s Jews of Bukhara were forced to wear a rope around their waists as a reminder that they could be hanged at any time. One historian, writing in a journal in 1903, noted their settling in Jerusalem: 'Jews, from Bokhara and Samarkand . . . They are the richest of all communities; and their houses, on a hill to the north of the city, are a great advance on the miserable hovels which are being erected by other communities. The rabbis dress most becomingly in long grey robes, with rough Astrakhan caps, and long close-fitting boots; while the women, except those who all too soon have adopted the clothes of the land, wear picturesque loose robes of most fantastic hues. Many of their houses are furnished with taste, especially in respect of carpets . . .' Around 100,000 Jews with Bukharan heritage live in Israel today. Many more Uzbek Jews left during the hardships after the Soviet Union collapsed in 1991. Today, there are only around 200 remaining Jews in Bukhara, with 50,000 or so residing in New York City.

I walked towards Siyob Bazaar, stepping through a late-afternoon light both fizzy and golden, a luminosity that Igor Savitsky, aesthete and founder of the great art museum, soaked up: 'Two years in Samarkand also helped me to appreciate the enormous meaning of colour. Colour and light – with which Samarkand and Central Asia are flooded . . .' Vendors at the bazaar were hauling boxes and packing up, their abundance still laid out on long tables: mulberries, grapes, walnuts, dates, prunes, raisins, almonds and pistachios. Piles of shiny maroon pomegranates – the juice of which Tamerlane's armies allegedly drank before going into battle – collectively tilted their crowns to the resplendent Bibi-Khanym Mosque, one of the most magnificent buildings in the world, silently exuding stir and beauty. Standing 40 metres high, it was financed by Tamerlane's victories in India. Christie found it 'Amazing, considering that he lived as far back as the fourteenth century, that so much remains of those architectural adornments added by him to Samarkand, which he made his capital.' One-eyed and with crippled limbs, some historians believe Tamerlane wanted to beautify his surroundings as he was not a handsome man, even refusing ever to look in a mirror, while others say it was simply his way of venerating God.

Dusk. The sun dipped and the clamour of the city began to sink with it. Suited men and schoolchildren with their mothers meandered through the mahallas heading home. I got to the Registan, the colossal square that is the heart of Samarkand and was the centre of Tamerlane's ancient empire, as darkness fell. Christie described a scene at the Registan, just before World War I when she visited, almost impossible to picture now: 'Food is appetisingly set out on brass trays, in the form of fried meat cakes, and bowls of rice . . . there was omelette aux fines herbes, which is made in a copper pan. Hard boiled eggs were also sold, dyed red and blue.' Now, the square is empty of food but filled with tourists, who had arrived with cameras just as it began lighting up. A thousand neon beams waved across the three madrassas that flank the square. Once the Registan was silent at night, now lights waved and pulsed. Future generations will likely never see it unaffected, naturally bathed in darkness. Tourism is the latest trade on the Silk Road and the city seems to know it, it has become more aware of itself, prouder. More self-conscious. But Samarkand will keep on changing, and in ten years from now we will likely look back again on what has been lost and what has been gained. Again, beware nostalgia.

EXPLODING WINTER MELONS

Between Samarkand and Kokand, where I was headed next, is melon land. During the late autumn harvest, small steel beds topped with little fabric canopies line the roads. Providing a place of rest, these make-do beds ensure the melon sellers are able to remain 'Wide awake as brokers from Bukhara', as the old Uzbek proverb goes. According to one exporter, Uzbekistan has 22,000 hectares of melon fields, producing 400–500,000 tonnes a year. There are 160 varieties of melon but it is the winter ones, harvested from mid-September onwards, that are treasured for their vitamins and antioxidants. Strapped to the rafters of specially made melon sheds, called qovunxona, with rope or netting, they ripen in slow motion over the cold months, skin wrinkling, flesh gaining maximum sucrose, becoming ever more melon-y. Cultivated that way, they are good to keep for almost a year. Historically that made them perfect Silk Road goods, suitable to travel overland, without perishing, across vast distances. One legend warned that particularly ripe melons could, however, spontaneously burst out on the steppe with the thundering hoof beats of horses. Ancient Uzbek kingdoms would send forth their prized winter melons, fruits of peculiar beauty, wrapped in cotton, as much coveted gifts. Slowly, they'd go by camel caravan to Russian tsars, Chinese emperors and to the Abbasid capital of Baghdad.

Many of the world's greatest travellers to Central Asia wrote winter melons into their stories. In Samarkand, Clavijo, the nobleman of Madrid and guest of Tamerlane, noted that, as well as palaces, there were great orchards, Persian-style gardens and ample melons: 'The melons of this countryside are abundant and very good, and at the season of Christmas there are so many melons . . . Every day camels bring in their loads of melons from the country and it is a wonder how many are sold and eaten in the market.'

Babur, great-great-great grandson of Tamerlane, born in Andijan in the Fergana Valley, was a victim of melon madness. On conquering northern India in 1526, and becoming its emperor, he bemoaned the south Asian climate in his memoir, *The Baburnama*, but mainly he lamented the lack of fruit: 'no grapes or muskmelons, no good fruits, no ice or cold water, no good bread or food in their bazaars'. Where he came from there were superior melons with 'skin yellow and puckered like shagreen leather . . . pulp four fingers thick'.

Studded with saucer-size porthole windows, Uzbekistan's melon sheds require good ventilation, therefore many have been built close to the 'city of winds' – Kokand – 300 miles to the east of Samarkand, deep in the heart of the Fergana Valley. Headed there by road, I went not in search of melons, winter or otherwise, but halva.

WORKSHOP

Searching for artisans

KOKAND, EAST UZBEKISTAN: Drowning out melodic morning bird song was the sound of smashing, splintering, wood. Bang, bang, bang. Crack! Wood on wood. The hammering reverberated around the usually tranquil Juma Mosque in Kokand. A momentary pause, and then it started up again. It was breakfast time in Kokand, city of winds and city of khans, gateway to the Fergana Valley, but Abdul Wahid had no time for tea. His rolling pin went up and down, again and again, splintering and crushing hundreds of almonds and pistachios. Lost in the rhythm of his work, under his breath he blessed each ingredient and process, 'bismillah, ar-rahman, ar-rahim' ('In the name of God, the Merciful and Compassionate…'), pouring out more almonds, occasionally throwing one upwards into his opened mouth. Finally, putting down the rolling pin, he ushered in his two young disciples, both no older than 20, who flip-flopped into the sparse kitchen in sandals. They were late and Wahid, dressed in trainers and a white laboratory coat, needed their help to lift and pour out the huge vats of creamy, nutty halva into shallow steel platters the size of car doors. Wahid's disciples carried the trays out into the cool morning air, setting them down onto a large marble counter in another room, complete with a wildly arabesque roof, tucked behind the mosque. Built in 1809 by Umar Khan, the complex's main draw is a huge wooden aivan (canopy) elaborately painted in rainbow colours in the Fergana style, held up by 98 redwood columns from India. A man-made forest of mind-bending colours.

Wahid is from a family of passionate confectioners and is a third-generation halva maker. Given the nod from the President nine years ago, he has been making halva at this mosque, now more museum with its knife workshops and little showrooms, ever since. Kokand is famous for halva and there are dozens of dedicated cooks in the city. Every week, with a little help from his trainees, Wahid makes over 200 kilos of halva in a room repurposed as a basic kitchen. 'Every cook has their own approach and recipe, but this is the best in Uzbekistan. This is Kokand halva.' Marbled like fine Italian paper, its beauty lies in the fact that within each square, each colourful ingredient sings out: cream-coloured almond, neon-green pistachio and dried maroon-brown persimmon. Little morsels of edible art. Wahid handed me a piece. Intensely buttery, each fruit and nut flavour was instantly recognisable and it was pleasingly nubby. I wonder if it was halva that Ella Christie ate in Samarkand: 'The bakers who are very clever at their trade, also make a cake of flour, honey, and pistachio nuts.' Quite possibly.

One of Uzbekistan's three great 19th-century khanates, along with Khiva and Bukhara, Kokand's city palace nearby, is where the tourist buses stop. Built in stages and completed in 1873, the Palace of Khudayar Khan has cool courtyards dotted with pomegranate trees and over 100 rooms, reflecting past powers. During the Kokand khanate, special envoys went to Istanbul to garner support from the sultans, against Russia, China, and the khans of Bukhara with whom they were at odds once they gained independence from the Bukharan Emirate. They carried gifts from Kokand: silks threaded with gold, shawls, pomegranates from Margilan, and precious zedoary brought in from China, cousin to turmeric and sometimes called 'mango ginger'. In Istanbul, cherished cargo was exchanged to be taken back to Kokand: clotted cream, honey, jam, salt, olive oil and horseshoe nails for their stallions.

Ella Christie arrived here travelling first by open carriage, through the desert steppe. She specifically feared a bee-size black spider which, capable of killing a camel in less than three hours, she saw once mummified in a bottle of spirits, but never alive. She then pootled, by slow train, into Kokand, never travelling faster than 20 miles-per-hour. On arrival, she found a 'garden city', famed for its mulberries and walnuts and silver-leaved willow trees, acacia trees and forests of poplars. A wealthy city, built on the cotton trade, she described a hard-to-imagine population that went free and easy on 'the most expensive brands of champagne that France can produce'. Today, it isn't easy to find a drink in Kokand.

During her visit, Christie, ever observant, discovered an early prototype of an 'Aldershot Oven'. This stove was a field oven, which according to the *Manual of Military Cooking* in 1910, could be erected in a trench and had the capability to cook dinners for '220 men'. In Kokand, a cook had slapped inside this oven 'loaves or meat cakes', presumably non bread and samsa. She was less impressed by a wandering 'refreshment seller' who, with cups barely washed, recycled an icy milk drink with any remaining ice or drops from a buyer added back to the pail.

Christie travelled, too, to Margilan, by train, home of ikat textile weaving, a part of the Fergana Valley, blessed with the best soil and the finest climate in Central Asia. It reminded her of northern Italy for its irrigation and agricultural fields.

SCORPIONS, PURPLE BASIL AND INDIGO

I stayed in Fergana city, a 15-minute drive away from Margilan, where the Uzbek obsession with fruit, flowers and herbs plays out along ordinary nondescript roads. You smell it before you see it. Filling borders along junctions and avenues are rows of neatly planted purple basil. From the beds where marigolds the colour of egg yolks are also planted, the purple leaves spice the air, a natural citywide air freshener, lifting up as the heat beats down.

In a taxi to Margilan, where I hoped to meet a master ikat weaver I'd met before called Fazlitdin Dadajanov, the driver told me that the following morning he'd swap his car for a truck and would drive Fergana-picked fruit all the way to Novosibirsk in Russia, nearly 2,000 miles north. The autumn roads in the Fergana Valley are busy at this time of year with lorry drivers hauling the season's harvest northwards. Vendors hawking scarlet pomegranates tempted me constantly. At any opportunity, a sweet messy ceremony would unfold: the car would stop, I would jump out, buy a bag of pomegranates, and with a pen knife the pomegranate would be quartered, and its seeds, cherry-sweet with a tiny drop of sour, released to be crunched and sucked like sweets.

I arrived to Margilan too late. Dadajanov was in Tajikistan. I'd missed him. His son did not speak much Russian or English, but he already had apprentices under him, children no older than ten, who knew how to greet people and serve tea in the Uzbek way – with charm and with one hand on their heart. Inside the workshop silk ikat hung in long panels. The faint clickety-clack of textile looms echoed. Dadajanov's son walked me through the workshop full of all the things I find completely irresistible, cotton and silk weaved with fabulous designs and patterns full of hidden messages and motifs. Dramatic shimmering designs in every colour, soft-edged, almost blurred patterns, to make the material look as though it is floating, cloud-like. Red bleeds into green, blue bleeds into yellow.

Ikat follows nature, its design reflecting fruit and botanics and the intensity of the land. Carnations and pomegranates are emblems of fruitfulness; decorating bed covers as part of the dowry for a newly married couple, they are stitched, too, onto ikat robes, suggesting strength and abundance. Scorpions embroidered around the ankles of trousers, and onto nomad felt blankets, are magical power symbols to protect the wearer from harm. Traditionally pomegranate was boiled with iron filings to create a black dye, while pistachios provided a form of tannin helping to fix colour. Other kitchen items were put to use: egg white to stiffen, gloss and glaze cloth, while Turkmen tribes added wheat sourdough and bone marrow to their powdered indigo dye which was laid in the sun to ferment. Code is applied to colour: red is said to be life-giving, yellow shows married status. Textiles enlivened the everyday: an embroidered bag to carry tea leaves, called a chaikhalta, dyed with madder and indigo; a lali posh, material for wrapping food, decorated with sun discs; a salt carrier, woven and narrow-necked, and block-printed soufreh, a clean fabric surface to prepare food upon.

Under Soviet rule, weaving families like Dadajanov's joined the masses in collectivised cooperatives, or left their profession entirely. Weaving skills were lost under pressure from Moscow to mechanise and economise. Synthetic dyes gradually replaced natural dyes and only a handful of families continued their craft, in secret hidden workshops. If they were caught they'd be arrested, or worse. In the 1920s, any talk of the 14th-century Sufi saint Bahauddin Naqshband, the patron saint of weavers, was banned. Stalin's 'Movement of the Godless' was intensified in the 1930s and pushed Islamic practices underground. Mosques were closed. Beards were shaved off. In 1927 thousands of women tore off and burned their veils in public squares.

Today, the revival of ikat weaving in the Fergana Valley follows a wider Islamic renaissance throughout Central Asia. Hundreds of mosques were destroyed during the Soviet era, but today in Margilan, like elsewhere in Central Asia, they are slowly being rebuilt. Today, silk unites the community in Margilan again. Many people who live here work as weavers. Others raise silkworms, feeding them on mulberry leaves (traditionally these were kept by women in a cloth pouch and snuggled next to breasts for warmth); and the most talented, like Dadajanov, sell their designs to overseas buyers. Some residents will tell you that the ancient mulberry trees have descended by those cultivated by Tamerlane's gardeners. Ikat is alive. It has history, it is active through everyday use. It exudes its own moods and muscle.

GRAPE TUNNELS AND BLACK LAKE MELONS

Margilan has long been known for silk, with bolts of it going to Marseilles, Istanbul, Moscow and cities in Iran and India, with one traveller in the 1930s referring to the entire population of the Fergana Valley as 'silk-wise'. But it is also a wonderful place for food. Daisy-shaped bread loaves, their fat petals dotted with sesame, were proudly displayed on wooden shelves lining the pavements. One stand called Shohona ('Royal'), its logo a gold crown, displayed hundreds of giant golden non bread – glazed, covered with sesame seeds, looking like sunflowers from afar. Grey doves picked on the fallen seeds. Some bread sellers engraved their mobile telephone numbers in the centre for easy reordering. At the bazaar, winter melons with fantastical names, roughly describing their appearance, were for sale. There is 'white feather', 'wolf head', 'golden eyebrow' and 'black lake'. Disappointment came at the semi-destruction of the Khonaqoh Mosque, which draws 4,000 faithful every Friday. It may be 'under state protection' but four years ago the old part – with unusual candy-cane style twisted columns that I went looking for with original photographs in hand – had been destroyed.

The 45-minute drive from Margilan to the small city of Rishton, home to 40,000 people and dozens of workshops that support an 800-year-old ceramic tradition, was out-of-the-ordinary, flamboyantly so. The way was lit, quite literally, by canopies of grapes – tunnels of hanging pink-ish and green grapes, arching and dangling over everyday life that went on below them. Men cycled and children played underneath their glow, shaded from the worst of the heat. How did they resist plucking them all day? It looked like one never-ending edible laburnum walk. With Arab dominance and the arrival of Islam in the 7th and 8th centuries, the growing of raisin grapes, rather than wine grapes, was encouraged. Still today high-sugar dried grapes, molasses and grape vinegar from this area are famous. But this enjoyable living grape trail was met by more heart-sinking and hurried rebuilding at Rishton. The bazaar had been temporarily moved into the park, whilst the centre of the city was a building site as all the facades of all the central streets were beautified in a bizarre Potemkin fashion. Behind these bland exteriors, I was told that the mahallas carried on as usual, for now.

In an unnamed plov and shashlik café in Rishton, I sat with master-ceramist Alisher Nazirov. I'd bought some plates and cups from his workshop and he'd generously suggested lunch. His work is on display at the Khan's palace in Kokand, he has a dedicated worldwide following, a league of apprentices and is especially popular in Japan where he once studied. 'Oral tradition says that ceramics such as these were things first made for kings and khans. When normal people visited him they would be so in awe of the ceramics that any fear of the king would disappear, but then they'd also forget why they came to see the king in the first place,' Nazirov said as we sprinkled chillies onto our plov. We ordered more tea and sat back at the dastarkhan. Separated by trellis screens, one man leant over and shook his fist at our winter melon, sliced up on the table. 'That rose melon is so sweet. If you have diabetes, like me, you cannot eat it.' He looked at the melon mournfully and returned to his shashlik.

Nazirov's workshop is an exquisite space, a vine-tangled courtyard filled with lagans (platters) for plov, ceramic bread bins and water jugs, the sort of things you don't buy, because they are heavy and unyielding, and then think about for months at home afterwards. Quails sang from huge hollowed-out gourd cages, bouncing from the ceiling. The local Rishton style is dominated by bluish-green hues, blue being the most important colour as it represents the cloudless sky and therefore, happiness.

Teapots and plates are decorated with pomegranate and flowers, and the legendary Huma bird, emblem of Uzbekistan. 'This bird is on the head of every person, it's like their luck. Every artist has their own style to draw this fantastical bird,' Nazirov said. He showed me an old-style ceramic plate, crafted with feet, platters for nomads that could be set down in a stable way for eating out on the steppe. As I picked up plates, running my fingers over designs of embossed dots, as detailed as braille, Nazirov sat on a floral-quilted tapchan and freestyled a new piece, with no sketch, no plan. He told me he had studied from a ceramicist who was a 13th-generation master. 'There are many masters here but the true masters are few. There are maybe six out of two-to-three hundred others. The tradition has now become a bit mixed up as so many try to do it.'

The common adversary of communism – and its attempts to crush Islamic traditions and faith – may have gone but in the Fergana Valley, as elsewhere, corruption and rows over ethnicity and divisions over land have taken its place. Tomorrow I'd leave for Osh in Kyrgyzstan, heart of the Fergana Valley, a place where ethnic jitters are prone to explode. I wanted to visit a friend with a high-altitude food story to tell.

Friday Mosque Halva

Inspired by Abdul Wahid's halva at the Juma ('Friday') Mosque in Kokand, this is a halva with nubs of dried fruit, creamy white chocolate and neon green pistachio slivers. Wahid used dried persimmons but as they are not always easy to find, I have used dates. Cranberries would work, too, if you'd prefer a sharp-sweet note. The honey makes this halva more fudge-like and less crumbly which is how I like it. These are ideal mini-treats for teatime.

MAKES ROUGHLY 25 PIECES

115g/1 cup pistachio kernels

40g/¼ cup dates, pitted

320g/2⅔ cups plain flour

150g/⅔ cup softened butter, cubed, plus a little extra for greasing

100g/⅓ cup honey

½ tsp vanilla extract

50g/2oz white chocolate, chopped roughly the same size as the pistachio kernels

¼ tsp fine sea salt

Preheat the oven to 120°C/250°F/gas mark ½ and line a 20cm/8in square baking tin with parchment.

Place the pistachios in a bowl of boiling water for 2 minutes, then drain them. Once cool enough to handle, rub them in a clean tea towel so the skins slip off. Place in the oven for a few minutes to dry them. Remove and when cool, add 85g/3oz (keeping back 30g/1oz) of the pistachios to a food processor and pulse with the dates until you have a gravelly mix.

Tip the flour into a large saucepan and place over a medium-high heat until it slowly toasts. Stir gently and constantly until it has taken on a milky coffee colour (keep a close eye so that it doesn't burn and become bitter) and once it smells nutty and toasty, remove it.

Once cool sift into a mixing bowl (sifting is important here or you'll have little pockets of flour in the finished halva). Add the butter, honey, vanilla, white chocolate, the pistachio and date mixture and salt, and combine well, stirring it all together. Roll to make a ball of dough.

Press the mixture into the prepared baking tin, getting it into the edges and flattening the top as you go. Once smooth, scatter and press into the top the remaining pistachios, halved, for decoration.

Cover the tin with cling film and place it in the fridge to set overnight. The next day, cut out squares of roughly 4cm/1½in. The halva will keep in an airtight container in the fridge for a couple of weeks.

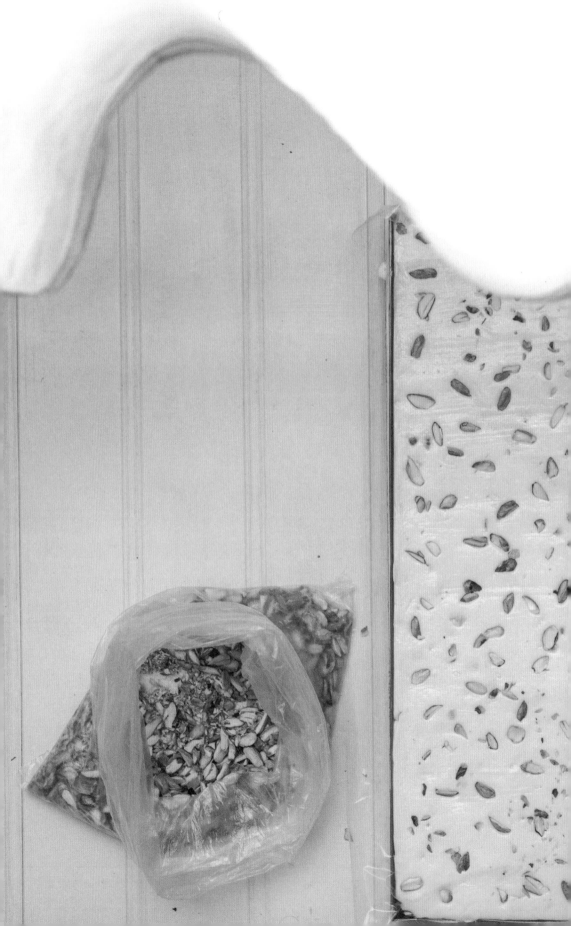

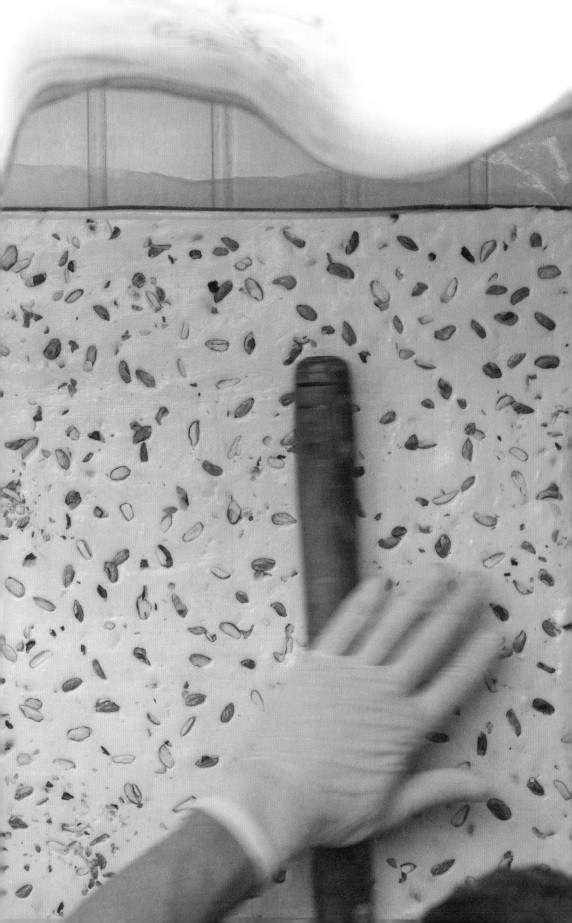

BASE CAMP

Musing on mountains and mountaineers

OSH, SOUTHWEST KYRGYZSTAN: The Throne of Solomon stands its ground above Osh. A jagged pile-up of grey rock, shadowing pilgrims 150 metres below, at the top is a prayer-room that a teenaged Babur, founder of the Mughal dynasty, diarist and devoted lover of melons, had built for himself in 1497. It is one of the holiest sites in Central Asia because some say the Prophet Muhammed prayed here, while others believe that it was here biblical Solomon ruled from his throne. In reality, Solomon's throne promises as much as it withholds.

Early one Sunday morning, I slipped upwards to the top, through the dusty, poorly tended-to graveyard, filled with Soviet stars and ashes and dirt, coming out just beyond the little sci-fi-looking museum, punched somewhat indecently, grotto-like, into the side of the holy hillside. At the top, under a giant Kyrgyz flag, the city fanned out below, hazy and low-slung. A woman manned a little stall selling water, prayer beads and miniature copies of the Qur'an. A few people prayed at Babur's small room.

Kyrgyzstan's second city is another outlier of Central Asia that doesn't look to the capital but rather to the places close to its borders – Andijan in Uzbekistan, Kashgar in China, the high roads to Tajikistan. From up high, Osh looks like a sleepy city but in June 2010, ethnic clashes between Kyrgyz and Uzbeks left hundreds dead, and makeshift refugee camps were set up over the border in Uzbekistan. Ethnic Uzbeks make up around 15 per cent of the population in Kyrgyzstan, but here it is an even mix, roughly half Uzbek, half Kyrgyz. The Dostyk border crossing, to Uzbekistan, is practically inside the city. You could not be closer. Osh, and the wider Fergana Valley, can be a litmus test around election times and during times of economic instability. If things are going to boil over, it is here that it tends to happen.

Ella Christie stopped at Osh, en route to Kashgar in Xinjiang, witnessing 'a wonder storm' of fork lightning striking over the Pamir Mountains. At the rambling bazaar she bought the skin of a panther cub and quoted Babur, who wrote in his book the Baburnama, 'The air of Osh is excellent . . . Its violets are particularly fragrant. It abounds in streams of running water.' Scenery that Christie recognised 400 years later.

At the bazaar I drank tea in a solemn rose-garlanded chaikhana where I suspected one gloomy table of men were sipping vodka – ak choi (which translates as 'white tea') – from teapots. The market scene, visible from the teahouse, was not unlike the one Christie painted a hundred years ago: apricots from Batken, known for their sweetness, were for sale by the barrow-load and egg shops, lined up one by one, each displayed the quality of their goods via penny-size holes which had been somehow been drilled into shells to show off the supremely orangey yolk inside. Other stalls were weighed down with golden squashes and bruise-coloured skinned sheep's heads. Wooden and glass armoires stood unattended, with small wheels of golden non bread inside. I had one more pot of green tea, bought a big bag of pistachios for a song, and left the bazaar, keen to get to the Turan mahalla, a neighbourhood that is almost entirely Uzbek, where my friend lives. In a taxi, the driver was chatty. 'Do you see any Kyrgyz graveyards here? No. That's because this is an Uzbek area and long before Kyrgyz nomads settled here in Osh, this was an Uzbek city.' I paid and got out.

MUSTARD FOR CLIMBERS

We stood for a moment in silence before a slow smile crinkled the skin around Imenjon Mahmudov's eyes. Taking my hands he leant forward to hug me. 'It's been so long. Now you are here,' he said ushering me towards a large wooden tapchan where tea and fruit had been set out, a welcoming dastarkhan. Above, ten baskets, each containing a quail, bounced and sang. More quails had just arrived, he told me, over there in a large cage. They'd provide eggs for going on top of plov. Other colourful birds chattered and sang in cages hung around the courtyard. Grandfather, father and the supervisor of a menagerie of birds, Imenjon is in his mid-70s now. He is slight, eats modestly and since I last met him he has grown a beard. Twenty generations ago, his family came here from Uzbekistan and he looks every part the Uzbek village elder. His family helps him out with his guesthouse. He prays five times a day, here on the tapchan where his prayer rug lives, amidst the clatter of everyday life.

I first met Imenjon a few years ago when I was on my way to Uzbekistan. It was just before the death of president Islam Karimov and foreigners were often bothered at land borders, usually asked to open laptops and show photographs, declare any medication. I don't remember much else about that crossing but I often look back nostalgically at my stay at Imenjon's guesthouse when we'd become friends. As well as the welcome, what stayed with me was a remarkable story of high-altitude cooking and mountaineering that he had told me. As we sat down again, we spoke more about his time spent working as a cook at the base camp of Peak Lenin, close to the border of Tajikistan.

At 7,134 metres Peak Lenin is one of the world's 'seven-thousanders' made difficult to climb by extreme weather. Avalanches are common. In July 1990, a team of 40 climbers, from five different countries, was killed by a landslide triggered by an earthquake. It was one of the worst tragedies in the history of Soviet mountaineering. As we drank tea, Imenjon recalled another catastrophe, when an entire team of eight Soviet women mountain climbers froze to death in August 1974, as they attempted to traverse Peak Lenin.

Many of the greatest Soviet mountaineers were fed by Imenjon. He had a few tricks, he told me, that he sent them on their way with. 'Garlic is very good for alpinists, it helps breathing. It has the same effect as menthol.' He then left the tapchan and went into the kitchen, and came out with a small glass pot.

'This is my homemade mustard. It was very good at clearing the heads and lungs of the climbers.' He put a sliver on a knife-edge and handed it to me. It tasted stimulatingly and nose-tingly hot.

Next, Imenjon brought his plov out to the dastarkhan. Whereas once plov was only eaten by the wealthy, today everyone eats it. Anthropologists suggest an Uzbek family of six will eat a tonne of rice a year mainly in plov – but not all plov is as good as this. Uzbek culture holds calorific food – the sort shunned by the west – in the highest esteem. I took a bite and it was every bit as good as I had remembered. Better, even. What makes it so special? Undoubtedly Imenjon's skill but also whole peeled garlic cloves which are scattered through – to be mashed with the back of a fork – strong cumin seeds that are well toasted, very fresh carrots and onions, and particularly sweet and plump raisins. Mainly though, it is the rice. Locally grown, in Uzgen, it is short, fat, reddish and supremely flavoursome. As we ate, I recalled the conversation we'd initially had when I was en route to Uzbekistan.

'This plov is the same that I cooked for two decades at the base camp of Peak Lenin. The Soviet mountaineers enjoyed eating it,' Imenjon had said.

'Did you cook for any famous climbers?' I asked.

'Yes, I did. Anatoli Boukreev, for example,' Imenjon replied.

He'd said this calmly, after thinking a while, but when I heard the name Boukreev, I had almost dropped my fork. There can be no overstating of Boukreev's accomplishments. Awarded for selfless and repeated rescue attempts on the upper slopes of Everest, in his obituary in *The Times* on 24th January 1998, he was called 'one of the toughest and greatest high-altitude mountaineers of his generation . . . once described as a lung with legs . . .' In 1987 he went up and down Peak Lenin in just 14 hours. Depicted in the 2015 blockbuster film *Everest*, Boukreev was a huge, heroic and handsome mountaineer and before he was killed by an avalanche on Christmas Day in Nepal, aged just 39, he'd made dozens of 7,000m and 8,000m ascents, almost always without supplemental oxygen.

As before, Imenjon showed me his Soviet-era books and photographs featuring these great climbers as his grandchildren snored.

Imenjon's plov is legendary to me but of course many mountain men and women cooked interesting meals in the high mountains of Central Asia. Perhaps the best story of high-altitude cooking is that of the red-bearded Scot Charles Adolphus Murray, British army officer and seventh Earl of Dunmore, who prepared a Christmas pudding in 1892 while pretending to be on a hunting mission (he was likely keeping an eye on the expanding Russian Empire). When he decided it was time to make this winter pudding, in a high-altitude yurt near a high pass not far from Osh, the temperature was –40°C. On his journey of 2,200 miles he crossed no fewer than 41 mountain passes.

This was his account published in 1893:

'First of all we took some dark-coloured Kirghiz flour and some baking-powder and the frozen yolks of six Kashgar eggs, which we scraped with a knife into a yellow powder, and after being well kneaded, this compound was rolled out, my telescope making a grand rolling-pin. We then stewed in a small Degchi [cooking utensil] all the Beg's apricots and raisins with some of my own honey. Another corner of the fire was occupied by a frying-pan, in which I fried the kernels of the pistachio nuts, in the only butter I could get, which I very carefully took out of a fresh tin of Sardines au Beurre. When the paste looked as like the beginning of a roly-poly pudding as we could make it, we poured the apricot, raisin and honey stew into the middle of it, then rolled it up and stuck the outside of it full of the fried kernels of the pistachio nuts, until the result looked like a new-born porcupine. We then proceeded to bake the whole thing as best we could, and I venture to say that no cook in Europe, on the 25th December, 1892, could have been as proud of his Christmas Pudding as I was of mine.

Although its manufacture was not the least interesting part of it, still the eating of it was more pleasurable than most enforced duties are usually, notwithstanding the slight suspicion of a flavour of sardines about it, which at any rate was a new departure in Christmas Puddings, and possessed the one great advantage and charm of novelty.'

Carrying dried apricots to prevent altitude sickness (and car sickness), travellers and climbers would also haul tins of smoked fish and biscuits. In the 19th century two travellers, remembered as the Littendales (Theresa and George), arrived to Osh. There, dressed in Harris Tweed and sheepskins, they shopped in the bazaar to supplement the dried ox tongue on which they'd stocked up in Georgia ('very portable and made a delightful change from the inevitable mutton we had to live upon later').

Early the next morning, it was time to go. I sat one last time with Imenjon on the tapchan. Above us the quails in their muslin-covered bell-shaped cages sang and the weak sun picked out the inlay detail of the carving on the etched wooden canopy above, all plant vines and flowers. The weather had changed overnight. Yesterday it was 30°C, now autumn had arrived with a frigid breeze. Imenjon was dressed in a thick red tracksuit and a beige knitted skullcap and his hands were busily peeling off the thick green tennis ball-like husks of walnuts. A small nutty carpet lay beside him. And it was to walnut forests, some say the biggest in the world, that I was now headed, an easy drive away. When autumn conditions are right, whole families head into the groves, for months at a time, to harvest.

Before I set off, a breakfast of vatrushka – fat rings of baked sweet dough filled with quark-like tvorog – as well as jam and bread was set down by Imenjon's granddaughter. As I ate, Imenjon pulled his prayer rug from the side of the dastarkhan, knelt towards Mecca, and began whispering his trust that there is but one God. Beside him, a thick duvet and pillow had been carefully placed in a neat pile, suggesting that he had slept out last night, under his beloved quails, and under the moon and stars high above Osh.

A Lamb and Quince Plov for Imenjon

Imenjon is a modest but terrific cook and his masterpiece is lamb and quince plov. This superior plov is similar to what he'd make for Soviet mountaineers up at Peak Lenin. Don't be shy on the garlic and make sure your cumin seeds are as fresh and punchy as possible. In Osh, Imenjon uses Uzgen rice, which is short grain and red-hued; here I've used basmati, quite different but it works well and is readily available (unlike Uzgen). It's important to use really fresh garlic for its pungency. Aromatic and rich, this is a dish for all the senses.

SERVES 4 GENEROUSLY

1 tsp cumin seeds

150ml/⅔ cup vegetable oil

2 large quinces, peeled, cored and cubed

500g/1lb 2oz lamb leg, cut into 4cm/1½in chunks

1½ tsp fine sea salt

2 large onions, cut into thin wedges

4 yellow carrots (regular carrots will do if you can't find yellow ones), cut into thick matchsticks

½ tsp cayenne pepper

½ tsp freshly ground black pepper

400g/2 cups basmati rice, rinsed

60g/2oz raisins

10 garlic cloves (the freshest you can find), peeled

Sea salt flakes, to season

Pink Pickled Onions (page 88) or a side salad, to serve

Warm Non Bread (page 120), to serve

Place a large lidded casserole or saucepan over a medium heat and toast the cumin seeds for a few minutes until they start to lightly colour and release their aroma. Remove the seeds and crush them gently to break them down, then set aside.

In the same pan, heat the vegetable oil over a medium heat. Fry the quince for around 20 minutes, stirring occasionally, until the cubes are soft and golden on all sides. Remove using a slotted spoon and set aside on a plate and cover with foil to keep warm. Keeping the oil in the pan, add the lamb and season with ½ teaspoon of salt. Fry the meat over a medium heat, until browned, then remove with a slotted spoon and keep it warm under the foil with the quince.

Turn up the heat and using the same oil once again, fry the onion and carrot until glossy and tender with another ½ teaspoon of salt. Sprinkle over the crushed cumin and the other spices and mix everything together.

Spread the rice in an even layer over the onion and carrot mixture, scatter over the raisins and then slowly pour in enough water to just cover the rice, sprinkling over the final ½ teaspoon of salt. Leaving the lid off, keep the heat high and boil away the water, this will take around 15 minutes.

When the rice is almost cooked, remove from the heat. Poke 10 holes in the rice with the handle of a wooden spoon and place a garlic clove into each hole. Add the lamb and quince on top of the rice and let it all steam – with the lid on – for about 15 minutes.

Plate up and sprinkle over some sea salt flakes. The Uzbek way to eat the garlic is to serve it on top and let the diner mash their own cloves with the back of a fork, stirring it through the rice as they eat.

Laza Hot Sauce

In a region not known for heat, laza is a welcome quirk of Central Asian cooking – a searingly red hot sauce. I'd eaten it in various places, not really knowing what it was but enjoying its piquancy. In Osh, I saw it cooked on the roadside in giant vats, the chillies piled high in enamel bathtubs, which gives you an idea of just how many go into this sauce. It goes well with the Cheat's Laghman (page 233), Grand Asia Express Samsa (page 214) as well as Emil's Lamb Plov (page 18).

MAKES 1 SMALL JAR

10 red chillies, deseeded and roughly chopped

2 shallots, roughly chopped

½ tsp sea salt

1 tomato, roughly chopped

4 garlic cloves, peeled

2 tbsp sesame oil

To sterilise the jar, preheat the oven to 140°C/275°F/gas mark 1. Wash the jar in warm, soapy water, rinse well and place it on a clean baking tray. Transfer to the oven for about 15 minutes, and then leave to cool. To sterilise the lid or rubber seal, boil them in a large saucepan for 5 minutes then drain and leave them to air dry on a rack.

Using a food processor whizz together the first five ingredients until everything is as fine as possible, then pour in the sesame oil and mix again. Spoon into the cooled, sterilised jar. It'll keep for a couple of weeks in the fridge.

TENT

Rambling through the world's largest walnut forest

ARSLANBOB, SOUTHWEST KYRGYZSTAN: If ever a forest were to flourish it would be here, below the 2,000-metre-high slopes of the Babash-Ata Mountains in southwest Kyrgyzstan, three hours north of Osh. Rain regularly thunders down feeding rich soil and rivers, and clean jags of warming sunlight penetrate the valleys with their life-giving rays, nourishing woodlands filled with pear, plum and wild apple trees. In these thick valleys is the world's largest walnut forest which, on a good year, can yield 1,500 tonnes of nuts. Each one a singular precious treasure: sweet and oily, tucked safely inside its own shell.

I arrived early October, at the official start of the annual harvest. Families from the large village of Arslanbob had already taken their tents and wagons into the woods where they'd stay for two months or until the snow comes. At the bazaar, children sat on sacks of nuts already gathered, above thick caramel-coloured mud that pooled and slopped over galoshes and boots. Fingers and palms of villagers in the bazaar and at the chaikhana, where nuts are swapped for money, were already stained a tell-tale brown from the walnut oil. It had rained hard all night and it had poured down when I'd come here in spring a few years back, too. This time, I stayed again with Nazira, a formidable grandmother of considerable spirit, who hugged me tightly on seeing me bedraggled at the steps to her large balconied house. Under a wooden canopy, she showed me that she had already laid out a thick layer of walnuts on a blanket, next to a large plate of bread for the birds because bread is never thrown away here. The next day, I went into the forest with Almaz, my gentle, softly spoken guide, whose name, he told me, means 'diamond'. Like Nazira, he is ethnically Uzbek. Uzbekistan is close here, only around 50 miles away.

After ten minutes walking upwards along muddy tracks into the woods, nature gained ground: first, a woody aroma lifted from the forest floor. Then, after half an hour more up boggy tracks, steep grey karst hills appeared through the mist, heaven-reaching pinnacles washed with rain, shining softly in shades of cream and pigeon-grey, looking as if a Chinese scroll painting had unfurled from the heavens to our feet. Twenty minutes more, curving paths urged us on further still to see what lay just out of sight, which was woven wattle fencing, a place of rest for birds, and man's eternal symbol of control over nature, the wooden stakes proof that something useful and of value lies within. Then, a little deeper still, and the unmistakable gnarly twisted branches of walnut trees. Some in groves so tight that sunlight cannot cut through. Some as old as 500 years. Children scuttled on the mulchy forest floor picking up fallen nuts. To know what is around that corner,

over that hill, through that field – that is the curiosity of walking, whatever the weather, and that was how, despite the hammering rain, we ended up spending all afternoon in the world's largest walnut forest which spreads over thousands of hectares.

FATHER OF THE GARDEN

As well as a sense of remoteness – in both space and time – there is an undeniable air of mystery and cult in this part of western Kyrgyzstan. Local lore has it that Prophet Muhammed tasked a servant to find the most beautiful place on earth. The land he found was here, with its mountains and rushing rivers. The Prophet agreed it was good but commented that there were no trees, so he gave his assistant a bag of nuts to scatter down from a mountain peak, thus creating the forest. The servant's name was Arslanbob, and the mountain crags he stood upon, which form the backdrop of the forests, became known as Babash-Ata, meaning 'father of the garden'. This tale fits the quasi-mystical atmosphere. And it is hard, in landscapes such as this, not to idealise it. But it is also more important not to be misled. While a few token animals had been slaughtered to mark the start of the harvest, and families had moved into the woods with their tents, weird weather had other plans for them.

'Ten years ago was the last truly good harvest. Last year was very bad, I couldn't even find two to three kilos to buy for myself,' Almaz said. Locals see the nuts as revenue and income but they also value walnuts in other ways, aware that they are healthful, with high concentrations of omega-3 fatty acids and antioxidants. They are used to supplement diets here and are pressed into oil. Plates of uncracked nuts go onto the dastarkhan every mealtime.

These enormous groves have witnessed many changes, environmental and man-made. Soviets collectivised the forest, trying to tame what they saw as wild, hostile even. During that time there was heavy timber extraction but the nut forests were eventually listed as protected areas in the 1940s. Before the Soviets, the Russian Empire annexed the khanate of Kokand and grew interested in detailing natural resources and climate, ordering explorers' reports which noted felling and fires. Today, the forest is state-owned, and divided up, with many families renting their portion of land, usually just a hectare or two, paying partly for it in walnut revenue. Tour operators may tout the walnut groves as unspoiled and pure, but the truth is they haven't been that way for decades.

Boots squelching, Almaz and I went deeper still through the slime and rain over tracks churned up by hooves of donkeys and horses, into the forest that is both innkeeper and inn. Fields had become a refuge for walnut families who were busy boiling water for tea, popping up tents and tarpaulin covers or dragging in wagons. But the numbers were small, nothing like the photographs I'd seen of previous years that depicted festival-like forest clearings with bonfires and singing. Shops had been arranged but were little more than a trestle table with a weighing scale and a few strings of sausages, largely run by women whose husbands were working in Russia. As with the rest of the country, here almost every family has at least one or two male relatives working there, sending money home. 'I was in Russia, my older brother was in Russia, every second man you meet here will have been there at some point. We don't need visas, we speak Russian, so we go,' Almaz said.

Remittance work in Russia is often tough, badly paid and with zero safeguarding, but this is dangerous work as well. Harnesses and ladders are rarely used, men shimmy up the trees using their legs and arms. Every year there is at least one death during the walnut harvest, men who have climbed too far along a branch, with their beating-sticks in hand, and have fallen far and fast to the forest floor. Non-fatal accidents nearly always mean broken limbs, resulting in lost earnings and hungry families. And if it is a poor harvest, there is no money, either. If it is a successful harvest, the profit can be good and the further the nuts travel they more value they gain. Here they sell for about $3 a kilo but by the time they're sold abroad, that price triples. In Bishkek, walnut sellers make deals with buyers from Iran, Turkey, Russia and China.

THE TREES DO NOT NEED US

Walnuts have long been traded in this part of the world, almost certainly along the Silk Road and as far back as the 4th century BC. And they have long been valued, too, found as grave offerings in tombs dating back to the Tang Dynasty (AD 618–907) at cemeteries in Turpan, Xinjiang. At the Chinese imperial court, walnuts would be swivelled in the palm of the hand like dice to calm nerves and stimulate blood circulation. Some harvesters recall the legend of Alexander the Great's soldiers, who lingered here a while before returning to Europe with walnuts in their pockets, possibly carrying kernels for Greece's first walnut forests.

Going deeper still, into a dark shady thicket, which smelled slightly of the sea and heavily of the earth, we skidded and slipped over streamlets of sludge, until a grove appeared where a tent, big enough for ten people, had been set up. We sloshed over. Turgunbay, whose hands were as rugged and lined as the giant trunks of trees, introduced himself. Rain, softer now, sputtered the tarpaulin. Dressed for the weather, in a thick wool jumper, a denim utility vest with ample pockets and a hat of Kyrgyz felt, he told us that he has been coming to this particular slice of the forest since 1963, the year he was born. As an only child he inherited the lot, almost three hectares (about 220 trees) and now he brings

his own family here every year. 'You could say that I was born here, and grew up here.' With a voice as deep as the sodden valley we stood in, he smiled easily and generously, eyes twinkling as he spoke, but he looked older than his years, the skin on his cheeks and brow both weathered.

'Back in 2002, that was the last good harvest. Then I got one tonne of walnuts. After that a maximum of 300 kilos a season. Last year, zero, nothing. So far this year, only one bag. The climate, the weather, it is changing. During spring this year, it was suddenly hot and walnuts fell down from the trees too early, then it snowed as well, which killed a lot of the apple trees.'

He is here, he told us with his wife, who was born in Tashkent, his son-in-law and nine grandchildren. While there aren't many nuts, they will stay the whole season to guard the trees from illegal loggers, as at this time of year there is a lot of traffic coming and going in the forest. When it snows it is safe, Turgunbay said, as then there are no cars. 'Only when the snow comes will we go back to the village. Only if we collect a lot of nuts during a season do we move, taking them down to the village, to sell them on immediately before returning back here.' He picked up a few walnuts from the ground and rolled them around his oil-stained palm. Each kernel and shell had slowly matured on its own branch, neatly packaged and contained by nature, with its own rich reserves of protein and goodness. Some fell down to the lap of the earth to the harvesters, but also to the squirrels and rodents, who'll take the nuts as their wintertime stock of food. The trees show us what nature does when left in peace. These trees do not need us.

'I respect the forest, I won't cut a live tree. We try to only take the dead wood. If we collect only two kilos of nuts this season anyway I will still be happy. It is good to be in nature, in clean air.'

'Does the rain bother you?'

'No, water is life,' Turgunbay said.

I gave him some pistachios and dried figs from the bazaar in Osh, and he insisted on putting some walnuts into my hand.

Men like Turgunbay understand the forest better than the rangers who freely come and go. By sleeping out in the forest, every year for several months over many decades, changes are sensed and observed. If Turgunbay has concluded that weather patterns are strange, and that the harvest has been affected, then there is a good chance that climate change is to blame. The lack of nuts – such primeval food – was surely a dire warning. Would the harvests ever come back and flourish as fruitfully as they once did? Are we losing them for ever?

Almaz and I turned back, talking more about nuts and village life. 'Those who don't have their own land in the forest, their own trees, they buy bags of nuts from others to process them, cracking them open with a hammer and cleaning them, which they can then charge more for. In the winter, people gather around a stove and do this together. When there is a lot of snow, there is not a lot going on. And now the harvests are poorer, their price increases again.'

Back at Nazira's guesthouse I ate, showered and slept cosily under a fluffy leopard print blanket, Turgunbay's walnuts, ten or so, drying in a little pile at the foot of the too-short single bed. Rain fell heavily outside.

As my taxi pulled away the next morning, Nazira leant over her balcony and blew me a kiss, 'Goodbye, Carolina!' I waved and wondered whether we'd meet again. I hoped so. Half an hour later, we were back into wider valleys, skidding past rice fields, rice that will go into plov. Just before the city of Jalal-Abad, the sun finally broke through the clouds and I sat with my eyes closed, thinking of the walnut forests, the warm rays pouring onto my face as we drove on. Easing out of the city, I heard revving and a car speeding towards the back of the taxi. I opened my eyes, looked over my shoulder and saw a white, polished top-spec 4x4 Mercedes and a man hanging out of the front passenger seat, with something long and black in his hand. A Kalashnikov. Then, a series of maniacal gunshots tore up into the air. Crackling in the sky. A wedding? A warning? A big cheese, for sure. My taxi driver just smiled, his face suggesting it was nothing to worry about.

I ran my fingers over the ridged contours of the marble-size walnuts in my jacket pocket and thought of what Nazira had said, 'Where there are nuts, there are people.' And that is part of the problem. People are taking more than the forest is able to give. Soil erosion from the overgrazing of cattle and chopping trees for fuel are both contributors to poor harvests, but the unseasonal rains and peculiar weather are likely caused by people everywhere, the result of climate change. Where there are nuts there are people, and where there are people there are problems. And, alas, this would not be the last firsthand account of unseasonal weather and unfruitful harvests that I would hear on this particular autumn journey.

Pancakes with Green Grape Conserve

Breakfast at Nazira's homestay, right by the world's largest walnut grove, was often light and fluffy homemade pancakes served warm with green grape conserve. I'd eat them huddled next to an electric heater if it was cold, or else outside on the tapchan surrounded by birdsong. Back home, they make a super weekend brunch and the moreish grape conserve is a flattering partner to porridge, overnight oats and plain yogurt. You can of course make the conserve ahead if you like.

MAKES 1 X 450ML JAR OF CONSERVE AND AROUND 8 PANCAKES

FOR THE CONSERVE

450g/1lb seedless green grapes, rinsed

5 tbsp water

450g/2¼ cups granulated sugar

Juice of 1 lemon

Knob of unsalted butter

FOR THE PANCAKES

100g/¾ cup self-raising flour

½ tsp bicarbonate of soda (baking soda)

Pinch of fine sea salt

1 tbsp caster (superfine) sugar

1 large egg, beaten

150ml/⅔ cup kefir

20g/1½ tbsp unsalted butter, melted and cooled, plus extra for frying

Put a plate in the freezer an hour or so before you start. To sterilise the jar, preheat the oven to 140°C/275°F/gas mark 1. Wash the jar in warm, soapy water, rinse well and place it on a clean baking tray. Transfer to the oven for about 15 minutes. To sterilise the lid or rubber seal, boil them in a large saucepan for 5 minutes then drain and leave them to air dry on a rack. Leave the jar in the warm oven until the conserve is ready to be potted up – it must go into a hot jar.

Place a preserving pan or a heavy-bottomed saucepan over a low heat and gently simmer the seedless grapes in about 5 tablespoons of water, until they begin breaking down. Add the sugar, lemon juice and butter (which will give sheen and stop scum forming), and heat very gently.

Keep stirring to dissolve the sugar – this will take around 10 minutes – ensuring it's fully dissolved or else the conserve will have a higher chance of burning. Remove from the heat and break up most of the grape mixture using a hand blender or the back of a spoon, leaving a few grapes whole. Return the pan to the heat and bring the mixture to a rolling boil – you're looking for a foaming mass of small bubbles – stir occasionally to ensure it isn't catching. When the bubbles have receded, take the pan off the heat. Test for a set by dropping a little of the conserve onto your freezer-chilled plate, wait for it to cool then nudge it with your fingertip. If it wrinkles when it's pushed, setting point has been achieved. Allow to cool for 10 minutes then pour it into the jar while still hot.

To make the pancakes, into a mixing bowl sift the flour and bicarbonate of soda with a pinch of salt, and stir in the sugar. In a jug, combine the egg, kefir and melted butter, and stir slowly into the flour mixture. You're looking for a yogurt-like consistency; lumps are fine at this stage but if it is too thick, add a tablespoon or so of milk. Don't over-mix the batter or else the pancakes will be dense rather than fluffy. Leave the mixture to stand for 5 minutes.

Melt a small knob of butter in a large frying pan over a medium heat. Using a ladle, pour 3 tablespoons or so of batter into the pan. Once bubbles form, flip the pancakes and continue cooking for 1–2 minutes until the pancakes are cooked. Serve immediately with the grape conserve poured over. Once opened, the conserve will keep in the fridge for a couple of weeks.

BAZAAR

Drifting past traders, hawkers and merchants

BISHKEK, NORTH KYRGYZSTAN: Kyrgyzstan might be landlocked but Bishkek, the country's capital, has a market forged entirely from shipping containers. Dordoi Bazaar, located on the outskirts of town, is made up of thousands of these steel boxes covering the equivalent of 160 rugby fields. Flipped on their sides and doubled up, they make efficient shops, rigged with lights and padlocked securely at night. Distinct in spirit and commerce, Kyrgyzstan's biggest bazaar offers particular insights into local trade wars, hospitality, food and the new Silk Road. Jalil Mukanbetov, a local friend, offered to lead me through this giant commercial labyrinth, which he calls the 'Dordoi Republic'.

Gold-painted statues of a man and two women flank the main entrance, a life-size monument to Central Asia's 'shuttle traders', entrepreneurs who commuted back and forth between the cities of the Soviet Union, and then later, the post-Soviet states, buying goods in one location and then selling them elsewhere for profit. Memorialised, too, in gold, are piles of bulging suitcase-size bags that each statue leans against. Made in China, these familiar-looking squares of checkered woven plastic with handles, are an instantly recognisable universal symbol of people on the move, of the entrepreneur and the newly arrived, of the traveller and migrant. Bags that crowd railway carriages, bus stations and market stalls the world over.

Inside, Jalil led the way, greeting a gang of retailers nimbly pulling down stock from upper containers, to their shop fronts below, hands and minds occupied with the task. 'My mother worked here, and my two uncles. But all together I would guess maybe 50 members of my extended family have worked at Dordoi. You could say I grew up here,' Jalil said.

We started in the China 'zone', which is the biggest and cheapest section of the market, before moving through to the European belt, which is smaller and more expensive, and then weaving back into China's lanes. For the uninitiated it was impossible to tell where one started and the other ended, most containers sold similar-looking leather and fur jackets, shoes and socks. Somewhere was the 'caravan' district whose name gives a nod to the old Silk Road. Through the alleys, tea ladies huffed, waltzing their trolleys set up for coffee with condensed milk and soup from thermos flasks, pushing deeper into the twisting gurgling intestines of the bazaar's ever-hungry belly.

Mid-week meant it was relatively quiet but at the weekend shoppers pile in from all quarters of Bishkek, searching for bargains and joining retailers from

Tajikistan and Uzbekistan, Kyrgyzstan's own shopkeepers who come to stock up, and wholesale traders from Kazakhstan, whose border is only 20 miles away. All are served by the 70,000 or so workers who are officially, and unofficially, employed by Dordoi: drivers, unpackers, cooks, shopkeepers, tea boys, toilet attendants, security, waitresses, exchange tellers and tailors. Pushers and pullers, handlers and dealers. All busy importing, exporting and re-exporting. What may look anarchic at first is actually a well-oiled operation. Money dictates order and the bazaar is far too profitable to be chaotic. Dordoi has its own football team and a mosque that is well attended on a Friday.

NEW SILK ROADS

'The China section is where you can see everything that life offers. Different people, different attitudes. Some people get really rich really quickly there and you can see how money changes them, just over one three-month season. They get exclusive access to a new thing from China, a certain pair of trainers, a handbag, and word gets out. Before everyone else can copy him, the seller gets rich. Then, their attitude changes,' Jalil said with a pair of football boots in his hand, now knocked down to $5. Above us hundreds of galoshes and plastic boots had been strung up, essential for the long Kyrgyz winter. At Jalil's uncle's container, boxes of fashionable boots and court shoes, with fur trims and patent flourishes, were being unpacked. All brought from Xinjiang in northwest China.

'Business is a risk. It's better to do it with family, you cannot do it alone. You need hands, and you need money. You sell together. If someone wants something and you've sold out, maybe your brother has stock. You need $30,000 to buy goods for a season, and together, we can collect it.' Jalil's uncle said, pouring us tea.

But travelling to China has become difficult. Impossible for some. A suicide bomber attacked the Chinese embassy in Bishkek in 2016, and now Chinese visas are harder to come by. Jalil's aunt joined us in the container, nodding as she sat down. Above the till on a shelf sat a framed hologram of a white mare and a Qur'an in Kyrgyz, Russian and Arabic. Traders used to travel to Urumqi, the capital of Xinjiang, by sleeper bus, where seats had been ripped out and bunk beds built in, the journey taking at least 30 hours. Then, as flying became cheaper, Dordoi's traders would go by plane to physically check the goods, with the stock following behind a few days later by truck. The route is over the remote Torugart Pass, a high-altitude border crossing in the Tian Shan mountain range connecting China and Kyrgyzstan, only snow-free during the short summer. It was not an easy journey.

Now, with visas stalled, trade happens online. 'I send a picture of what I want, they send the goods. This only works if you have a good relationship with the seller and there is trust. It is still best to travel to China to check the stock from all sides but that is difficult now,' said the uncle.

Another man inside the container chipped in. 'Business used to be better. Ten years ago it cost twice what it does today to set up here, that's because business was so good.' Some say the problem is Kazakhstan. Khorgos, on the China-Kazakh border, used to be a simple crossing place, now it is an enormous dry port, a giant duty-free trade zone, part of China's massive country-spanning Belt and Road Initiative, also known as the New Silk Road, a hugely ambitious development campaign to boost trade and growth across Asia, Africa and Europe. As we left the shop, two men in black leather jackets arrived looking to buy shoes in bulk for their shop in Khujand, northern Tajikistan, 450 miles away.

Another woman waved Jalil hello. 'I have so many relatives here, I have forgotten that one's name,' he chuckled. The kindness of a close-knit community meant slow progress through the China zone as we regularly stopped for tea. By one container, a pair of fluffy caramel-brown socks caught my eye. They had come from Mongolia and were knitted from camel fur. As soon as I picked a pair up, the trader appeared. 'Where to? To Moscow?' he asked, assuming I wanted to trade.

Stopping in front of an empty exchange booth, we read out the currencies of the merchants: Chinese yuan, Kazakh tenge, Russian rubles, Uzbek sum and Kyrgyz som. Before the use of plastic payment cards, Jalil said the market swam with cash and buyers would carry bulging bags of banknotes. The cash tellers in the exchange booths were far busier then. 'There was a time when my mother told me not to go near those foreign exchange counters. Occasionally they'd be raided by gunmen and bullets would fly.'

TOLSTOY, TRUCKERS AND TRADERS

Lunchtime arrived and a world of culinary enterprise went on the move. Prams operated as moveable cafés, with Thermoses filled with tea and blankets swaddling freshly baked samsa and pies. Trolleys of kumys, fermented mare's milk, went whizzing by, white and splashing. Kyrgyz believe kumys is a cure for a whole host of ailments from digestive issues and anaemia to typhoid and nervous conditions. Leo Tolstoy and Maxim Gorky both took kumys 'rest cures' at Russian sanatoriums drinking nothing but mare's milk several times a day, for months. Some say Bishkek takes its name from the wooden spoon used to stir kumys.

A Dungan woman called Fatima, slowly steered her food trolley past us, ushering shoppers to 'make the way free!' Dungans, a Muslim minority ethnic group with communities in Kyrgyzstan and Kazakhstan, have closely preserved their culture, especially their food heritage. Despite arriving 150 years ago, they eat with chopsticks rather than forks and use distinctly Chinese flavours and ingredients in their cooking. Fatima's takeaway plates were wrapped with all the ingredients necessary for a ready-meal of ashlan-fu, the most famous Dungan dish of all. Each one contained noodles, vegetables, sliced-up omelette and a sachet of vinegary sauce. 'Just add water,' she said pointing at the plates.

Trailing behind Fatima was a blind beggar with a singing voice as powerful as Pavarotti. Dressed in a kalpak, the traditional felt Kyrgyz hat, he was led at each elbow by an assistant. The trio shuffled slowly, each holding out a hand for banknotes, blocking the lane and stalling a huffy pickle hawker and a pomegranate juice pusher whose stereo speakers, attached to his cart, threatened to drown out the beggar. A trolley of plov got stuck in the melee. Two dozen boiled eggs had been artfully arranged in a semi-circle around the rice, which gave the appearance of a white-toothed smile. One man angrily barged past, yelling in Kyrgyz, his cheeks as pink as the dripping flesh of his cut-open watermelons. Central Asian tastes, cultures and flavours on the move.

'There is one legendary samsa place, let's go,' Jalil said, steering me down a side lane. Tucked between the China and European zones, a man squatted by his tiny oven. Half-Turkish, half-Dagestani but a Kyrgyz citizen, he told us that his boss, the owner of the samsa business, is Uyghur. Square rather than triangular, the cook had arranged his samsa in lines so their corners pointed upwards like little a mountain range. Flaky, hot and moreish, mine cost less than a postage stamp back home, and was just one of 200 or so samsa that he will pull out of the oven this lunchtime.

CONTAINER COUNTRY

Appetites piqued, the smell of shashlik smoke led us past a haberdashery section, then wedding dresses and bottles of badger oil ('old medicine,' said Jalil), potted plants and chrysanthemums. Outside, we settled on a café called Arua where we sat upstairs to eat with a panoramic view of the rusty containers. Over ruby-coloured borscht and pelmeni dumplings, served by an Uzbek waitress, Jalil told me about his Stalin-loving grandfather, a man who had little respect for the 'citizens' of Bishkek, preferring instead village life. And, we spoke about literature and Chingiz Aitmatov, Kyrgyzstan's literary great who specialised in man's search for meaning. The café was busy with women we guessed were from the North Caucasus. They spoke to one another softly in Russian, their hands glittering with jewels, pouring one another tea. As with the traders, Russian was the common language in the café.

'In Kyrgyzstan, you know we have a lot of tea traditions. If you drink tea with an enemy, remember to only ever serve them with your left hand,' Jalil said, his right elbow lifting to pour us more tea. Below, traders had begun barring and bolting their containers. Here since daybreak, most business had been done by mid-afternoon. Container country was starting to close.

Back outside, past aisles selling kitchen utensils, all from China, a crew of drivers sat chatting under a notice advertising logistics and haulage for the countries that trade with the bazaar: China, Turkey, Russia and Kazakhstan. Some of them would overnight here, retiring to one of the tiny hotels clustered around the huge car park. In many ways, this grimy terminal, filled with exhaust fumes, cigarette butts and tea-sipping men, is the new Silk Road in essence. Today's trucks are yesterday's goods-carrying camels. Exchange counters have taken the place of moneychangers and the hotels – appearing like small Japanese capsule hotels – have taken the place of the old brick-wall inns and caravanserai. Here, as on the old Silk Road, other countries come to the city. Chinese- and Turkish-made goods arrive, then from here they move to other Central Asian cities, and into Russia. Dordoi is far less racketeering than it once was, Jalil said, but there are still fewer checks and less interrogation here than at any border control.

We went inside one of the hotels, curious to see. A man mopped white tiles and the receptionist was friendly. I asked where their guests come from. 'We mainly have Russians, Turkmens and Kazakhs staying here but also drivers from countries further away, like Ukraine. A café nearby stays open late so they eat there. A room costs eight dollars a night, per person.' Doors to several rooms were open, they looked clean and ordered. Pinned to the back of the doors were small posters advertising barbershops, dubious-looking massage services and local taxis. There are at least six other hotels in the bazaar, the receptionist said.

'The market takes a lot out of you,' Jalil said as we slumped tiredly against a wall waiting for a taxi out. Shadows lengthened across the dusty lane as this world within a world closed up for good. The beggars had gone, so too had the food trolleys. A fleet of Grand Asia Express buses wheezed out from the depot, heading to towns elsewhere in Kyrgyzstan. Every seat was taken. Long-distance drivers steering freight trucks followed them, one by one, their eyes catching ours out of windows over the windscreen rubbers and sun visors. Each one just beginning their long road journey, each one with a route planned out in their heads, a mental map of stops and towns. Each one a snapshot of a life that we shall never know.

Grand Asia Express Samsa

Essentially triangular Central Asian turnovers, samsa are eaten everywhere and are typically filled with lamb, potato or pumpkin. At Dordoi Bazaar, I had an unusual variation, a square chicken samsa that was light and flaky, its filling steaming and puffing as I bit into it. It is a perfect snack eaten hot on the spot. Here's a quick recipe named after the legions of trucks and truckers that arrive and depart from Dordoi Bazaar, picking up a samsa or two for their long border-crossing journeys. The onion seeds make a nice addition but they are optional.

MAKES 12 LARGE SAMSA

400g/14oz chicken breasts

1 tsp olive oil

Sea salt and freshly ground black pepper

2 medium-size potatoes, peeled and roughly chopped

1 medium onion, roughly chopped

1 tsp ground cumin

1 x 500g/1lb 2oz packet of puff pastry

1 egg, beaten, for an egg wash

1 tbsp onion seeds (optional)

Preheat the oven to 180°C/350°F/gas mark 4. Prepare a small roasting tin by lining it with tin foil.

Put the chicken breasts in the tin, rub them with olive oil, and season with a pinch of salt and pepper. Roast them in the oven for 25 minutes, or until cooked through. Set aside to cool, then roughly chop.

Bring a medium saucepan of salted water to a boil and cook the potatoes for 15 minutes, or until soft. Drain and set aside to cool.

Pulse the onion in a food processor until very fine, then add the cooled potatoes, and pulse again. Add the chicken, cumin, a good pinch of salt and pepper, and pulse again to bring the mixture together – you may need to scrape the sides of the bowl down as you go.

Preheat the oven to 200°C/400°F/gas mark 6. Line a large baking tray (or 2 smaller trays) with greaseproof paper.

On a lightly floured surface, cut the pastry into quarters, then cut each quarter into thirds. Roll out each piece of pastry so that you have 12 rectangles, roughly 17 x 10cm (7 x 4in). Drop 40g/2 tbsp of the mixture onto one end of each rectangle, leaving a border around the edge. Brush the edges of the pastry with a little of the egg, then fold the other half over the top, pressing the edges together to seal well. Repeat with the remaining pastry. Brush the top of each samsa with egg and scatter over the onion seeds, if using. Place the samsas on the tray and bake for around 25–30 minutes until cooked through and completely golden.

Non Puju

Non bread is Central Asian but the flavours of the beef stew here are Chinese and when put together they make up this unusual, rustic and full-flavoured Dungan dish. In the 19th century Muslim Dungans in China tried to establish an independent homeland but their attempts were quickly quashed. To escape persecution many tried to flee, with some crossing the Tian Shan Mountains and settling in Central Asia, where many became esteemed farmers. A handful of Dungan-only villages are in existence in modern-day Kyrgyzstan today. One is Milyanfan, a village just outside Bishkek, where many city-dwellers go at the weekends just to eat ashlan-fu (page 218).

For the non bread, follow the recipe on page 120, just omit the raisins and walnuts.

SERVES 2 GENEROUSLY

450g/1lb lean beef steak, such as sirloin or flank

1 tsp fine sea salt

Freshly ground black pepper

1 tbsp vegetable oil

¾ tbsp Chinese five-spice

½ fresh red chilli, finely chopped

½ fresh green chilli, finely chopped

2 tbsp tomato purée (paste)

1 tbsp soy sauce

150g/5oz canned chopped tomatoes

100ml/⅖ cup beef stock

Non Bread (page 120, leave out the raisins and walnuts), to serve

½ handful of coriander (cilantro) leaves, to garnish

1 tbsp sesame seeds, to garnish

Fresh red or green chilli, deseeded and sliced, to garnish (optional)

About 30 minutes before you start cooking, put the beef in the freezer. During this time, it won't freeze, but it will firm up. Remove from the freezer (one at a time if using smaller steaks) and slice as thinly as you can using a sharp knife. Trim off the fat and discard. Put the sliced steak in a bowl and season with a teaspoon of fine sea salt and freshly ground black pepper, to taste.

Heat the oil in a frying pan over a high heat and add the five-spice and chillies, and cook for less than a minute, just to release the scent. Keeping the heat high, add the steak to the pan and flash fry for a few minutes until browned, adding a bit more oil if necessary. Scoop the steak out of the pan and into a bowl, and set aside.

Turn the heat down to medium, add the tomato purée, frying it for a minute or two. As the colour of the purée darkens and it starts to stick ever so slightly to the bottom of the pan, add the soy sauce, chopped tomatoes and beef stock. Cook for another 5–10 minutes until the mixture thickens and reduces slightly.

Add the steak and any resting juices back into the pan and stir it around, coating it in the thick, glossy sauce. Taste and adjust the seasoning if it needs it.

Pile the saucy beef on top of the non bread, scattering over a few coriander leaves and sesame seeds. If you like heat, you could also top with a few more slices of fresh chilli. Slice the non puju as you would a pizza, take it to the table and let people help themselves.

Alternative Ashlan-Fu

It is not easy to make the classic Dungan dish ashlan-fu – cool noodles served in a spicy vinaigrette broth, topped with shreds of omelette, vegetables and chives – as cooks traditionally prepare two types of homemade noodles for it. In Karakol, close to Issyk-Kul, there is 'ashlan-fu alley' where a string of competing cafés all sell their own versions. At a counter there, I placed my order and watched as a server put thin wheat noodles into a bowl, then thick white starchy noodles on top of those, before adding a scattering of stir-fried vegetables and pouring over the spicy tangy broth. A final flourish saw a handful of sliced omelette and chives sprinkled on top. I took my seat at a counter and greedily scooped up the ashlan-fu with some puffy fried bread sold alongside it.

This is an inauthentic version to try at home, prepared with ready-made noodles, which does share the same vinegary flavours to proper ashlan-fu. While this is a dish typically eaten cold, there is, of course, nothing stopping you from eating it lukewarm, as I tend to do. It is especially useful for hangovers given that it is salty, spicy and moreish.

SERVES 2 GENEROUSLY

100g/3½oz egg noodles

100g/3½oz rice or glass noodles

4 tbsp Chinkiang black rice vinegar

450ml/2 cups vegetable stock

1 tsp granulated sugar

4 tbsp soy sauce

2 tbsp vegetable oil

1 red or green (bell) pepper, diced

1 carrot, diced

1 small onion, diced

1 tomato, diced

1 fresh red or green chilli, deseeded and diced

Pinch of sea salt

½ tsp ground Sichuan pepper

2 garlic cloves, peeled and crushed

Knob of butter

1 large egg, beaten

Handful of chives, chopped

Have all your ingredients prepped before you start as this dish cooks quite quickly. First of all, cook both the noodles according to their packet instructions, then drain and immediately cool with water to stop them cooking further. Set them aside. Make the broth by combining the vinegar, 150ml/⅔ cup of the vegetable stock, sugar and soy sauce, and whisk until the sugar dissolves.

In a wok or large frying pan, heat the oil over a medium heat and fry all of the vegetables, except for the garlic and the chives, adding a generous pinch of salt along with the Sichuan pepper, then cook the vegetables until tender, about 20 minutes. When they're done, add the garlic, fry for a minute, then pour in the remaining stock and simmer over a low heat as you make the omelette.

Add a knob of butter to a frying pan and place over a medium heat. Mix the beaten egg with half the chives and pour into the pan to make a thin omelette. Remove from the heat and chop it into postage stamp-size pieces.

Take two large bowls and put the egg noodles to one side and the rice or glass noodles to the other. Pour over the vegetable mixture, then the vinegar mix and scatter over the chopped omelette and the remaining chives.

Serve when cool.

DACHA

Swimming in the lake

ISSYK-KUL, NORTHEAST KYRGYZSTAN: 'Comfort me with apples,' said
the Song of Solomon and there is much pleasure to be had biting into a sun-
flushed apple plucked from a bending branch. From Bishkek, I'd travelled east
by taxi to the southern shore of Issyk-Kul, the world's second largest alpine lake
after Titicaca in Bolivia, arriving in time for the apple harvest. The orchard I sat
in, with trees planted in neat rows, produces two tonnes of fruit a year but it is
not a commercial business, rather a private garden belonging to Anna and Sergei,
whose family history here goes back seven generations – the details of which came
out the following night, over plum brandy at the kitchen table.

Beyond the orchard, the sleepy lakeside village of Tamga is all confetti-coloured
wooden cottages decorated with lacy curtains, timber cladding and picket fences.
Hundreds of stag-headed branches, heavy with jumbles of apples, lined the quiet
lanes. Rugs had been draped over bonnets of cars, a final airing against dust and
moths, before the long winter. The whole village was a mountain-ringed appley
heaven. Tamga had been built alongside a Russian military post in the 19th
century and had once been a solely Russian village, although ethnic Russians,
like Anna and Sergei, are a minority today. The lane their house is on, translates
literally as 'under the mountains' because the mountains, shady and snow-covered
year-round, almost look close enough to touch. Where Anna and Sergei live, on
the quiet and remote southern shore of Issyk-Kul, could not be more different
to the built-up northern shore dominated by the beach resort of Cholpon Ata.
There, on the main strip, a ten-minute walk from the beach, loud Russian pop
music pumps out of packed cafés and bars. Between the strip and beach, men file
into convenience stores to down quick nips of vodka.

Anna and Sergei's homestead was an indoors-outdoors set up of wooden
dacha-esque huts and garden pavilions, all set within the orchard, managed by
Sergei who usually carried around with him a hammer or drill. My bedroom was
a small chalet and as well as a bed inside, there was a small bunk on the porch for
sleeping out under the stars. After I dropped my bag there, Anna ushered me
into a detached wooden house, complete with a summer kitchen, set in the apple
garden. Sunlight flooded in, and the odd bee buzzed behind the lacy curtains.
Otherwise, it was silent. For lunch, Anna had covered a wooden table with a
hand-stitched tablecloth, and had set out a bowl of hot chilli-laden laza for the
freshly made potato manti to be dipped into, alongside a cooling bowl of sour
cream. A basket of bread, a plate of dill-flecked tomatoes, a pot of green tea, jars
of homemade jam and pickles. I read a book and relaxed in a way that I hadn't

for weeks, while outside clouds bloomed and tall birch trees cast long shadows, suggesting late afternoon.

Before darkness fell, I went back into the orchard, planted by Sergei's parents decades ago, and sat on a bench, under a spreading tree that dropped the occasional apple to the cidery floor. I picked one up. The apple filled my palm perfectly with its symmetrical shape. Its skin, half-flushed with broken stripes of red, green and purple, was smooth and dry but dotted with tiny russet specks of beading. Underneath, a little indented basin held the eye where the petals had dropped off and the fruit had formed. It had a stout little stalk, and a sage-green leaf. The chewy skin had a revitalising acidity that gave way to creamy white flesh, fine-textured with no fluff. I bit right down to the orange-brown seeds. The apple tasted a little like pear drops. The garden was full of visitors. Caterpillars and birds during the day and apple-loving mice and voles who'd scrump for fallen fruit under moonlight. It seemed I was the only person paying to stay.

TSAR'S CURLS AND LAKESIDE LAVENDER

The following day, Sergei drove me out to the lake, passing by Tamga's military sanatorium. Murals of doctors with syringes, swimmers and rowing boats hinted at what went on inside. More of a medical centre than a spa, it was built for army men, boxers and pilots who came here to get their teeth and eyes fixed, to work out and to have electrotherapy. Its grandest building housed a huge boxing ring on one floor and a vast swimming pool on another with glass walls offering views out to the valley. This was where Sergei's parents, who'd planted the apple trees, worked. His mother in the canteen, his father as an on-site carpenter.

Closer to the water, sea buckthorn grew between sharp thorns, its berries going into tea, vodka and jam, not to be confused with ephedra berries, Sergei said, which also grow here and go into illegal amphetamines. We drove away from the lake, heading inland. Ravines met gorges met gullies. All was the colour of coral, the colour of Arizona. Fairytale canyons reached towards the heavens. I had no idea this landscape existed here. We parked, got out and walked. Water pooled around the sharp escarpments – there are often spring downpours – and by the lagoons grew tall and sturdy reeds with which the Kyrgyz line their yurts. There was not a soul around, so we yelled to test the echo of the canyons, sending unblinking cigarette-size lizards, under rocks. With no man-made constructions around, it was impossible to get a sense of scale; we were simply dwarfed by ridges and slopes hued in peach, yellow, beige and red.

'Plenty of food here in this canyon,' Sergei said, pointing out wild garlic, dog rose, sharp lemony barberries (ideal for plov) and lavender as we walked. 'We burn this wild sage and the smoke protects the house,' he added stroking its

ВЫШЕ

БЫСТРЕЕ,

downy leaves, before pointing to a little dandelion-like plant, busy puffing away in the wind, known as 'tsar's curls'. Such a landscape might be the backdrop of an oil painting by the Russian artist Vasily Vereshchagin whose 'Turkestan Series' was shown in London in the late 19th century. He came here, and painted Issyk-Kul at sunset. He also painted a reimagining of a pile of skulls, heads that had been lopped off by emperor warlord Tamerlane, likely inspired by the sort of grave markers we noted in the distance, which also look like Scottish cairns. In the ochre-coloured canyons, Sergei saw the outlines of animals in the rocks: a Bactrian camel, a horse, a dog, a pig.

That night, I was invited by Anna into the main house, a traditional Russian-style family home surrounded by flowers and topped with carved eaves. In the kitchen, I met her parents, Antoli and Lyudmila. Both had cornflower-blue eyes, the colour of the lake. Lyudmila was dressed in a thick, fluffy dressing gown and booties. Outside, the little burn that bubbles behind the birch trees was all that could be heard, along with a faraway dog howling its moon chorus. Together, we all huddled around the small table. It was warm in the small kitchen. It smelled of comfort, family and potatoes.

'Plum brandy, homemade!' I was poured one glass, then another. A kitten took refuge by the stove, and a television on the wall played a Russian variety show. Over two more glasses of brandy, Lyudmila told me their story.

In 1887 their ancestors moved to Karakol, an hour's drive east from here, to the very outermost edge of the Russian Empire, from Smolensk, in western Russia and Georgia's capital, Tbilisi. Back then, Karakol was a military garrison. 'As the empire grew people went further and further, a lot of people came here, for the lake, for the mountains, for the climate. But still, all these years on, here we are seen as Russian, and in Russia, we are seen as Kyrgyz,' Lyudmila said, her eyes sparkling above sharp cheekbones. Earlier, leaning on a giant plov kazan set in the garden, next to a tandoor oven, Anna had said something telling: 'We have a different kitchen here. A kitchen more Asian than Russian. I cook local food – plov, dimlama, laghman. Big dishes. We cook in another way.'

Lyudmila continued, 'We stayed in 1991 when the Soviet Union fell because we believed things would get better. But they didn't. Now, of 5,000 people here in Tamga, only 500 Russians are left. The same story in Karakol, where we live,' Lyudmila said glumly, tucking a strand of silver hair behind her ear. Karakol was previously named Przhevalsk after the Russian explorer Nikolai Przhevalsky, who, born in Smolensk, died in Karakol in 1888. A monument to him, along with a two-humped Bactrian camel, stands in Alexander Garden, St Petersburg.

'Why did you choose to stay when so many others left?' I asked. 'The living is easier here, the climate, the clean air, the fruit. Industrial Russia is hard. Here, all the seasons are beautiful,' came the answer.

Most Kyrgyz and Russians get along well, relying on one another as in any society. But Kyrgyzstan, as with most post-Soviet states, is nation-building and rebranding its history and that does not always include Russians. But Russian is still spoken widely, Kyrgyzstan sends much manpower to Moscow and Kyrgyz football fans often support Russia during the World Cup matches. It's never been straightforward. A last plum brandy sealed the evening and I returned to my room wondering about this double life and of the future.

The following morning, Anna served me her famous zapekanka in the wooden summerhouse. This was a slice of plain rectangular cake, half the size of a paperback book, light yet somehow dense, topped with sour cream and enlivened by a syrupy homemade strawberry jam cut with sharp lemon. It was exquisite, especially eaten amid the sun-dappled orchard. Later, I looked back upon it with great longing.

Sergei took me on one last trip, out to the Barskoon Valley, keen to show me a gorge where waterfalls thunder. In the valley, teams of chestnut horses galloped in their dozens past emerald-green hills and trucks huffed up and down to the Kumtor gold mine, so large, apparently, that it can be seen from space. Mint and rosemary went underfoot as we walked to see the waterfall. Sergei, fit as a boxer but softly spoken, with an easy laugh and a rare gentleness, rhapsodised about the falls. But it was lost on me, as waterfalls generally are. As a postscript, he showed me something far more thrilling. 'And, here, on this rock, is Yuri.' And, there he was, unexpected and magnificent. Yuri Gagarin's face painted gold and carved into a rock the size of a small car, a red space helmet on his head, immortalised here, close to the southern shore of Issyk-Kul. Along with Soviet leaders, he'd recuperated on the northern shore where the big sanatoriums still are today. And I was headed there next, with that in mind.

Later that day, Sergei arranged a taxi to take me to the northern shore of the lake. The driver told me he'd worked as a pilot during the Soviet period and had moved here in the late 1960s, staying on after the collapse of the Soviet Union. He'd stayed, he said, simply because 'It was a better life than back in Siberia, in Omsk.' We drove past the lake, its shores dotted with apricot, plum and pear trees, their leaves, red, gold and green. Trees here produce so much fruit that most of it is sent to Russia. It was not hard to see why people would choose to stay here, in peace and quiet, by the lake fed by meltwater from the mountains. It is, undoubtedly, one of the most beautiful places on earth. Hauntingly so.

TORPEDO TESTING AND PSYCHEDELIC SALADS

A quick suck of breath as the cold water hit my chest, then into Issyk-Kul I went. The water was freezing, goosebump-inducing, casting further doubt on local lore that states this inland sea is warm as it reaches down to the earth's molten core. There are many names for the lake. Kyrgyz people sometimes call it the 'earth's eye', the Chinese 'warm sea', while to Russians it is 'the pearl of Kirghizia'.

I'd dabbled initially at the edge of the northern shore of the lake. Running my fingers through the sand, as if panning for gold, with the hulking Aurora sanatorium behind me. Then, I'd followed two other women, who'd made a great show at the water's chill, into the waves. Before long, we were floating and swimming with different strokes. Warm enough once in. What else on earth, that costs nothing, is more freeing? Walking, of course, but not much else. By the water, I met three other women, colleagues from Chelyabinsk in central Russia, who had travelled for two days overland on buses to get here for their three-day holiday. Each had an air of utmost relaxation about them despite the long journey and short stay, and each carried a carton of kefir in their hands. On the sand, a Kyrgyz woman threw bread skywards to the gulls. The water was clear to at least 20 metres. It made the silver ring on my left hand sparkle good as new.

Years ago, the eastern section of the lake was subject to torpedo testing by the Soviets, making it a no-go zone for foreigners, although some surprisingly famous westerners did come. American writers Arthur Miller and James Baldwin, authors of *Death of a Salesman* and *Giovanni's Room*, respectively, arrived in the autumn of 1986, along with Peter Ustinov, the actor and writer, all invited by renowned local novelist Chingiz Aitmatov who had assured them that the meeting would be independent and not fuelled by government propaganda. The intellectuals had gathered on Issyk-Kul, to discuss global issues following a failed arms control meeting between Mikhail Gorbachev and President Reagan in Iceland. Ustinov was quoted as saying the Issyk-Kul group had included people other than 'the usual fellow-travelers', which seemed fair. Alongside the American writers was Zülfü Livaneli, the Turkish composer, and Afewerk Tekle, the Ethiopian painter. They had all stayed at a health resort on the lakeshores.

I shook the beads of water from my hair, and two more women in bikinis approached the water cautiously, before sliding in as smoothly as seals. The water was cold but this side of the lake got all the sun. On a lounger, a man lay starfished, his back covered with bruised purple rings. Another woman had traces of paraffin wax on her arms, clues that most beachgoers had been at the Aurora sanatorium behind us.

Resembling a banked cruise ship, with a smaller, tip-tilted black dreadnought crowning its roof, the brutalist-style sanatorium was built in 1978 for the Communist Party elite and recovering cosmonauts. The architect may have drawn inspiration from Chingiz Aitmatov's novel *The White Ship*, according to some reports. It does make a visual impression, one of bulk and importance. During the Soviet era, millions of people went to sanatoriums not so much to holiday but for self-improvement. Passes and vouchers in hand, they arrived ready for their subsidised stay, eating healthful foods, socialising with people from elsewhere in the USSR, and taking advantage of a chance to experience the Soviet ideal of exposure to the elements, water, clean air and forests, which in turn would make them stronger, healthier Soviet citizens. Everything at the sanatorium was carefully designed and under supervision. Diet, exercise, rest, sunbathing, even sleep, was monitored. To holiday at a sanatorium was to show loyalty to the motherland. Many of the guests at the state-owned Aurora were older, holidaying now as they did back then, together, as comrades.

Lunchtime. I dried off and went inside. The swirling carpets went on forever through the mint-green corridors. No one bothered me, so I followed a trail of pot plants, viewing the photographs of former guests that lined the walls. Boris Yeltsin, dozens of cosmonauts, the sort of model workers and high-ranking Soviet nomenklatura who tended to get all the caviar in life. The sanatorium smelled musty but it exuded cleanliness, and was decorated with expensive chandeliers, marble, statuettes and giant chessboards. A sort of ersatz fantasia blending Soviet solemnity with Oriental luxuriance. Bas-reliefs of women carrying jars and waves, a visual metaphor for wellness and plenty. The coffee shop, cinema, billiards hall and dining room retained their original wood panelling.

The restaurant was a throwback in time, the decor unchanged since the 1980s. I clumsily talked my way into the kitchen and was shown the Soviet-era ovens, pasta rolling machines and enamel pots. All original. The cooks laughed and waved, it was cheery and busy. A happy place. I sat and ate my blini, beetroot in mayonnaise, cabbage and grated carrot salads, all neon with dill, and I ate the mashed potato and fish set before me. I tried to pay, and tried again, but nobody would accept my money. I explained I wasn't staying, but still the staff would not budge. I was a guest, an outsider, and they wanted to show me kindness, through food, through feeding me. I left the sanatorium, walking under a mural of a map of the lake and a pearl showing the location of Aurora.

I took a taxi back to the capital, Bishkek, with the driver singing lullabies the whole way. I fell asleep, then awoke to see sun-lit plastic picnic gazebos by sparkling streams, golden birch trees glowing and shashlik smoke corkscrewing skywards. A good road, an easy driver. Rest before travelling on to Tajikistan.

Anna's Breakfast Zapekanka

This light cake is a rendition of Anna's simple breakfast zapekanka served in her garden-orchard. It marries beautifully with a not-too-sweet conserve. It's a handy recipe for when you have people staying over and you'd like to serve something a bit different at the breakfast table. It also works for afternoon tea. Tvorog, similar to quark, can be bought from Polish shops or in large supermarkets.

MAKES 1 CAKE

100g/1 stick unsalted butter, softened, plus extra for greasing

100g/½ cup granulated sugar

275g/1 cup full-fat tvorog

2 medium eggs

1 tsp vanilla extract

1 tbsp sour cream

200g/1½ cups plain flour

1 tsp baking powder

½ tsp fine sea salt

Sour cream, to serve

Thin jam or conserve, to serve

Preheat the oven to 170°C/325°F/gas mark 3 and grease a 1kg/2lb loaf tin with a little butter.

In a large bowl, cream the butter and sugar until light and fluffy, then add the tvorog, eggs, vanilla and 1 tablespoon of sour cream. Mix well, it will have the consistency of cottage cheese at this stage. Then, sift in the flour and baking powder, add the salt, and mix to combine. It will be quite a thick batter but transfer it to the tin and smooth off the top as best you can (a palette or butter knife that's been run under the tap works well).

Bake for 50 minutes to 1 hour but check on it about halfway through. If the top of the cake looks to be catching, remove it from the oven and tent it with tin foil then return to the oven for the remaining time.

Once golden on top and a skewer comes out clean, remove from the oven, leave in the tin until it's completely cool, then remove. To serve, add a generous spoonful of sour cream and pour over a little jam or conserve. To store the zapekanka keep it wrapped in foil, then to serve again warm it gently in the oven.

Cheat's Laghman

Laghman is a Uyghur noodle dish topped with a mild stew of meat and vegetables. Uyghur cooks rightly demand that the noodles should be hand-pulled, but they are pros at the delicate and tricky art of pulling and flinging noodles, and if you're not, well, it is challenging to put it mildly. This version (reluctantly) cheats on the noodles but brings you the warming flavours of laghman, a dish served throughout Central Asia, popular with everyone from yesterday's commissars to today's chess players.

SERVES 4

275g/10oz thick egg noodles

2 tbsp sunflower oil

500g/1lb 2oz lamb leg steak, cut into bite-size chunks

Salt and freshly ground black pepper, to season

1 onion, diced

2–4 garlic cloves (dial up or down depending on taste), peeled and thinly sliced

1 tsp cumin seeds

150g/5oz Chinese (Napa) cabbage, chopped into bite-size pieces

1 red (bell) pepper, chopped into 2cm/1in pieces

1 green (bell) pepper, chopped into 2cm/1in pieces

1 fresh red chilli, deseeded and sliced thinly

2 tbsp tomato purée (paste)

350ml/1½ cups beef stock

1 tbsp sesame seeds, to garnish

Chives, to garnish (optional)

Have all your ingredients ready to go before you start, then cook the noodles according to the packet instructions.

Add 1 tablespoon of oil to a wok or large frying pan and place over a medium heat. Season the lamb well with salt and pepper before frying it for 5 minutes – keep it moving in the pan, or else it'll stick. When almost cooked through, remove and cover with tin foil to keep it juicy.

Add another tablespoon of oil and keep the wok or pan over a medium heat. Fry the onion with the garlic and cumin seeds for a few minutes, stirring all the time. Add all the other vegetables along with the tomato purée and fry over a medium-high heat for about 20 minutes, until the vegetables have softened. Add the stock and bring to a boil, letting it bubble away for another 10 minutes, so that it begins to thicken. Add the lamb back to the pan, along with its juices to warm through, check the seasoning and remove from heat.

Serve the noodles in large bowls, with the stew on top, sprinkling over some sesame seeds and chives, if using.

OPERA HOUSE

Reminiscing in the capital

DUSHANBE, WEST TAJIKISTAN: Bunches of red roses for sale in musty underpasses. Banners of Lenin in souvenir shops. Sputtering fountains. Mountain views. Dry, dehydrated air that makes your face tight, lips dry and throat sore. Those things I recognised. But since my last visit, five years ago, something in Dushanbe, Tajikistan's diminutive capital, had changed. The city had become less fixed. More mechanised and faster. Louder.

Disorientated, I wandered to familiar places, nostalgia steering meals and moods. At the Ukrainian restaurant, Traktir Konservator, I ordered a bowl of crimson borscht, ladled out alongside a plate of plump garlicky pampushki (bread rolls). It was as good as I remembered. Across the road, by the opera and ballet square, I walked into the pastel-painted but undeniably bleak Hotel Vakhsh. Its corridors, lit by bare light bulbs, were still painted a swampy green and above the main stairwell a window of blue and yellow stained glass glowed churchlike, also untouched. Harbouring the same old inertia, the hotel is a perfect place to stay if you're hankering after a sharp Soviet flashback, one of sporadic plumbing, saggy beds and suspicious comings and goings late at night. I wondered if they still took jewellery as a deposit on a room, as a stone-faced receptionist had suggested on my first ever visit a decade ago. The hotel's fabric and spirit appeared resolutely fixed, reassuringly unaffected.

Countless other Soviet-era structures, though, have been flattened for good. Called Stalinabad from 1929 to 1960, hundreds of Russian engineers, architects and industrialists arrived here, to work at the far edge of the Soviet Union until it collapsed in 1991, after which many quickly left. Nowadays, many in the capital aspire to a modern way of life, not a Soviet past. So, gone is the old Jami cinema, named after the Sufi writer Nur ad-Din Abd ar-Rahman Jami, and gone, too, is the old Mayakovsky Theatre, which housed Tajikistan's first cinema and its first radio-broadcasting centre.

When Dushanbe was declared the capital in 1924 it was little more than a village of a couple of thousand. Today, construction sites edge most of the major roads. A city far smaller than Tashkent, the changes are startling and obvious. Yet, this is no boomtown. Many of the shiniest apartment blocks and office buildings, such as Dushanbe Plaza, a monolithic 22-storey wedding-cake construction, lie empty or else are only partly used. These buildings, especially those that huddle around President Emomali Rahmon's urban dacha, are Potemkin pleasures. Built to please the president's eye, to give the illusion of a wealthy city, to mask and hide poverty.

Extravagant facades and triumphant architecture built as a way of cloaking housing crises. Witnessing this brings to mind the forceful, and slightly sinister-sounding, words inscribed on Tamerlane's summer palace in Shakhrisabz, Uzbekistan: 'Those who doubt our power, see our buildings.' Underused and expensive buildings jar in a country where poverty remains the enemy for most. Crippled by a five-year civil war at the onset of its independence in 1991, between pro-government forces, Islamists and pro-democracy groups, Tajikistan today is shackled by Russia, heavily depended upon for work opportunities and security, and debts to China, mounting ever upwards as Beijing builds roads, tunnels and power infrastructure.

And yet despite all the changes, the city's main thoroughfare, Rudaki Avenue, remains one of the handsomest and loveliest streets in Central Asia. An artery cutting through the centre of the city, running from the train station in the south to the cement factory to the north, it is lined with statues and parks and is partly canopied by mature trees, providing shade from the strong sun in summer. Come evening, it is a lovers' lane, of sorts, filled with strolling couples.

Named after the 10th-century master of classical Persian literature and Tajik poetry, Abu Abdollah Ja'far ibn Muhammad Rudaki, it is a physical reminder, too, of Tajikistan's historical and linguistic connections to Persia. Many Tajiks can quote Omar Khayyam and poets such as Ferdowsi. The Tajik language is closely linked to Persian and is the language you hear in Samarkand and Bukhara, across the border in Uzbekistan, where thousands of Tajiks live today and thousands more trace their roots. Along with the Qur'an, books of Rudaki's poems remain the most purchased and read here.

Options for evening entertainment in Dushanbe are limited, so at the Ayni Opera and Ballet Theatre, opposite the Hotel Vakhsh, I bought a ticket for a concert that evening that promised classical music from two American musicians who were on a 'Silk Road Tour.' Built in 1942, the opera house has been thoroughly spruced up, but as a protected building of 'cultural significance', it retains its original grandeur. I pocketed the ticket.

Along with the opera house, Rokhat chaikhana, on Rudaki Avenue, is another survivor of the construction boom. Proof, perhaps, of the power of the teahouse. Open-fronted, tall as a four-storey apartment building, and with a Persian-style painted roof supported by wide white columns, it was designed by architects in the 1950s adept at combining eastern comfort with Soviet brute immensity. I sat upstairs, pouring green tea from a little pot as autumn sunlight flooded warmly onto my back. Couples dined together, other lives and loves being played out to the unmistakable and eerie theme tune of *Twin Peaks*. Gentle, hardworking and sober-looking waiters sloped across the polished floor, serving bowls of lunchtime laghman and baskets of bread.

THE SUN SHINES OVER TASHKURGAN

Ten minutes before the concert was due to start, the taxi driver grumbled as we sat locked in traffic, the engine running. Roads had been sealed off by baton-wielding policemen who were unhurriedly redirecting traffic. President Emomali Rahmon, the former boss of a cotton collective and in power since 1992, was on the move, and soon enough his all-black motorcade cruised through the city centre. With the whole of central Dushanbe at a halt, I'd not be the only one late for the concert. Then, finally, we were off, moving slowly down Rudaki Avenue, past the glittering statue of Ismoil Somoni, emir of the Samanid Empire (AD 819–999). This Persian dynasty, remembered for leadership, scientific advances, poetry and trade, has become part of Tajikistan's nation-building post-independence and is celebrated. The currency is named after Somoni, and there is Ismoil Somoni Peak, formerly known as Communism Peak, the highest mountain in Tajikistan.

I sprinted up the front steps of the opera house, then walked up the red carpet alongside other ticket-holders, everyone well-dressed for the occasion, passing ornate stucco walls decorated with golden-framed portraits of musicians, ballerinas and choreographers. Faces and fashions of another time. In the auditorium, the ceiling glowed with gold, pink and mint-green florals and paisley designs, another nod to Tajikistan's historic links to Persia. The lights remained on for the performance and we began with Grieg and Debussy, then moved onto Gershwin's 'An American in Paris'. Occasionally, a local cello player, whose stand was way too low for her, joined the American violinist and pianist. 'The Sun Shines Over Tashkurgan', composed by Chen Gang and based on a traditional Tajik folk song, stirred the audience. The town of Tashkurgan, in Xinjiang, is an ancient stop on the modern Karakoram Highway that follows an old Silk Road route from China. In Tashkurgan, the sort of place where clear-cut definitions of east and west, and Europe and Asia, matter less, people may introduce themselves as descendants of Alexander the Great, and their light skin and fair hair hints at this. Some historians believe that the Stone Tower Greco-Egyptian geographer Ptolemy believed marked the midpoint on the ancient Silk Road was in Tashkurgan, while others say it was Osh or Tashkent.

At the end of the concert, women stood in the audience, clapping, waving their programmes, their pearls and diamante glittering in the light. Nobody threw roses onto the stage, as they might do in Russia, but when a bunch of flowers was carried onto the stage, it was clear that the American musicians had already left. There was no interval, and no bar so I sloped into a nearby café for a beer, where I listened to night-time drag racers tearing down Rudaki. I'd heard the same screeching and revving from my grim little bedroom at the Hotel Vakhsh years ago. In 1924 there were only two cars in Dushanbe, a fact hard to imagine today.

The following day, I went to Mehrgon Market, a sort-of replacement for the Green Bazaar, close to Rudaki Avenue, which had been knocked down, one of the most controversial, and talked about, changes to take place in the city. I have only vague memories of visiting it in 2009 but wandering through the new bazaar, more sanitised high-rise mall than traditional whirling and low-slung Central Asian market, I wondered what had been gained by knocking it down. Inside, it was quiet, the lanes of fruit and nuts mainly manned by people scrolling on their mobile telephones.

Outside, a convention of honey sellers had gathered, proudly displaying their amber-hued jars and wooden honeycomb frames, bringing a welcome dash of nature, real life and enthusiasm to the scene. They were in town for three days, they explained, to introduce their exceptionally fresh and grassy-tasting honey to the residents of Dushanbe. They'd come from the Rasht Valley, east of Dushanbe, where mountains surround fruit-filled valleys. Tajikistan's landmass is 93 per cent mountains, and less than 10 per cent of the land is suitable for growing crops, so fertile valleys are rare. The honey sellers told me to go and see it for myself. I said I would, not least as I'd had a similar tip-off. Many farmers and naturalists fill the bountiful valleys of Rasht but there is one man, I'd been told by friends, to go and meet. A poet, musician and renowned botanist named Mirzoshah Akobirov. Stay with him, they'd said. Stay with him in his village of Jafr, eat with him, listen to his stories and hear his songs. I bought a paper map of the Rasht Valley from a bookshop on Rudaki Avenue, and left Dushanbe.

Melon, Yogurt and Hazelnut Pudding

Visitors to Central Asia are always bowled over by the melons, but because they are the best in the world, very little tends to be done with them. They are simply carved up into juicy crescents and eaten. Therefore, I was interested to find out about a dish using melons in the qurutob cafés close to Mekhkalon Mosque in Dushanbe. Unlike qurutob, which is a savoury salad with flatbread and a yogurt sauce, fatir maska is sweet. A southern Tajik speciality from the Khatlon region, shredded fatir bread is fried lightly in butter, and is served with chopped melon scattered on top. This is a take on traditional fatir maska, a great way to get melons on the table. You'll need four sundae or dessert glasses ideally for serving these.

MAKES 4 INDIVIDUAL PUDDINGS

1 sheet of filo pastry

20g/1½ tbsp unsalted butter, melted

50g/⅓ cup blanched hazelnuts

60g/1 cup soft breadcrumbs

25g/1¾ tbsp golden caster sugar

1 Galia melon or similar

100g/½ cup natural yogurt

Preheat the oven to 200°C/400°F/gas mark 6 and line a baking tray with greaseproof paper.

Brush the filo sheet with the butter, lay on the baking tray and bake for 3–4 minutes until golden (keep a close eye as it can colour quickly). Remove from the oven and when cool, break into large shards.

Preheat your grill. Smash the hazelnuts using a pestle and mortar, just to break them up a bit rather than turning them into dust. Mix with the breadcrumbs and spread thinly onto a baking tray. Sprinkle over the sugar and grill until golden, this should only take a couple of minutes – give them a stir around halfway through to allow for the under-layer to colour.

Using a melon baller to create spheres and put them into the glasses, filling two-thirds, pour over the yogurt, then scatter over the hazelnut-sugar-breadcrumb mix and artfully arrange the buttery filo shards on top.

Prunes Cloaked in Chocolate

Boxes of prunes dipped in chocolate are for sale in Dushanbe's smarter shops and I love their sweet, bitter flavour. These are ideal for a mid-afternoon pick-me-up with a cup of coffee.

MAKES 25 SWEETS

100g/3½ oz dark chocolate
(70 per cent cocoa solids)

25 partially rehydrated dried
prunes, stones removed

25 blanched whole hazelnuts

Line a platter or baking tray with parchment. Snap the chocolate into pieces and add them to a heatproof bowl. Place the bowl over a saucepan of simmering water, being careful not to let the base of the bowl touch the water. Once melted, remove from the heat and stir gently until the chocolate is completely smooth.

Dip each prune in the melted chocolate, press a hazelnut onto the chocolate coating and set each one carefully – so as not to remove too much chocolate – on the platter or baking tray to set. Once they're all assembled, put the tray into the fridge to set for 20 minutes.

Dushanbe Sambusa with Chickpea, Spinach and Mint

Flaky and buttery samsa, Central Asia's beloved turnovers, are known in Tajikistan as sambusa. Elsewhere in the region fillings are typically beef, lamb, pumpkin, spinach or potatoes but in Dushanbe there are chickpea ones and in the springtime, herb-filled variations. This recipe combines the two. Samsa or sambusa are always eaten with green tea, this is especially the case if they're lamb as tea cuts through the fat.

MAKES 15 SAMSA

1 small onion, roughly chopped

1 x 400g/14oz can chickpeas (garbanzo beans), drained

3 tbsp mint leaves, roughly chopped

Handful of spinach

1 tsp fine sea salt

1 tsp black pepper

1 tsp ground cumin

1 tsp dill seeds (optional)

1 x 320g/11oz packet of puff pastry

1 small egg, beaten

1 tsp black sesame seeds, to garnish (optional)

Flaky sea salt and freshly ground black pepper, to garnish (optional)

Preheat the oven to 200°C/400°F/gas mark 6 and line a large baking tray (or two smaller trays) with greaseproof paper.

Into a food processor add the onion, and pulse a few times, then add 100g/3½oz of chickpeas, the mint and spinach, and pulse so it comes together. Put the mixture into a large bowl and mix in the salt, pepper, spices, dill seeds, if using, and the remaining unpulsed chickpeas.

Lightly flour the work surface and the pastry, and roll it out to 37 x 28cm/ 14½ x 8in. Using an 8cm/3in cutter, stamp out 15 rounds then put a teaspoon of the filling in the middle of each one and bring up the edges to create a triangle shape. Press to seal, creating a samosa-style triangle. Repeat with the remaining pastry.

Place on the baking tray seam-side down. Brush each one with the egg wash and scatter over the black sesame seeds or a sprinkle of flaky sea salt and a few grindings of black pepper, if you like. Bake for 15 minutes, then when the pastry has fully risen, lower the oven temperature to its lowest setting and bake for a further 10–15 minutes, until the layers are dry and crispy.

BOTANICAL GARDEN

Philosophising in a mountain orchard

RASHT VALLEY, CENTRAL TAJIKISTAN: Mirzoshah Akobirov's orchard in the small village of Jafr in the Rasht Valley felt far from Dushanbe. Above a carpet of golden leaves, two men were high up ladders collecting apples to go into crates and wheelbarrows below while pairs of women huddled under a wooden gazebo, octagonal and crowned by curved Marco Polo sheep horns, sorting and boxing the fruit ready for sale.

It had taken half a day to get here from the capital, bumping eastwards in the back of an old Toyota with a cracked windscreen and poor suspension. Yet, once past a string of derelict factories that nudged the city limits, we were under the shadows of sharp escarpments and towering mountainsides, a landscape not short of heart stopping. The dusty mountain roads were dramatic, mainly switchbacks and blind corners. On one bend my driver, keen-eyed and steady, narrowly avoided tumbling rock fall from a steep hillside but passengers up ahead in another car had been less lucky and huddled together underneath the bluff, visibly shaken. We continued on. Children ran up to the car calling out to us to buy hawthorn berries they'd strung on thread and hung around their necks, each orange-yellow fruit a shiny bead. Mid-way, we stopped at a market to buy bags of white mulberries and persimmons. Hamlets of mud-brick houses and ancient gnarly mulberry trees appeared, the mountain foothills glowing with autumn colours of red, gold and green.

Such bucolic scenery made it hard to imagine that the Rasht Valley saw some of the fiercest fighting during Tajikistan's civil war in the early 1990s and that many opposition fighters hid out here. The valley still occasionally makes the news for harbouring alleged militants and combatants. I'd stopped at the town of Gharm, where I had to pay the driver and then find a local taxi for the last leg, as is often the way here. In Gharm those grim details felt a little keener. I stopped to look at the painted roof of a chaikhana on the main road, but was told it had become a 'nightclub', not a good place for a foreigner to visit. At a restaurant run by a friendly woman called Pahmina, I ate lamb and turnip soup in the main dining room while gruff army men stomped past, choosing to sit in private curtained-off booths.

It was, therefore, a relief to arrive at Mirzoshah's tranquil orchard. Under one particularly abundant tree lay a carpet of apples, their skins lined with red and green stripes so perfect they looked as though they had been drawn on. I picked one up.

'You can only eat that particular apple here. I went to a small forest not far away from here and there was a rare and unusual apple tree, all on its own. I took cuttings and grew my own tree here. It had no recorded identity, so I named it after my father, Iskander. It is one of twelve apples I have named,' Mirzoshah said. These particular apples are the last in the season to be harvested, sold in Dushanbe during the cold months. I bit into it. Firm-textured with flesh cream tinged with green, it was crisp and sweet. As a winter variety, these are hardy and heroic apples. It made sense he'd named them after his father, himself a survivor.

In July 1949, a giant fist punched up through the earth hitting the southern edge of the Tian Shan Mountains. In the earthquake's wake, tonnes of soil and clay were sheared, creating landslides that killed thousands in the villages of the Rasht Valley. In the village of Jafr only eight people survived and among them was Mirzoshah's father. Up in the mountains, Iskander Akobirov was just far away enough from the impact of the landslides. He was the only one of his family to survive. Now, people come to the orchard to collect cuttings in order to grow their own Iskander trees, Mirzoshah explained. The apples, therefore, acting not only as a family memory, but one of shared remembrance, too.

At Mirzoshah's house, a short drive away, we stepped inside the family museum he had built for visitors. A caged chukar partridge clucked and gurgled a welcome. 'He does that when he sees a new person,' Mirzoshah said. Inside, two framed photographs, next to an ancient leather-bound Qur'an and a clock that told the wrong time, stood out. Both were of Iskander Akobirov but they could not have been more different. One showed a young but serious clean-cut moustachioed man, his uniform covered with medals, his head shaved. A photograph from the Second World War when his father had fought for the USSR in Berlin, dodging the gunshots and artillery that had killed two of his brothers. And, next to it, another framed photograph, of a Tajik elder. A practising Muslim and man of God, with a long white sweeping beard, striped robe and rounded skullcap. The photographs showed the same man in youth, and in old age, during the Soviet Union, and after it. Clearly identifiable by the same kind eyes. It didn't take much to work out that Mirzoshah's father could not have been home long very long before he narrowly escaped the enormous earthquake that killed so many. Later, he married Mirzoshah's mother and went on to have nine children. 'He didn't speak much about the war in Germany,' Mirzoshah said taking his car keys out of the pockets of his boiler suit.

We travelled down a track in his four-wheel-drive back to the orchard. Mirzoshah drove surely and carefully, his quick hazel eyes watching the road under his rain hat, his cowboy boots fixed on the pedals. As we chatted he listened carefully to every word I said and considered every answer he gave. I liked him instantly. Poetic, gentle, empathetic and insatiably curious, he was quite typical of many Tajiks I had met but it was obvious he was a unique character, a free thinker.

The orchard remained a flurry of activity with Mirzoshah's sons busily sorting and boxing up Golden Delight and Ruxhora apples, red as blushing cheeks. Crates were packed next to the gazebo. Where we stopped to talk, rosehips grew in tangles around wooden beehives at our feet, and one tree had six different types of apple grafted onto it, all red and all seasonal.

'I had the idea for this garden when I was 20. I didn't want to work within the government structures in Dushanbe. If you had such dreams of course it was impossible to put them into action back then and anyway the government thought I was a fool for wanting land for a garden. But there was nothing here. It was like a desert. The earthquake had destroyed everything. I learned how to love the land again from my father and started to create this garden. This is a sanctuary for all the fruit of the region. I have 64 types of apples, 36 different pears and 22 varieties of apricots. In the state gardens, there are lots of workers but here it is only me and my family. I have nine children, six sons and three daughters, exactly the same as my father. In the end, the authorities were amazed I had cultivated such a unique collection.' An exceptionally talented botanist and gardener, Mirzoshah told me he had recently been awarded the title First Gardner of Tajikistan, by the Minister of Agriculture.

THE SEASONS COME, THE SEASONS GO

We moved to a dastarkhan that had been set up for lunch at a wooden tapchan. Chewy honeycomb from the garden was laid out along with a plate of golubtsi, stuffed cabbage leaves with lamb, barley soup and tomato salad. The dastarkhan was covered with bowls of raisins, dates, almonds, whole dried apricots, red and green apples. Pomegranates and red grapes. Non bread, freshly baked. The scene brought to mind the Tajik proverb on what is needed for a good life: 'a garden and a breath of wind'.

Of all of these delights, it was the Gharm pear I'll always remember, which in true Mirzoshoh style is not grown anywhere else. Grainy and small, it was hard and exceptionally crisp. Each cold, lemony-sharp bite stung slightly at the very back of the jaw, right under the ears, but then a lingering sugary blissful sweet aftertaste burst forth. Its flesh was pure white, the same colour as the fresh snow draped over the peaks of the Peter I Range that hovered in the distance, sun colouring the tops. A sure sign that winter was on its way.

'You can't find those pears anywhere else, only here.' And, this is pear country. Historians believe that pears, like their botanical cousins, apples, originated in Central Asia, also growing in the Tian Shan range, where there are groves of *Malus sieversii*, the likely ancestors of almost all apples eaten today. Like the walnuts of Arslanbob, they have long been valued, and like those nuts, whole dried pears were discovered in tombs dating back to the 4th–8th centuries AD, in the ancient Astana Cemetery near Turpan in Xinjiang. We ate slowly, taking our time, but as soon as Mirzoshah's sons had served the food, they were back to stripping apples from trees.

'What is your favourite season?' I asked as we moved on to tea. Mirzoshah's eyes lit up. Apparently, this was a good question.

'I love every season and I'll tell you why. I love spring because after a heavy winter, we see life. Early spring, I do the planting, hopeful that sowing will be harvested in the autumn. Everything is green. I love summer because we have lots of guests, we're outside in the garden together, and just starting to see the fruit come through. I love autumn because then we see the fruit of our labour, when the harvest happens you're happy to see what you've got. And, winter, I love winter because there is no work, so I sit inside and read books, think and write Tajik poetry.'

Mirzoshah puts his guests up in a little stand-alone house, right by the orchard, a pit-loo down a lane and a summer shower for the warmer months. At one end of the sleeping room was a selection of Tajik musical instruments, stringed tanburs, dutars, rubobs and drums. Inside, as soon as the sun dipped, it was absolutely teeth-chatteringly cold, despite the little electric heater. I slept in all my clothes, on a pile of thin stuffed mattresses, with thick polyester fleece blankets as covers.

UNDER THE CROP CIRCLES

The next day, we drove along a track and up into a steep-sided valley where hundreds more fruit trees clustered under the moving shadows of milk-coloured clouds. There, with only a solar-powered radio, a bag of walnuts and flashlight for company, we met one of Mirzoshah's brothers, Hussein. Until the snow sets in, Hussein camps out, on duty and keeping watch.

'If someone is not here the bears will eat everything. I have to stay and look out. They come right down from the hills sometimes.' He took off his white skullcap, placed it upside down on the grass and poured a handful of walnuts into it, encouraging me to eat. We sat in the sun with Mirzoshah and I asked Hussein how he would deter a bear, should he see one. 'It's easy. I shine the flashlight at him, and he runs off.' Night watch for bears, without a shotgun. I hoped the solar power panel, no bigger than an A4 folder, was up to the job.

Sat on the hillside, we ate the walnuts and scanned the sky in search of vultures and eagles. 'Look', said Hussein, 'over at the edge of that hill, can you see?' It wasn't a bird but rather a brown or black oval-shaped creature tumbling and waddling down the hill then over a spur, and back again. Its movements gave it away.

'It is very rare to see a bear just like that,' Mirzoshah said calmly. A few hundred metres away it wasn't nearby but it was close enough. Hussein's eyes were amazingly sharp to have spotted him. They had to be. I cracked open another walnut. The nuts were yellow and creamy, soft and young with a bitter aftertaste.

'He won't come down now. He'll wait until it's dark. The bigger problem is wolves because they are quick. They outrun the bears.' Hussein said with a sigh. Mirzoshah laughed. The land on the hillside does not belong to the brothers, but they manage it, cultivating the trees. At 1,400 metres it was already cold, and soon there would be a metre of snow.

Back in the car, we thrashed down the side of the valley following a rough track, stopping before two huge discs like giant crop circles on the steep side of the valley. Mirzoshah had planted dozens of small trees in a bicycle spoke formation, each one meeting a central point. There wasn't much to see now, but next summer when the walnut, peach, plum, apricot, pear trees blossom and fruit, the hillside will look like living embroidery. At the centre, he'd planted a wild almond tree.

'The view changes each season, the snow line, the trees, the colour of the water. But the climate has been changing, too. There is less snow every year and if there is less snow, there is less water. From May to October this year we saw no rain. This has not happened in 60 years, in my lifetime. The climate, the weather, it is changing,' Mirzoshah said.

I had heard those exact same words 'the climate, the weather, it is changing' from the walnut harvesters across the border in Kyrgyzstan, who also spoke of climate fears. Mirzoshah knows the land intimately. Every day he lives connected to it as a protector and preserver of soil, landscape and nature. If he is worried, we must listen. And, with him, we must worry, too.

That evening, the temperature dropped sharply and the dastarkhan, with all of its plates and baskets of fruit, honey, nuts and bread, had been moved inside onto the floor of the cabin where I slept. For dinner, Mirzoshah arrived, dressed warmly in a felt skullcap, a thick woollen jumper and jeans, carrying a bicycle wheel-size platter of qurutob, a national dish combining shards of flatbread with onions, tomatoes and cucumbers, and a thick tangy yogurt sauce. It is a dish for all seasons and it has long played a key role in feeding the country. On top of the platter sat a single red chilli pepper for a dash of colour and a hint of piquancy.

By the warmth of the electric heater, we ate together, tearing up a huge non bread the size of a hula hoop – the biggest I'd ever seen – and using it to scoop up the salad. Mirzoshah brought his cupped hands up to his hairline and passed them over his face to his chin, the Muslim way of giving thanks to God. Then, without a hint of awkwardness, he wandered over to the musical instruments propped against the wall, picked up a tanbur and a plectrum, sat on the windowsill, rested the instrument on his lap, and sang. Soulful Tajik songs he'd written himself, no doubt about the beauty, hardships and pain of the valley. I lounged like a sultan and listened indulgently. It was mind-bendingly beautiful, Sufi-esque, gentle, melodic music. Sleep-inducing. Mirzoshah said goodnight and left and I bundled up to sleep, poetry wandering in my mind as my eyes grew heavy, W.B. Yeats, 'The silver apples of the moon, the golden apples of the sun'. Then I thought of something Mirzoshah had rhapsodised earlier in the orchard:

'For hundreds of years our culture, that is Tajik culture, has had links to Persia, Afghanistan and Uzbekistan. Values change, but our culture is not and has never been Russian. I told my sons not to go to Moscow and work there like everyone else. I didn't go to Russia to work. I stayed here and I worked our land. And they should stay here, where they are from. I wanted my children to be immersed here, in this land, more than anything.' This rejection of dependence on Russia was relayed firmly. Kitchen gardens and orchards have never just been a simple pleasure. Where they were able to grow in this mountainous land, they supplied a vital lifeline for people recovering from the civil war, providing personal and on-hand relief, and some income. There was much purpose to staying here, and to ensuring a continuity of Tajik life. Mirzoshah was resolute. 'My sons may eat less bread here, but this is their homeland.'

A Kind of Qurutob

Qurutob, typically a salad of tomatoes, cucumbers, onions, fresh herbs and flatbread, takes its name from qurut (dried milk curds), as watered-down qurut is used as a kind of salad dressing although sometimes yogurt takes its place. It is a national dish and it is one of the very best things to eat in Tajikistan, especially in the hot months. There are many variations, but qurutob is always served in vast quantities as a shared dish, in a giant round wooden bowl, with everyone helping themselves, often using a piece of non bread as a scoop. Whole cafés in Dushanbe are dedicated to qurutob but the finest version I ate was the one on a floor cushion, just before Mirzoshah sang his mournful Tajik songs (see page 251).

SERVES 4

FOR THE DRESSING

150g/1½ cups Greek yogurt

1 garlic clove, crushed

Juice of ½ lemon

½ tsp fine sea salt

½ tsp freshly ground black pepper

2 tbsp extra-virgin olive oil

FOR THE SALAD

1 pitta bread, untoasted and roughly chopped

1 tbsp extra-virgin olive oil

¼ tsp fine sea salt

5 tomatoes, chopped

1 cucumber, chopped

1 small white onion, grated

1 fresh whole green or red chilli, to garnish

Flaky sea salt and freshly ground black pepper, to taste

Chives, chopped, to garnish

Pitta breads or Non Bread (page 120), to serve (optional)

Make the dressing first by combining all the ingredients in a jug, whisking until smooth.

Preheat the grill. Drizzle the pitta bread pieces with the oil and sprinkle them with salt, and then put them under the grill for a few minutes (tossing once). When cool, gently mix with the tomatoes and set aside.

To assemble the salad, you're looking to create five segments with the whole platter covered. Firstly, combine the cucumber with the onion and pile it up in the middle of the platter, putting your chilli on top for decoration. Then, thinking of a compass, put the yogurt dressing north and south, and the tomato and pitta mix at east and west. Season with salt and pepper and scatter over the chives.

Bring the platter to the table and let everyone help themselves with a spoon, or by scooping up with extra pitta or non bread. The idea is that you mix the ingredients as you eat, taking a little of the different segments for each bite.

Autumnal Soup with Rice, Barley and Lamb

In autumn, at almost any dastarkhan in Tajikistan, you will be served a thick, warming soup full of lamb and fresh vegetables, often so hearty that it is the main event. This is a version of the soup I ate with Mirzoshah at his apple orchard, sunshine warming our backs as we ate, snow-capped mountains hovering in the distance.

SERVES 4

2 tsp olive oil

300g/10½oz lamb neck fillet or lamb leg, trimmed of fat and cut into bite-size pieces

Sea salt and freshly ground pepper

½ large onion, finely chopped

50g/¼ cup wholegrain or brown basmati rice, rinsed

50g/¼ cup pearl barley, rinsed

500g/1lb 2oz mixed root vegetables (I used swede (rutabaga) and carrot as well as potatoes), peeled and cubed

½ tsp ground allspice

¼ tsp cayenne pepper

700ml/3 cups lamb stock

1 fresh bay leaf

Handful of flat-leaf parsley, chopped, to garnish

Non Bread (page 120), to serve

Heat I teaspoon of the oil in a casserole or large saucepan. Season the lamb generously with salt and pepper, then fry over a high heat for a few minutes until browned. Add the other teaspoon of oil, along with the onion, rice and barley, then gently fry for I minute. Add the vegetables and spices, season, and cook for 2 more minutes, before adding the stock and bay leaf. Bring to a boil, then simmer gently, with the lid on but stirring occasionally, for 40–50 minutes, or until the pearl barley is cooked but still has bite. Check the seasoning.

When it's cooked, spoon about a quarter of the soup (but not the bay leaf) into a separate pan or bowl. Purée with a stick blender then stir it back into the rest of the soup. Again, check the seasoning. Ladle into bowls, scatter over the parsley and serve with warm non bread.

SANATORIUM

Falling down a rabbit hole

GISSAR MOUNTAINS, WEST TAJIKISTAN: First the taxi driver's cupped hands went over his face in prayer, 'Bismillah, ar-Rahman, ar-Rahim' ('In the name of God, the Merciful, the Compassionate . . .'), then arms of other drivers stretched in through the car window for handshakes and well wishes. As roads in Tajikistan are usually high-altitude, and occasionally lethal, every time, ahead of departure, there is this ritual. We edged away from Dushanbe's taxi stand by the belching cement factory on Rudaki Avenue, travelling in the direction of the Gissar mountain range. Our destination was Khoja Obi Garm, a Soviet-era sanatorium that locals call 'the magic mountain'. I had no idea what to expect. Contact had proved impossible by telephone so I decided to just show up in the hope of overnighting. It was less than an hour's drive away and once we were out of the city's churning traffic, the driver zoomed along, keen, I guessed, to get back in time for Friday afternoon prayers.

Skirting past the president's 'dacha for guests', and strings of shashlik restaurants with gazebos overhanging the thrashing Varzob River, we began the steep climb up, switchback after switchback, the tyres hazardously close to mountainsides. Cherry-red, burnt-orange and moss-green leaves floated on the air, autumn colours deep and brilliant.

Then, there it was, Khoja Obi Garm, with space enough for 770 people. Monstrous and magnificent in its scale, set almost 2,000 metres up, it appeared like a banked battleship. We circled up and up further still, before finally reaching it. I got out, and entered what looked like a giant secret military lair. The entrance was not obvious, there were no signs, just taxi drivers waiting for a fare back to Dushanbe, leaning on their cars smoking. I walked down paths and up stairs, under the building's giant concrete vertebrae, passing beneath a panel of identical honeycomb-like windows. Bedrooms faced the surrounding mountains, views of nature being useful for wellbeing. Soviet sanatoriums were built for citizens as an ideological monument, reflecting the might and power of the USSR. Here, the original sanatorium opened in 1934, a little further down the hill as a plaque on a wall read, with the main section built later, in 1982. Today, the sanatorium was in utter disrepair. Dangerous, even. Lumps of concrete that had fallen from outdoor stairways and walls lay scattered about. 'Brutalist' only began to sum it up. I eventually found the entrance by a five-storey-size portrait of President Rahmon, stern-faced and photoshopped in front of a field of poppies.

Inside, there were none of the marble pillars, grand balustrades or heavy chandeliers found at Kyrgyzstan's Aurora sanatorium on Issyk-Kul but the reception, on the third floor, was busy. Groups of women sat on rows of chairs, the stainless-steel sort you find in railway station waiting rooms, drinking green tea and watching Tajik singers perform on television. They all wore bright headscarfs, fluffy dressing gowns and slippers. The men, mainly tall and thin white-bearded elders, wore their velvet chapan robes and skullcaps. Everyone exuded a sort of solemn patience. No one rushed, and no one chatted into a mobile phone. There seemed to be little contact with the outside world.

A receptionist with amber eyes and skin the colour of skimmed milk checked me in, took my passport and handed me two coupons. One for food and one for my 'luxe' bedroom. I asked where the other guests were from. 'Oh, all over. Tajikistan, Afghanistan, Russia, Lithuania, Sudan.' A group of polished Californians arrived behind me, confusion spread across their faces. Their tour guide smiled weakly. Of Iranian heritage they were visiting academics on a day trip from Dushanbe, they said. No, they weren't overnighting, they added. Above the reception, clocks told the time for Moscow and New York and a poster advertised the centre's dental treatments. Beyond reception, the corridors were mainly empty.

My bedroom, as I expected, was quasi-Soviet. Exuding a slept-in smell and the air of an old boarding house, radiators pumped out heat relentlessly, with no way to turn them down or off. The bathroom had a strange, sulphur-like odour. From the window, framed by curtains with a gold fringe, I had half a view of the mountainside, and half a view of pigeons messily nesting on the weathered windowsill. The sanatorium made little attempt to merge with its natural surroundings. Either way, it was time to explore.

MAGIC MOUNTAIN, RADON DREAMS

Cracked tiles underfoot, I walked downstairs to the third floor and back to the reception area where it seemed most life was. The windows, floor to ceiling on the stairwell, were unwashed and opaque but managed to show off and frame the glorious yellow and orange leaves of trees outside. Potted plants lined the corridors. It felt like a distinctly out-of-time house of mirrors, a strange hideaway of sorts. With every step, unsmiling maids watched me closely.

On the third floor, a doctor introduced himself as Mirali. He offered to show me around. He was a tall man, in his late fifties, wearing a white doctor's jacket and too-big trousers which he'd wrapped tight on his hips with a leather belt. He'd worked here for nine years during the Soviet Union era, and for the past six years, and in between at a hospital in Dushanbe. 'The sanatorium was built by the Soviets, but the French designed it. People come here from all over the world. Afghanistan, Luxembourg, Russia, Sudan.' Sudan, again. Of course it sounds unlikely but some African students come to Central Asia to study medicine. It was possible a few made it here. Down darkened corridors and unmarked doors, we passed patients carrying booklets, records of their personal treatments. Then a whoosh of hot air as Mirali opened the door straight onto a steam room, where a man was poaching the pink folds of his considerable body. 'Let's not infringe on privacy too much,' I asked, looking away. Mirali took no notice, and opened every door, duty-bound, it seemed, in giving me a tour. Inside the empty swimming pool, closed now for winter, our voices echoed.

'The water comes from a natural spring and it is 97 degrees, pumped up from just over there,' Mirali said pointing to a green roof outside, by the water source. The sanatorium was built here because the water is radioactive with radon, a by-product of uranium, believed by those who work here as having healing powers, though it is generally doubted by doctors in the west, some of whom link it to lung cancer. We stood in front of the empty cracked radon baths, their taps completely corroded by the radioactive water. 'Is this the same water in the guest room bathrooms?' I asked, already fearing the answer. 'Yes, radon water is included in the price, it's used for the showers. Radon baths are very good for you, but only ten minutes at a time.'

All around, in the little cells and physiotherapy rooms, lined with Oriental blood-red rugs and lacy white curtains, patients were steamed, douched and dunked in the special water. In one room, the door was opened on another man having an 'aero-massage for the nervous-system'. By a banya, there were fat massage chairs like the ones you find in airports. In another large room, men laid on coffin-like beds, shrouded in thin white sheets, dozing with acupuncture needles sticking into their backs and legs, tended to by doctors wearing white scrubs. Human anatomy maps hung on the walls. Matronly women, the size of Soviet shot-putters, manned the desks, while men in white coats came and went administering oil massages and leg stretching. Along a dimly lit corridor, lined by unmarked doors, we met another doctor, much younger than Mirali, called Sharaf. He too was eager to tell me about the effects and benefits of radon. 'We all use it. Always have. It is good for you.'

Most come here to escape the heat of Dushanbe – the mercury climbs to 45°C in summer – and then are prescribed a catalogue of treatments for ailments they didn't know they had. The sanatorium was a social world, too, isolated from the rest of society. The café-kiosks offered some privacy, with curtains cordoning people off in booths. A portrait of President Rahmon hung in every large room, his eyes watching. I had heard rumours of drug addicts going cold turkey here, up on the magic mountain, locked in rooms to battle it out.

MILK DAYS AND APPLE DAYS

For dinner, the idea was that we'd all come together, men and women, old and young, but food coupon in hand, I had trouble finding the restaurant. Lifts led to unlit floors. Suddenly, there was no one to ask. Most people were already dining in the main canteen but as I'd booked a luxe room my coupon said to go to the dining room. I wanted to see, and eat in, the mess-hall canteen and regretted not going for half-luxe. Eventually I found my spot, and was seated with four others; two couples, on a round table. The youngest pair had been married for just four days. He, a soldier, had been shaken up on the Afghan border and was here for his nerves, she, sullen and dressed in a sparkly blue headscarf, looked as if it had all gone badly wrong already. They looked like children. The other couple were jolly middle-aged professionals from Dushanbe who spoke good English. The table was a lazy Susan, so we spun to one another teapots, baskets of bread and beetroot salads laced with mayonnaise. As the line between hospital and holiday camp at Khoja Obi Garm was blurred, the kitchen was not quite the pharmacy I expected, instead turning out typical dishes: lamb soup, an unidentified fish in batter and for pudding, a plate of persimmons, some Russian cheesecake-flavoured chocolates and more tea. All perfectly fine. During the Soviet period, 'milk days' were prescribed for those with heart problems, and 'apple days' for digestive issues. Still, our dishes would have been washed in radon water, so there was that.

After dinner, I roamed down other stale corridors listening out for the entertainment which Mirali had said would be a concert. I located it by the general canteen. Sloping in, a little late, I found a small auditorium with a roof that had been painted the same Persian floral style as the opera house in Dushanbe. The stage was backed by a white satin curtain. None of the chairs matched. A woman walked on stage, her long black hair pulled tightly back, gold hoop earrings shining. She wore a full-length grey military-style winter coat, trousers and flat black shoes giving her the stern appearance of a border guard. A young man, dressed in a grey flannel suit, then came behind her and positioned himself by a Korg keyboard set atop a speaker. The lights were dimmed. There were flashes of gold teeth as patients chatted in semi-darkness. Then, disco lights came on above the singer, the keyboard started up, and the singer began to sway side to side, eyes closed, preparing to start. Psyching herself up. Then, she stopped moving, lifted the microphone slowly to her mouth and unleashed the power of ancient Tajik singing traditions. With the range of a Bollywood playback singer, she sung mournful songs with the intensity of a blues guitarist, full of longing. Never moving an inch, and all the while keeping her eyes tightly shut. A sonic soundscape ripped through the sanatorium. Audience members slowly filtered onto the stage and deferentially placed bank notes gently in her the pockets of her grey wool coat, almost bowing to her as they passed by. It became obvious that the singer kept her eyes closed as she was blind.

Women gradually got up from their chairs and danced in their long ikat-print dresses, hands spinning above their heads, all quick wrist movements. Men joined in but there was no contact between the sexes. Women danced with one another, the men with their sons, friends and brothers. A few Uzbeks became animated when a song they recognised was performed. Afterwards we all moved out into the freezing mountain air, and took to our luxe or half-luxe beds. Mine, being luxe, was covered with a red and pink polyester satin throw full of static electricity.

In the morning, I radon-showered, at speed, and left Khoja Obi Garm, wondering how much longer it will manage to limp along. Colossal and crumbling, it was certainly no spa but it did offer a timeless, eerie world, merging, I suspected, hospital with holiday camp; sanatorium with asylum. The po-faced young couple I met at dinner had chosen to stay, so maybe it would appeal to some sections of the next generation. It is certainly a curiosity, sold as a utopia, marketed as the magic mountain. Tajiks have turned their backs on it as a Soviet construct and have created something else instead. They come for the treatments, but also for the singing in the evening, to relax and socialise. To be together, somewhere different. As with the torn-down Lenin statues, what is the alternative? Either destroy the sanatorium and let it enter a historical void, or keep it as heritage. The sanatorium did feel orphaned, and would need millions to refurbish it, but it also appealed in a strange unique way. And, really all that misses the main point anyway. The sanatorium, a giant Soviet ideological retreat, actually masked the main reason Tajiks visit. It is built on the site of a holy spring, so in order to Sovietise and strip the holiness away, a sanatorium was built. Today it is a place faded by poverty but brightened by song and philosophy. And it haunted me, Khoja Obi Garm. Back home, I rewatched the recordings I took of the blind singer performing her powerful songs. And, I still sometimes have strange watery radon dreams.

A Soviet Sanatorium Appetiser

Psychedelic-looking salads of shredded orange carrots and ruby-red beetroot rule sanatorium dining rooms in Central Asia. And for good reason. Rich in antioxidants, fibre and vitamins, beetroot leaves contain more iron than spinach and in ancient times they'd be used to wrap wounds as bandages. While beetroot is traditionally simply shredded, and dressed in a little vinaigrette, this is more of a dip, showcasing the tangy, pleasantly sweet flavour and deep colour of fresh beetroots. It works well as a side dish.

SERVES 4 AS PART OF A MEZE PLATTER

345g/12oz beetroot (beets)

5 prunes, stones removed

50g/½ cup chopped walnuts, toasted

½ tsp sea salt

1 tsp freshly ground black pepper

1 tbsp sunflower oil

1 garlic clove, roughly chopped

2 tbsp mayonnaise

2 tbsp fresh dill fronds,
to garnish

Preheat the oven to 180°C/350°F/gas mark 4.

Wash the beetroot, pat dry and wrap it in tin foil. Place on a baking tray and roast for 1 hour, or until tender. When cool enough to handle, peel and add it to a food processor, along with all the other ingredients – except for the mayonnaise and dill – and pulse. Swirl through the mayonnaise and dress with dill.

CABIN

Walking the Seven Lakes

FANN MOUNTAINS, WEST TAJIKISTAN: Seven Lakes are a chain of pale turquoise pools in Tajikistan's Fann Mountains, and I'd arrived there, having travelled by car for four hours or so westwards from the capital, as I wanted to walk. It was the very tail end of the hiking season and the few guesthouses that dot the valleys close to the lakes had closed for winter, but one remained open, by the fourth lake. I had taken a little stone cabin for a few nights, lit by candle at night when the power inevitably packed up, and heated well by a log-fed Russian stove. A mountain shepherd dog called Safir, only a year old but already standing level with my hips, guarded the guesthouse. He'd had his ears lopped off, which I hated to see, in case of a wolf attack, although he didn't wear a spiked collar like some mountain dogs in Turkey do. Despite bearing his teeth at me when we first met, we quickly made friends and he'd wait outside my room in the morning, following me to the main house, which he wasn't allowed into, where for breakfast I'd eat rice pudding, with unpitted cherry jam, and pour myself rough instant coffee that had been brought by someone from Belarus. Outside on the summer tapchan, under which Safir would tuck himself into a giant ball, large non bread fresh from the tandoor was left to cool.

The younger men of the family were all in Novosibirsk working on a construction site, and left behind to run the business was an older man, his wife and their school-age grandchildren. They felt safer with Safir. At night, with zero light pollution for miles around, the sky shone brightly with stars. I never once heard a wolf howl.

ON THE THIRD DAY, I WALKED

Starting a new walk feels like a gift waiting to be unwrapped, it is unknown, and you have no idea what it will be. But if you walk, you know it will deliver delight and liberation and an escape into somewhere else, somewhere not imagined yet. It will unknot stress, and if you're lucky, there will be some form of communion with the land. As Patrick Leigh Fermor used to say 'solvitur ambulando' ('it is solved by walking').

Each lake, surrounded by dark-brown and grey escarpments, looked like glass, not a single rumple or ripple denting its turquoise surface. And the lakes really were turquoise, each one lodged in its own yawning valley. I walked into the landscape, following the path, unwinding as I went, finding calm. Knowing only that I would cover 14 miles that day. In leaf-dappled villages, donkeys were laden with coal and firewood – the poor long-eared workers of the world – and women sat on stone walls chatting or threshing small fields. Remoteness means that community is relied upon here. Bartering for agriculture and water, and following traditional hospitality, waving hello, smiling to strangers. In the winter, villagers are snowed in together for weeks, in their mud and stone houses. This sense of helping one another is important, too, as no men of working age could be seen anywhere. Only mothers, young children and elders. All the men were in Russia, working to send money home. Remittances make up around half of Tajikistan's GDP. On thin mountain paths that link the lakes, young boys rode donkeys, their saddles always a fabulous knitted or woven fabric, driving their goats between villages. 'Heh! Heh! Heh!', they sang as they went.

I walked on until the footpaths began to feel like freedom. Into the endless variations of nature: fruit trees, herds of mountain goats, clouds of grey and white, golden and red leaves, silver river valleys. Spiky mountains overhead. Thin new saplings had been planted by villages, their trunks wrapped in rainbow-coloured ikat fabrics, not so that they grow straight but to deter cows and sheep grazing on them. Everything was peaceful and quiet.

By one lake, I stopped to take off a layer and to eat. It was hot on the move and a shirt for now was enough. Dried purple figs, pistachios, jet black wrinkled prunes, each eaten like candy for energy. I bit into one of Mirzoshah's special Gharm pears, enjoying the warmth of the sun – surely one of the oldest most primeval pleasures to be had in life. The autumn leaves shone.

Then, a kitten came tumbling down the path, towards the lake. Rolling about and unsure of itself, it was just a couple of weeks into this world at most. Without its mother, it followed its heart, then fell down to its belly, got up again, and waddled towards the shade and safety of a rock high above a sparkling lake. It was lost. I stood watching its movements, guessing it must have come from one of the nearby hamlets where women were busy airing rugs. As I lifted my arm to take another bite of the pear a strange feathery shadow cast across my elbow up to my face blotting out the sun for a second. I held the pear, looked away from the kitten, upwards, and as if in a dream, saw an eagle, no more than ten metres away, its twig-like talons hanging down from its enormous body, and in it came, down and down, swooping, dipping directly for the kitten. But something spooked the eagle and it soared upwards again. The kitten, now fast, and somehow surer of itself, darted under the rock, and stayed there. I sat on a rock and marvelled at what I'd witnessed, so unexpected and fast and unforgettable. Then, I finished my fruit snacks, and moved on.

Each aqua-blue lake was given up by the valley one by one, until three hours before sunset, I reached the seventh lake, completely ringed by mountains that spurred thoughts of going further. To see what is beyond that mountain, what peak, what glacier, what unseen sky. A little boathouse and foundations for three more had been built at its shore. I pulled my gloves on and my jacket hood over my hat, for now, later in the day and at higher altitude, it was cold. I'd walked there on rough tracks, across river plains, but the mountainside roads were new, carved wider to accommodate cars. Change will come here soon and I imagined that in the summer it was already a very different scene. These thoughts undid the tenderness collected on the trail. Of course others want to see, want to come, and come they should, but boathouses, picnic tables and jetties are permanent, they will not walk away at sundown. They will become part of the experience, part of the view. For now, though, it looked like the end of the end of the world, or a fairytale.

I turned back.

JOURNEY AS CRADLE, FOOD AS COMFORT

I needed to walk fast to get back before dark and often going downhill is harder on the knees than going up. By one small village, a man in a smart puffa jacket introduced himself as Said, and told me he was visiting friends and family in the village he grew up in for the first time in five months. He had an easy smile and a light step, the assurance of a self-made man. He told me he worked at a train station in a commuter town in the Moscow orbit, selling roses that have been imported from Ecuador. 'Business is good,' he said. 'Russians love roses.'

Said's wife and their three children live in the nearby city of Penjikent while he works five months on and two months off in Russia. At 42 years old, Said is one of thousands of men who travel to Russia from Tajikistan each year to find work and to send money back home. Some have a tough time, shovelling snow and cleaning streets for a couple of hundred dollars a month, and enduring harassment from the authorities and thugs is not uncommon. But it's not the whole picture, either. Said, who had worked in Russia for 12 years, was full of praise, as are many. Jobs in Tajikistan, especially in isolated villages and valleys such as these, are scarce and poorly paid, and Said explained that Russia, and the migrant labour channel, had given him a chance in life, an income for his family as well as a sense of pride. He earns ten times there, what he could earn here, if a job was available.

Our stroll down the valley also showed the downside of the migrant worker route. 'These villages are finished,' Said said. 'Nobody can afford to live here'.

And for a moment, a twinge of melancholy showed through Said's confidence. Perhaps, then, it is only tourism that can save them.

Back at my little cabin, the stove by the bed had been lit, as had candles on the tiny wooden windowsill. I peeled my muddy boots off, stripped off the sweaty walking kit and put on all of my other clothes immediately to warm up. It was far too cold to shower. At the main house, off the kitchen, a little glass-fronted cabin served as the dining room, where breakfast was also taken. Safir, the giant mountain pup, was sitting in a tight knot on a mat, his little docked ears twitching at the sound of food being prepared. He eyed me wolfishly. Inside, the dastarkhan had been set and an electric heater glowed invitingly under a poster of Mecca. I sat on a sparkly cushion and tucked my legs under the low table. A teenage boy came in, knelt on the floor and set down a hot pot of green tea, a cold Russian beer, then a basket of fresh bread pulled fresh out of the tandoor in the courtyard that afternoon. The boy smiled under his long eyelashes, left the room, then returned with a bowl of lamb, rice and barley soup. The heater hummed satisfyingly. This is the wonder of these little guesthouses in this part of the world. You are cooked for, not cooked at.

Next, a platter of Tajik pilaf with beef, carrots and little pea-size triangles of lemon strewn through it. What did the pilaf taste like? I remember it clearly as it was so good. The rice was nutty, soothing and starchy. The meat tasted home-raised and the crunchy carrots were earthy and fresh. The thin-skinned lemon slivers added a refreshingly acidic, and aromatic, dash. Hot and nourishing, the food instantly dropped my shoulders, made my eyelids heavy and relaxed tired muscles. Nothing is better than a warm room, a beer and a hot dinner after a long walk. Nothing. Journey as cradle, food as comfort.

Outside, it rained hard. Safir had moved to wrap himself tightly by the clay tandoor which still had a few fiery orange embers in it. His coat was so thick that the cold and wet didn't bother him. It had poured the previous three days, it would rain again tomorrow, to walk through rainstorms for seven hours wouldn't have been much fun. It had been a miracle and a joy to hike in such warm and welcoming sunshine. In the morning, it would be time, again, to go.

Seven Lakes Pilaf with Beef and Lemon

While researching this book in Tajikistan, I became obsessed with local lemons. Grown in the warm south, they are juice-heavy, thin-skinned and smooth as plums. Their flavour, without strong acidity, has a deliciously unexpected hint of tangerine. Harvested in autumn, they go liberally into salads and rice dishes. I didn't know at the time, but they are the same lemons as the Meyer variety, originally from China, which became wildly popular in the USA when introduced there. Legendary cook Alice Waters, owner of Chez Panisse in Berkeley, California, used this particular citrus fruit in her famous lemon meringue pie.

This beef pilaf is dashed with little nuggets of lemon, skin and all, providing a welcome sour note. It is based on the pilaf served at the guesthouse where I stayed in the Fann Mountains. If you cannot find Meyer lemons, regular unwaxed lemons, or even preserved lemons, will make a perfectly acceptable substitute. This is a slow-cooked dish, best done when you have ample time as the beef shin takes a while to tenderise.

SERVES 6

400g/14oz beef shin (shank), diced	½ tsp paprika
Salt and freshly ground black pepper, to season	½ tsp black pepper
	400g/2 cups basmati rice, rinsed
50g/3½ tbsp butter	125g/¾ cup chickpeas (garbanzo beans)
50ml/3 tbsp sunflower oil	50g/⅓ cup raisins
2 large onions, sliced	6 garlic cloves, peeled
2 bay leaves	¼ unwaxed lemon (skin left on), cut into pea-size pieces
120ml/½ cup water	
4 carrots, cut into thick matchsticks	Non Bread (page 120), to serve
1 tsp cumin seeds	½ onion, sliced paper-thin, to serve

Season the beef with salt and pepper. Heat the butter in a casserole or large saucepan over a medium-high heat and brown the beef. Remove from the pan with a slotted spoon and place on a plate covering the meat with tin foil to keep warm.

Lower the heat to medium, add the sunflower oil and fry the onions until translucent but not browned. Return the beef to the pan, along with any juices, add the bay leaves and the water. Bring to a boil, then turn the heat to the lowest setting, cover the pan with a lid and gently simmer for 1½–2 hours until the meat is soft and tender.

Spread the carrots in a layer over the beef mixture. Scatter over the spices and pepper, cover and cook for a further 10 minutes.

Add the rice in a layer on top of the carrots, and scatter over the chickpeas and raisins. Season very generously with salt and very slowly pour over enough boiling water to just cover the top of mixture. Increase the heat and leave the pan uncovered until most of the water has boiled away.

Make 6 holes in the rice using the handle of a wooden spoon and place a garlic clove in each hole. Cover the pan and cook at a low simmer for 5 minutes. Turn off the heat and without removing the lid, leave the dish to steam undisturbed for a further 10 minutes. If the rice isn't cooked, add another splash of boiling water and cover again. Serve the layers in reverse – first spooning the rice, chickpeas and raisins onto a platter, then the carrot layer and finally the meat on the top with the lemon pieces scattered over. Serve with some non bread and slices of raw onion.

Pink Radish Chaka

The small city of Penjikent is the jumping-off spot for treks into the Fann Mountains, also pairing well with a visit to nearby Samarkand if the border to Uzbekistan is open. As well as ruins of a major Sogdian town just on the outskirts, and good museums, there are also a couple of covered bazaars. Both have stalls selling giant tubs of chaka, cousin of suzma (yogurt cheese), made with thick yogurt and/or cultured milk. Sometimes beetroot is used for a dash of colour, but usually it is plain. I like it with radishes, when in season, but also with dill, Turkish red pepper and coriander. This is an easy-to-make version and is ideal as part of a larger meze lunch platter, but just remember you need to start this the day before you want to serve it.

MAKES 1 BOWL TO SERVE 4 AS PART OF A MEZE

500g/2 cups Greek yogurt

Pinch of sea salt

1 tbsp dill fronds, chopped

Handful of pink radishes, thinly sliced

½ tsp pul biber (Turkish red pepper flakes)

1 tbsp extra-virgin olive oil

Strain the yogurt 24 hours ahead of serving the chaka. Season the yogurt with a pinch of salt then place it in the middle of a muslin or cheesecloth, bringing the corners of the fabric together to create a ball of yogurt. Secure with an elastic band and hang it over a bowl to drain, in a cool place for 24 hours. If you have a wire rack-style fridge shelf, tie the muslin or cloth to the shelf and place a bowl below, or hanging it from a tap can work well.

After 24 hours, remove the yogurt from the fabric (discarding the drained-off liquid) and stir through the dill. Decorate the top with radishes, scatter over the pul biber and add a drizzle of olive oil.

CITADEL

Reaching the end

KHUJAND, NORTH TAJIKISTAN: The way to Khujand, Tajikistan's second city, which Soviet maps call Leninabad, was high-altitude and dizzying. The driver I'd agreed a fare with in the little city of Penjikent, close to the Seven Lakes, had just returned from a seven-year stint working in Moscow. He'd ploughed his savings into a secondhand boxy black Mercedes which he steered confidently and carefully away from the city, taking us out past juniper trees and northwards in the direction of the Tajik part of the Fergana Valley. The top-spec executive Mercedes from the 1990s is the sort that are discarded by Europeans after 150,000 miles, and bought by Central Asians who run them until they have done nearly one million miles. Soon, we began climbing, up and up, on looping windswept mountain roads, tyres sending dust over unmarked edges, dropping down dozens of metres below.

Oncoming traffic, not continuous but careening, jangled nerves and made palms sweaty. The driver remained unfazed. Then, for five miles, we went juddering in hushed silence through the poorly lit and uneven Shahriston Tunnel. Scooped out of the mountainside by the China Road and Bridge Corporation as 'a highway rehabilitation project', it had cost tens of millions of dollars to build, funded by grants and loans from Beijing. Clamping my eyes shut, I reopened them to see flashing headlights, fog-like exhaust smoke swirling and giant potholes being dodged by cars as they blindly overtook one another. I tried to block out thoughts of crashes, breaking down and rockslides. Giddy, I pressed the light on my watch and saw the date was Halloween. I snapped my eyes shut again.

I wanted my last stop of the journey to be back in the verdant and lush knot of the Fergana Valley, shared by northern Tajikistan, eastern Uzbekistan and southern Kyrgyzstan. The very heartland of Central Asia. A flourishing belt of rushing water channels, villages of silkworm breeders, vine planted gardens, abundant hollows and crops of barley, maize, millet, tobacco, vegetables and fruit. Many towns and cities in the Fergana Valley were once the old staging posts of the Silk Roads but Khujand long commanded the entrance to the valley, taxing those who filed in and building grand mosques and palaces on the takings, only to have them flattened in the 13th century by marauding Mongols. In this tightly packed, populous nook of Central Asia, the people of the Fergana Valley seemed to have more in common with the inhabitants living in their companion cities, than with those in their own capitals. To reach Kokand in Uzbekistan's section of the Fergana Valley, from Khujand, takes two hours but before time-saving tunnels were built, it could take a whole day to drive from Khujand to Dushanbe.

Gradually, the peaks of the Zarafshan Range, a natural buffer for the northern region of Tajikistan during the bloody civil war, gave way to flatter land and an endless procession of cotton fields, those bucolic-looking acres of back-breaking human toil. Apricot trees edged fields of wheat and rice, all fed by gushing brooks and channels of the Syr Darya River. On the outskirts of Khujand, men dozed in cabbage patches.

Khujand offered a gentle reintroduction to city life after the mind-freeing wilderness of the Fann Mountains and its glittering blue lakes. In temperament and spirit it seemed different from Dushanbe, displaying less of the capital's 'blow-down and rebuild' fever. It felt modest and wholly unaccustomed to visitors. In the main square, outdoor speakers piped melancholic music from the Kamoli Khujandi Theatre. Otherwise, it was so quiet that it was hard to think of Khujand as a city at all. Lonely unmanned bookstalls stood on street corners displaying Russian and Tajik novels and textbooks. Old samovars, from the Russian city of Tula, the world-centre of samovar production, were elegantly displayed by old men in flat caps in the main square. There was an air of country charm and a whiff of intelligentsia.

GEORGIAN FOOD, PERSIAN POETRY, RUSSIAN POP

Fusing oriental and Soviet styles, Panjshanbe Bazaar is the beating heart of Khujand. Huge buttermilk-coloured columns arch up to meet painted wooden rafters, the ribs around the bazaar's huge trading belly. Built in 1964, Panjshanbe means Thursday in Tajik, traditionally market day. Passing through the pink neoclassical entrance, flanked by two gold statuettes of shoppers, the market reflects the region's abundance. Past Greenleaf tea bags, crystallised navat sugar and three-in-one coffee sachets, a giant hall opens up, food again providing a porthole into other worlds.

In the middle of the market steel rigging had been set up and from it, winter melons, harvested from mid-September, were suspended in their thousands. Strapped to the rafters with netting, they hung there ripening in slow motion over the cold months, all the while skins shrivelling, getting softer and sweeter. Panjshanbe was ramshackle but wonderful. Women had fashioned counters from peeling wooden plasterboard where they displayed their non bread, wrapped in bundles of three, ready for sale. Korean pickle sellers were especially busy, dishing out salads of vinegary cauliflower and grated carrots for lunchtime shoppers. The salad displays were teetering. Giant vats of pickles arranged at browsing height were set on top of washing-up dishes, which in turn sat on top of giant empty paint buckets. All around, handshakes sealed wholesale deals in the crush.

Back past the fruit lanes, a trader handed me a strip of dried melon studded with raisins that had been rolled up into a bite-size energy ball. 'Tajik Snickers', he said. Central Asian snacks on-the-go, the sort possibly tried by Marco Polo. He wrote of something similar in his book *The Description of the World*: 'They [pieces of melon] are preserved as follows: a melon is sliced, just as we do with pumpkin, then these slices are rolled and dried in the sun; and finally they are sent for sale to other countries, where they are in great demand for they are as sweet as honey.'

Appetite piqued, I went in search of lunch. Khujand excels in shashlik restaurants, but I made Omar Khayyam, a Tajik-Georgian restaurant, my spot during the few days I stayed. Over a glass of rough Georgian red, I ordered salads with thin-skinned lemons diced and dashed through green leaves, a plate of cheesy khachapuri and a bowl of khinkali. While the decor reflected Tajikistan's links to Persia, with paintings depicting the astronomer-poet, Omar Khayyam, the Russian soft-porn pop videos on the television reminded diners of more recent cultural links. Georgian food, Persian poets and Russian pop music, where else in the world could you find such a trio of dining companions?

Taste buds still dancing, I left Omar Khayyam walking through the backstreets behind the restaurant in search of a Russian church shown on my map of the city. It wasn't hard to find. The keeper, a gruff woman whose hands were busy wrestling a kindle of kittens, nodded at a basket of headscarves, and told me that on Sunday nowadays they only get 35 worshippers at the most. I put a scarf on. I sloped inside to look at the iconostasis alone. It felt a sad place, one of ghosts and shattered fortunes.

Back towards the main square is the reconstructed citadel marking the spot of Alexander the Great's settlement. Inside the regional museum, set within the rebuilt city walls, are fantastic murals detailing the military leader's life. One shows the funeral procession, Alexander's hand hanging down empty, a sign that he left no formal heir. This student of Aristotle, lover of literature who hailed from Macedonia, died in Babylon at a banquet at the age of 32, some scholars believe it was a fever, others blame his heavy drinking habit and claim he was poisoned by fermented white hellebore (a poisonous plant in the buttercup family), mixed in wine. No one really knows. But here he is fondly remembered. Alexander or Iskander is a name you constantly hear today in Central Asia more than 2,000 years after his death. Lakes, baby boys and mountains all bear his name.

At dusk, I stood on the banks of the Syr Darya, the ancient Jaxartes, full of promise but still as glass. It carried no boats and no trade. Crows filled the sky as the sun dipped and cable cars set off, sluggishly travelling above the river headed towards the old Leninabad hotel, close to Khujand's main street, also named after the Soviet leader. With the river so empty and the city so quiet, it wasn't hard to picture Alexander's army coming down to the embankment here. Khujand was where Alexander built his furthest Greek settlement in Central Asia, in 329 BC, naming it Alexandria Eschate ('Farthest Alexandria'). It was here that he watched his troops rowing over to the north bank of the Jaxartes, afloat on ox skins, attacking the Scythians who were known for their archery. It was a tough battle and word came back that the desert scrub beyond was not worth fighting for. They retreated. Alexander decided that this faraway outpost was it, and here he stopped. Then, the world's most famous warrior and ruler, wheeled out to northern India, having claimed huge victories across the Persian territories.

The last of the sun briefly lit up the dry mountains behind Khujand, monstrous and scaly as dragons' backs, then, darkness fell. Alexander had found this far enough to come, and so did I. It was time to go home.

Preserved Lemon and Wild Rocket Salad

In the world of food there are known unknowns, that is things you know about but have not yet tried; and there are unknown unknowns, things you never knew at all. For me, the Tajik lemon, often a light orange colour, was a magical unknown unknown. Sweet, smooth-skinned and heavy in the hand, in Khujand they are sliced straight into salads. When I stopped to admire and photograph a stall of them at the city's fantastical Panjshanbe Bazaar, the young female vendor forced a lemon into my hand and would take no money for it as much as I insisted. I got the impression she was proud of the lemons and wanted me to have it. As most of us cannot access Tajik or Meyer lemons, preserved lemon is a good alternative. This dish makes firm friends with both plov and shashlik.

SERVES 4

2 preserved lemons

Handful of cherry tomatoes, halved

1 tsp cumin seeds, toasted

140g/7 ½ cups wild rocket (arugula)

2 tbsp flat-leaf parsley, chopped

50ml/3 tbsp extra-virgin olive oil

A few dill fronds, to garnish (optional)

Rinse the preserved lemons, cut them into quarters and then slice them very thinly (discarding any pips). Combine all other ingredients into a large bowl, add the lemon, toss to mix and garnish with dill, if using.

Pickled Cauliflower

Khujand's Panjshanbe Bazaar, like all good Central Asian food markets, has a wide selection of Korean-style salads. You can always smell them – potently vinegary and sour - before you see them.

MAKES 1 X 1 LITRE/2 PINT JAR

1 tsp coriander seeds

1 tsp yellow mustard seeds

½ tsp black peppercorns

230ml/1 cup white wine vinegar

70ml/⅓ cup rice vinegar

3 tbsp caster sugar

300ml/1¼ cups water

2 tbsp fine sea salt

2 garlic cloves, peeled and sliced

1 small head of cauliflower, leaves discarded and florets cut into 2cm/1in pieces

1 tsp Korean gochugaru chilli flakes

A few coriander (cilantro) leaves (optional)

To sterilise the jar, preheat the oven to 140°C/275°F/gas mark 1. Wash the jar in warm, soapy water, rinse well and place it on a clean baking tray. Transfer to the oven for about 15 minutes. To sterilise the lid or rubber seal, boil them in a large saucepan for 5 minutes then drain and leave them to air dry on a rack. Leave the jar in the warm oven until the pickle is ready to be potted up.

Put the coriander seeds, mustard seeds and black peppercorns into a medium saucepan. Toast the spices over a medium heat until fragrant, just for a minute or so, then add the vinegars, sugar, water and salt, and bring to a gentle boil stirring until the sugar has completely dissolved.

Carefully add the garlic slices to the hot, sterilised jar, followed by the cauliflower. Pour over the hot vinegary mix and leave to cool (with the lid off). Once cooled, gently stir through the Korean chilli flakes and coriander leaves, if using. Tightly lid your jar and place it in the fridge, letting the flavours develop for a few days before eating. This will keep in the fridge for a month.

EPILOGUE

'That's the trouble with wandering, it has no end.'

Gertrude Bell, diary entry, 1914

In mid-November, I returned home to Edinburgh as autumn made way for winter. During short dark days, I began reconstructing the journey I'd taken, the people I'd met and the stories I'd heard. What I found, during the spring and autumn of 2019, while charting a rough course from the shores of the Caspian Sea to the sun-ripened knot of the Fergana Valley, was slippery and disarming; life-affirming and heartening.

I'd set off to better understand this vast heartland of Asia, using food as a jumping-off point. I wanted to see the region with new eyes and to gauge how food forges and shapes the landscape and reflects history. To test how it can open doors to other lives and worlds. And I wanted to record the changes I'd witnessed too, over a decade of travelling to and from Central Asia.

Edible pleasures of great generosity flowed. From Pavlodar's prom-queen cake shop, Krendel, brimming with almost every sugary fancy under the sun, to tasting honey deep in the Kyzylkum desert. I had heard about mosque kitchens way out west in the desert steppe in Kazakhstan, out past the oil fields, but I could never have imagined the outlandish remoteness of them, nor predicted how pivotal the role of food is to pilgrims who make long journeys to get there. At the generous iftar feast during Ramadan at the Uyghur Mosque in Almaty, I listened to firsthand accounts of families separated by the crackdown on Muslims across the border in China. Tiny springtime strawberries, flavourful pomegranates and curious winter melons were seasonal companions.

But disorientation, and some disappointment, bedevilled the journeys. In remote windblown Aralsk, close to the Aral Sea in Kazakhstan, there was a sense of dissolving into a scorched landscape. The desiccation of the Aral Sea, a result of the Soviets diverting the Syr Darya and Amu Darya rivers to irrigate cotton fields, may have happened decades ago but the ecological fallout – health problems and environmental destruction – continues, even if there are signs of hope on the north shore. Elsewhere, farmers and harvesters, who, like their forefathers intimately know and work the land, spoke matter-of-factly about climate change in remote orchards in Tajikistan and the walnut forests of Kyrgyzstan, their terrain a frontline and a litmus test for the climate emergency. Nur-Sultan's bewildering architecture seemed both old-school Soviet in its scope and heft but also cutting-edge and futuristic, an effort, reflected across the region, to build a new identity. Elsewhere, in Dushanbe, and many of Uzbekistan's cities and towns, old traditional mahallas had been torn down, threatening traditional ways of life and family histories.

And, nearly 30 years after the Soviet Union fractured and disintegrated, Russia's ongoing influence cannot be denied. In each country, Russian is still widely spoken. Migrant workers, from all the countries that I travelled to, still go to Russia to work and send money home. In Tajikistan those remittances make up half the GDP. The Russian hangover exists in architecture, too, in circuses and cinemas, in cathedrals and churches, in opera and ballet theatres. But Russia no longer has a monopoly in the region over its business, trade and security affairs. China is the new force, with its cheap and large loans and ambitious trade projects that are reshaping pathways and routes across the land.

Disorientation was offset by mealtimes. A long bar session in Shymkent to shake off the stresses of the road, a familiar breakfast canteen to sooth a fever, a Turkish go-to spot in Tashkent to talk. Homestays where you know you will be cooked for, and cared for. Reliable, familiar flavours and dishes to depend upon: comforting plov, juicy melon, the crunch and bite of fresh salads, non bread, flaky samsa, sizzling shashlik. Good vodka, good beer. It's true that few outsiders travel to this region for its cuisine, but food – given the right consideration and thought – opens up compelling aspects of Central Asia that have been so often passed over.

If a journey, in the end, returns us home, then when we reach it, we carry pieces of places visited with us. Memories are not all we are left with because when we travel, we ourselves return changed. Indebted and connected to other places and other people. Marcel Proust knew this when he wrote: 'The real voyage of discovery consists not in seeking new landscapes, but in having new eyes.' Meetings on the road, chanced and determined, often change the way we see things.

A FERRIS WHEEL, A FLAG AND A FEAST

In the south of the Kyrgyz capital, Bishkek, a rusty ferris wheel eased upwards in front of the Tian Shan Mountains. Its gondolas, corrugated and painted sugary pink, appeared like rotating fairy cakes. At the centre of the wheel, Kyrgyzstan's red flag flapped slowly in the breeze.

In 2016, I'd taken a dizzying ride on the wheel before a friend took me for lunch at the home of a couple she wanted me to meet. Back on the ground, heads dizzy, we wobbled across a busy street to a peeling Soviet-built apartment block, one of a dozen or so identical high-rises that make up the Asanbai micro-district. A juddering lift took us up seven floors, then we knocked and waited. A small dark-haired woman with a round friendly face opened a heavy steel door.

'Come in, we've been waiting for you. I'm Janyl, the wife of Bek Mirza,' she said to me. Aside from a few short entries in Kyrgyz encyclopaedias Bek Mirza is little-known, but he is actually a modern-day Kyrgyz hero.

Bek Mirza greeted us with a firm handshake. Behind him were rows of hardback books in a myriad of colours. His face was broad with high cheekbones, framed by a spiked helmet of silver hair. Asking us to sit, he began his story. In 1991, when the Soviet Union fell and Kyrgyzstan became newly independent, there was a nationwide contest to design a new flag. Six hundred people entered. 'We were a five-man team and we worked day and night, for two months, here in this apartment. It was intense. None of us really slept. We worked non-stop on hundreds of different designs.' He spoke animatedly slapping the cheeks of his face as if what happened years ago, still hadn't quite sunk in. It wasn't hard to picture the scene: the fizz of energy that must have been in the air as the group sketched and smoked and philosophised late into the night with Bek Mirza leading the way as chief artist.

Declaring lunch, Janyl led us to the kitchen table to hear the rest of the story. As we unfolded napkins to eat mutton cooked in butter and wild garlic, Bek Mirza unfurled draft sketches of the flag. One design had two snow leopards curling around one another, like a black and white yin and yang. Another design was powder blue. That colour was dismissed as some Kyrgyz complained that blue was the colour of death. To Bek Mirza and his team, red was too Soviet, but they conceded. The design that won Bek Mirza the competition is the one that exists today, the one in the centre of the ferris wheel in the park opposite. It is bright red with a golden sun at its centre. The sun has 40 rays, representing the 40 tribes of Kyrgyzstan. In the centre of the sun is a tunduk, the wooden crown of a yurt that forms an opening to let smoke out, a nod to the Kyrgyz nomads.

Janyl got up and brought back to the table a plate of fresh doughnut-like borsok and a box of expensive-looking Russian chocolates. More green tea was poured. As we ate, Bek Mirza described the defining moment when he ascended the grand white presidential building in the city centre in 1992, replacing the Soviet flag with his own. 'It was a very emotional and proud time. We were independent. We were new.' Janyl chipped in, 'The flag binds people together. It stops ethnic conflict. If we see it at the Olympics we still feel great pride.'

Then, out came a bottle of Kyrgyz cognac poured into four glasses. 'You could say, there was life before the flag, and then life after the flag,' Bek Mirza said.

And, you could also say that you can learn a lot over a good lunch.

GLOSSARY

Ak – white

Aksakal – white beard, an elder

Ashlan-fu – a spicy Dungan (Muslim-Chinese minority) noodle dish

Aul – village

Ayran – salty watery yogurt

Basmachi – Muslim guerrilla fighters

Batyr – knight warrior hero in epic tales and poetry

Beg (also bey, or bek) – tribal aristocrat, gentleman

Beshbarmak – flat noodles with horsemeat

Bliny – Russian-style pancake

Borscht – hearty sour beetroot soup

Buzkashi – traditional horseback game played with a headless goat or sheep carcass, also known as kokpar

Caravanserai – traditional travellers' inn with courtyard

Chai – tea

Chaikhana – teahouse

Chapan – cloak, typically stripy and padded

Chorsu – four-ways, crossroad

Dacha – holiday home, usually wooden in the countryside

Darya – river

Dastarkhan – literally 'tablecloth', a dining place where meals are served and eaten

Dungan – Muslim-Chinese minority group (who settled in Central Asia in the 19th century)

Dutar – two-stringed instrument

Gulag – a system of labour camps maintained in the Soviet Union

Hauz – pool

Ikat – resist dye technique used to pattern textiles

Jailoo – summer pasture

Jaxartes – historical name for the Syr Darya river

Juma/Jami – Friday, usually in context of a mosque in a city which draws Friday worshippers

Kalpak – traditional felt hat

Kara – black

Karlag – a chain of labour camps

Kasha – porridge

Kazan – large cauldron used to cook plov

-kent – suffix meaning 'town of'

Khanate – the area governed by a khan (ruler)

Khinkali – Georgian dumplings shaped like money bags

Khunon – open Uzbek dumplings

Kobyz – Kazakh musical instrument

Kolkhoz – collective farm

Kompot – fruit juice

Kufic – Arabic script, calligraphy

Kum – desert (sands)

Kumis (or kumys) – fermented mare's milk

Kurgan – burial mound

Kyzyl – red

Laghman – noodles

Madrassah – Islamic school

Mahalla – urban neighbourhood

Manti – stuffed dumplings

Mastava – rice soup

Mazar – graveyard or mausoleum

Muezzin – the person who calls the faithful to prayer

Mufti – Islamic spiritual leader or legal expert on Islam

Navruz/Nawruz – New Year festival marking spring

Nomenklatura – people within the Soviet Union who held various key bureaucratic positions

Non – bread

Oblast – region, province

Oxus – historical name for the Amu Darya river

Pelmeni – small dumplings

Piala – handle-less teacup

Pishkek – churn for making kumis

Plov – similar to pilau, a rice dish with carrots and meat

Qurut – dried milk curds

Qurutob – a Tajik salad, of tomatoes, cucumbers, onions, fresh herbs and flatbread

Rayon – district

Registan – 'sandy place', square

Samsa – turnover typically filled with lamb or vegetables

Samovar – literally, 'self-boiler', an urn used to boil water for tea

Saxaul – desert bush, used for fuel

Serai – palace

Shubat – camel's milk

Smetana – sour cream

Sufi – a mystical tradition of Islam

Suzani – embroidered fabrics

Suzma – strained yogurt

Tapchan – tea bed

Tazy – breed of dog

Toi – celebration (especially weddings)

Turkestan – land of the Turks, Central Asia and Xinjiang

Tvorog – a little like farmer's cheese or cottage cheese

INDEX

RECOMMENDED READING

By no means comprehensive, this is a list of favourite books and online resources on Central Asia.

CENTRAL ASIA
(General, non-fiction)

Baumer, Christopher, *The History of Central Asia:* Volumes 1, 2 & 3 (I. B. Tauris, various).

Blanch, Lesley, *From Wilder Shores: The Tables of My Travel* (John Murray, 1989).

Chaubin, Frédéric, *CCCP: Cosmic Communist Constructions Photographed* (Taschen, 2011).

Christie, Ella, *Through Khiva to Golden Samarkand: The remarkable story of a woman's adventurous journey alone through the deserts of Central Asia to the heart of Turkestan* (Trotamundas Press, 2009).

Duguid, Naomi and Alford, Jeffrey, *Beyond the Great Wall* (Artisan Publishers, 2008).

Eden, Caroline and Ford, Eleanor, *Samarkand: Recipes and Stories from Central Asia and the Caucasus* (Kyle Books, 2016).

Eden, Caroline, *The Land of the Anka Bird* (Cornucopia Books, 2020).

Forbes, Rosita, *Forbidden Road, Kabul to Samarkand: The Classic 1930s Account of Afghan Travel* (The Long Riders' Guild Press, 2001).

Frankopan, Peter, *The Silk Roads: A New History of the World* (Bloomsbury, 2015).

Harvey, Janet, *Traditional Textiles of Central Asia* (Thames & Hudson, 1997).

Hedin, Sven, *The Trail of War: On the Track of Big Horse in Central Asia* (Tauris Parke Paperbacks, 2009).

Herwig, Christopher, *Soviet Bus Stops* (FUEL Publishing, 2015).

Hopkirk, Kathleen, *Central Asia: Through Writers' Eyes* (Eland, 2014).

Lioy, Stephen et al, *Central Asia* (Lonely Planet, 2018).

Maclean, Fitzroy, *To the Back of Beyond: Illustrated Companion to Central Asia and Mongolia* (Jonathan Cape Ltd, 1974).

Maillart, Ella, *Turkestan Solo: A Journey Through Central Asia* (Tauris Parke Paperbacks, 2005).

Mathews, Chloe Dewe, *Caspian: The Elements* (Aperture, 2018).

Meller, Susan, *Russian Textiles: Printed Cloth for the Bazaars of Central Asia* (Henry N. Abrams, 2007).

Metcalfe, Daniel, *Out of Steppe: The Lost People of Central Asia* (Hutchinson, 2009).

Omidi, Maryam, *Holidays in Soviet Sanatoriums* (FUEL, 2017).

Omrani, Bijan, *Asia Overland: Tales of Travel on the Trans-Siberian & Silk Road* (Odyssey Publications, 2010).

Whitfield, Susan, *Silk Roads: Peoples, Cultures, Landscapes* (University of California Press, 2019).

Whittell, Giles *Extreme Continental: Blowing Hot and Cold Through Central Asia* (Orion, 1995).

CENTRAL ASIA (Fiction)

Aitmatov, Chingiz, *Jamilia* (Telegram, 2007).

Aitmatov, Chingiz, *The Day Lasts More than a Hundred Years* (John Wiley, 1988).

Ismailov, Hamid, *The Devils' Dance* (Tilted Axis Press, 2018).

Ismailov, Hamid, *The Railway* (Vintage, 2007).

Ismailov, Hamid and Fairweather-Vega, Shelley (translator), *Of Strangers and Bees* (Tilted Axis Press, 2019).

Maalouf, Amin, *Samarkand* (Abacus, 1994).

Qodiriy, Abdullah and Reese, Mark Edward (translator), *Bygone Days: O'tkan Kunlar* (Bowker, 2019).

KAZAKHSTAN

Applebaum, Anne, *Gulag: History of the Soviet Camps* (Bantam Doubleday, 2003).

Brummell, Paul, *Kazakhstan* (Bradt Travel Guides, 2018).

Lillis, Joanna, *Dark Shadows: Inside the Secret World of Kazakhstan* (I.B. Tauris, 2018).

Meuser, Philipp, *Astana: Architectural Guide* (DOM Publishers, 2015).

Schreiber, Dagmar and Tredinnick, Jeremy, *Kazakhstan: Nomadic Routes from Caspian to Altai* (Odyssey Publications, 2018).

Shayakhmetov, Mukhamet, *The Silent Steppe: The Story of a Kazakh Nomad Under Stalin,* (Stacey International, 2006).

Wardell, J.W., *In the Kirghiz Steppes* (The Galley Press, 1961).

UZBEKISTAN

Burnes, Alexander, *Travels into Bokhara* (Eland Publishing, 2012).

Burton, Audrey, *The Bukharans: A Dynastic, Diplomatic, and Commercial History, 1550–1702* (Palgrave MacMillan, 1997).

Mayhew, Bradley and MacLeod, Calum, *Uzbekistan: The Golden Road to Samarkand* (Odyssey Publications, 2014).

Murray, Craig, *Murder in Samarkand: A British Ambassador's Controversial Defiance of Tyranny in the War on Terror* (Mainstream Publishing, 2007).

KYRGYZSTAN

Antipina, Klavdiya, *Kyrgyzstan* (Skira Editore, 2007).

Stewart, Rowan and Weldon, Susie, *Kyrgyz Republic: Heart of Central Asia* (Odyssey Publications, 2008).

Morton, Margaret, *Cities of the Dead: The Ancestral Cemeteries of Kyrgyzstan* (University of Washington Press, 2014).

TAJIKISTAN

Oudenhoven, Frederik van and Haider Jamila, *With Our Own Hands: A Celebration of Food and Life in the Pamir Mountains of Afghanistan and Tajikistan* (LM Publishers; Multilingual edition, 2015).

Middleton, Robert and Thomas, Huw, *Tajikistan and the High Pamirs* (Odyssey Publications, 2012).

Whitlock, Monica, *Beyond the Oxus* (John Murray, 2002).

WEBSITES

These are the essential few you need for keeping up with the news and for potential trip planning.

Caravanistan: This is the website you need to put an independent trip together. Covering Central Asia and several neighbouring countries, Steven and Saule, who run the site, work hard to keep it as balanced, vital and up-to-date as possible. A brilliant website and thoroughly recommended. caravanistan.com

PAMIRS: Huge resource on all things Pamiri – travel, culture, photographs – originally set up by Robert Middleton, an authority on Tajikistan for many years. pamirs.org

Teppa Tours: Community-based tourism in southern Tajikistan. southtajikistan.com

The Central Asia & South Caucasus Bulletin: Independent and committed to covering the news without bias, the Central Asia & South Caucasus Bulletin has been reporting on the region, which stretches from the Pamir Mountains to the Black Sea, since September 2010. Payable subscription service. thebulletin.news

Eurasianet: Providing excellent on-the-ground reporting from the South Caucasus and Central Asia. eurasianet.org

RFE/RL: Free Media In Unfree Societies – RFE/RL journalists report the news in 22 countries where free press is banned by the government or not fully established. A very good source for Central Asia. rferl.org

MAGAZINES

Cornucopia magazine. Every issue is an absolute joy and I heartily recommend it to anyone with even a passing interest in the Turkic-speaking world. cornucopia.net

For general reference and inspiration, I often look to the beautifully produced but sadly discontinued magazine, which I was lucky to work on for a while, *Steppe – A Central Asian Panorama*, edited by Lucy Kelaart.

SOURCES AND BOOKS CONSULTED

Research for *Red Sands* has involved a wide range of books, newspapers, journals, websites and magazines.

I am indebted to several writers, journalists and historians, but three in particular: firstly, Joanna Lillis for her reporting on Central Asia in various media including *The Economist* but especially for her excellent book on Kazakhstan, *Dark Shadows*. Also, Peter Leonard, Central Asia editor at Eurasianet and James Kilner at the *Central Asia & South Caucasus Bulletin*.

PRELUDE AND SETTING

Stark, Freya, 'Morning Over the Oxus', *The Times* (10th August 1968), p. 23.

MICRO-DISTRICT

Yankelevich, Matevi, 'Eve Sussman', *BOMB*, No. 117 (New Art Publications, Fall 2011), pp. 36–44.

Whitfield, Peter, *Travel: A Literary History* (The Bodleian Library, 2011), pp.85.

Anthony Jenkinson's Explorations, on the Land Route to China, 1558-1560, depts. washington.edu/silkroad/texts/jenkinson/bukhara.html

Aktau, the Kazakh city born in no-man's land, www.efe.com/efe/english/patrocinada/aktau-the-kazakh-city-born-in-no-man-s-land/50000268-3717058

OIL FIELD

Lillis, Joanna, 'The Gulag Archipelago', *Dark Shadows: Inside the Secret World of Kazakhstan* (I.B. Tauris, 2018), p.138.

Zonn, Igor S., Kosarev, Aleksey N., Glantz, Michael, *The Caspian Sea Encyclopedia* (Springer, 2010).

Pinkham, Sophie, 'Decomposition of Words', *The Times Literary Supplement* (22nd June 2018).

'Mullah fish', *The Economist* (2nd December 1989), p. 110.

Is the Caspian a sea or a lake?, www.economist.com/the-economist-explains/2018/08/16/is-the-caspian-a-sea-or-a-lake

Carving up the Caspian Sea, moneyweek.com/494788/carving-up-the-caspian-sea/

Kazakhstan seeks sweet spot in US-China-Russia power game, asia.nikkei.com/Spotlight/Asia-Insight/Kazakhstan-seeks-sweet-spot-in-US-China-Russia-power-game

Aktau – city by the sea, astanatimes.com/2017/11/aktau-city-by-the-sea

Caspian Sea: Five countries sign deal to end dispute, bbc.co.uk/news/world-45162282

Contarini, Ambrogio, iranicaonline.org/articles/contarini-ambrogio-1429-99-venetian-merchant-and-diplomat-author-of-a-noteworthy-report-on-persia-under-the-aq-qoyunlu

Rites of way: behind the pilgrimage revival, theguardian.com/books/2012/jun/15/rites-of-way-pilgrimage-walks

How Many Humps on a Camel? In Kazakhstan, It's Complicated, nytimes.com/2019/09/01/world/europe/how-many-humps-on-a-camel-in-kazakhstan-its-complicated.html

KONDITOREI

Lillis, Joanna, *Dark Shadows: Inside the Secret World of Kazakhstan* (I.B. Tauris, 2018).

Wardell, J.W., *In the Kirghiz Steppes* (The Galley Press, 1961).

SKYSCRAPER

Brummell, Paul, *Kazakhstan* (Bradt Travel Guides, 2018).

Meuser, Philipp, *Astana: Architectural Guide* (DOM Publishers, 2015).

Schreiber, Dagmar and Tredinnick, Jeremy, *Kazakhstan: Nomadic Routes from Caspian to Altai* (Odyssey Publications, 2018).

KARLAG

Applebaum, Anne, *Gulag: History of the Soviet Camps* (Bantam Doubleday, 2003).

Barnes, Steven A., *Death and Redemption: The Gulag and the Shaping of Soviet Society*, (Princeton University Press, 2011).

Blanch, Lesley, *Journey into the Mind's Eye*, (Eland, 2001).

Lillis, Joanna, Chapter 13 of *Dark Shadows: Inside the Secret World of Kazakhstan* (I.B. Tauris, 2018).

Pianciola, Niccolo, *The Collectivization Famine in Kazakhstan, 1931–1933*, Vol. 25, No. 3/4, (Harvard Ukrainian Studies, 2001), pp. 237–251.

Maya Plisetskaya, ballerina – obituary, www.telegraph.co.uk/news/obituaries/11581731/Maya-Plisetskaya-ballerina-obituary.html

Meeting of the ALZHIR prisoners in 1989, e-history.kz/en/publications/view/2363

Celebrating the 80th birthday of Valentina Tereshkova, blog.sciencemuseum.org.uk/the-queen-of-space-valentina-tereshkova-celebrates-her-80th-birthday-at-the-science-museum/

MILK FACTORY

Brown, Kate, 'Gridded Lives: Why Kazakhstan and Montana Are Nearly the Same Place', *The American Historical Review* (2001), Vol. 106, No. 1, pp. 17–48.

Kurlansky, Mark, *Milk! A 10,000-Year Food Fracas* (Bloomsbury Publishing, 2018).

Lillis, Joanna, *Dark Shadows: Inside the Secret World of Kazakhstan* (I.B. Tauris, 2018).

Polo, Marco, *The Travels of Marco Polo: The Complete Yule Cordier Edition* (Dover Publications; New ed of 1903 ed edition, 2003).

Germany holds kumys festival, astanatimes.com/2018/05/germany-holds-kumys-festival/

Saumal to make fresh Kazakh mare's milk widely available, astanatimes.com/2019/05/saumal-to-make-fresh-kazakh-mares-milk-widely-available/

Kurt – a stone that saved lives, e-history.kz/en/publications/view/1139

Food and Drink in the Mongol Empire, ancient.eu/article/1451/food--drink-in-the-mongol-empire/

COSMODROME

Siddiqi, Asif A., *The Red Rockets' Glare: Spaceflight and the Russian Imagination, 1857-1957* (Cambridge University Press, 2019).

Turkina, Olesya, *Soviet Space Dogs* (FUEL, 2014).

The First Woman in Space, blog.sciencemuseum.org.uk/the-first-woman-in-space/

Space Food, discoverspace.org/discover/el-pomar-space-gallery/space-food

'Space Men Make Landing in Desert', *The Times* (16th August 1962), p. 10.

DAM

Tazy: Speedy Dog of the Steppes in a Race Against Extinction, blog.nationalgeographic.org/2016/01/15/tazy-speedy-dog-of-the-steppes-in-a-race-against-extinction/

The country that brought a sea back to life, bbc.com/future/article/20180719-how-kazakhstan-brought-the-aral-sea-back-to-life

Once Written Off for Dead, the Aral Sea Is Now Full of Life, nationalgeographic.com/news/2018/03/north-aral-sea-restoration-fish-kazakhstan

WRITER'S HOSTEL

Feinstein, Elaine, *Anna of all the Russias: The Life of a Poet under Stalin* (Orion, 2005).

Glaessner, Sian, 'Anna Akhmatova in Tashkent', *Steppe Magazine* (2009), issue 7.

Manley, Rebecca, *To the Tashkent Station* (Cornell University Press, 2009).

Reeder, Roberta, *The Complete Poems of Anna Akhmatova*, (Canongate Books, 2000).

Sahadeo, Jeff, *Russian Colonial Society in Tashkent 186–1923* (Indiana University Press, 2007).

Uzbek Students Riot Over Price Rises, nytimes.com/1992/01/18/world/uzbek-students-riot-over-price-rises.html

Shostakovich's symphony played by a starving orchestra, bbc.co.uk/news/magazine-34292312

STOLOVAYA

Geist, Edward, 'Cooking Bolshevik: Anastas Mikoian and the Making of the "Book about Delicious and Healthy Food"', *Russian Review* (2012), Vol. 71, No. 2, pp. 295–313.

MAHALLA

Tashkent City: is 'progress' worth the price being paid in Uzbekistan?, theguardian.com/cities/2017/oct/18/people-paying-tashkent-gentrification-mahallas

GALLERY

Friends of Nukus Museum, *Homage to Savitsky: Collecting 20th-Century Russian and Uzbek Art* (Arnoldsche Publishers, 2015).

Babanazarova, Marinika, 'Remembering Savitsky', *Steppe Magazine* (2007), Issue 3.

The lost Louvre of Uzbekistan: the museum that hid art banned by Stalin, theguardian.com/artanddesign/2019/may/21/lost-louvre-uzbekistan-savitsky-museum-banned-art-stalin

STUPA

Higham, Charles, *Encyclopedia of Ancient Asian Civilizations* (Facts on File, 2004).

Taliban Jars Central Asia, csmonitor.com/1998/0814/081498.intl.intl.1.html

Twenty Years After Pullout, Soviet-Afghan Conflict Still Haunts, rferl.org/a/Twenty_Years_After_Pullout_SovietAfghan_Conflict_Still_Haunts/1493064.html

Afghan notebook: A last bar of Russian chocolate, bbc.co.uk/news/world-asia-26124556

Kara Tepe, livius.org/articles/place/kara-tepe/

Uzbekistan's best kept secret, news.bbc.co.uk/1/hi/programmes/from_our_own_correspondent/3630167.stm

FORT

Haynes, Roslynn D., *Desert: Nature and Culture* (Reaktion Books, 2013).

Hopkirk, Kathleen, *Central Asia Through Writers' Eyes* (Eland, 1993).

Gintzburger, Gustave, *Rangelands of the Arid and Semi-arid Zones in Uzbekistan* (Quae, 2003).

Middleton, Nick, *Deserts: A Very Short Introduction* (Oxford University Press, 2009).

MOSQUE

Bernbaum, Edwin, 'Sacred Mountains: Themes and Teachings', *Mountain Research and Development* (2006), Vol. 26, No. 4, pp. 304–309.

Tyler, Christian, 'The Turks of China: The plight of the Uighurs of Xinjiang' (2004), *Cornucopia Magazine*, Issue 31.

How One of the World's Hottest Cities Became a Hub for Grape Growing, vice.com/en_uk/article/nzkd8w/how-one-of-the-worlds-hottest-cities-became-a-hub-for-grape-growing

China detains Uighurs for growing beards or visiting foreign websites, leak reveals, theguardian.com/world/2020/feb/18/china-detains-uighurs-for-growing-beards-or-visiting-foreign-websites-leak-reveals

China has destroyed Uighur families, including mine, theguardian.com/world/commentisfree/2019/sep/25/china-has-destroyed-uighur-families-including-mine-guterres-must-act

China Uighurs: Detained for beards, veils and internet browsing, bbc.co.uk/news/world-asia-china-51520622

The world knows what is happening to the Uighurs, theguardian.com/world/2019/jul/27/the-world-knows-what-is-happening-to-the-uighurs-why-has-it-been-so-slow-to-act

REGISTAN

Christie, Ella, *Through Khiva to Golden Samarkand: The remarkable story of a woman's adventurous journey alone through the deserts of Central Asia to the heart of Turkestan* (Trotamundas Press, 2009).

de Clavijo, Ruy Gonzalez, *Embassy to Tamerlane, 1403–1406* (Hardinge Simpole, 2009).

Marozzi, Justin, *Tamerlane: Sword of Islam, Conqueror of the World* (HarperCollins, 2004).

Masterman, E. W. G., 'The Jews in Modern Palestine', *The Biblical World* (1903), Vol. 21, No. I, pp. 17–27.

Mayhew, Bradley and MacLeod, Calum, *Uzbekistan: The Golden Road to Samarkand* (Odyssey Publications, 2014).

Vámbéry, Arminius, *Travels in Central Asia* (Harper & Brothers,1865).

The President Wants Big(gish), Not-So-Fat Uzbek Weddings, rferl.org/a/the-president-wants-big(gish)-not-so-fat-uzbek-weddings/29447162.html

Bulldozing History: Ancient Uzbek City's UNESCO Status At Risk, rferl.org/a/bulldozing-history-ancient-uzbek-city-unesco-status-at-risk/28392139.html

Last Jews of Bukhara fear their community will fade away, theguardian.com/world/2019/dec/24/jews-bukhara-uzbekistanfear-community-will-fade-away

The magic of Uzbek winter melons: gifts 'of rare and strange beauty', ft.com/content/f595028a-10aa-11ea-a225-db2f231cfeae

The Conqueror Who Longed for Melons, atlasobscura.com/articles/babur-mughlai-food-india

In Search of Ibn Battuta's Melon, aramcoworld.com/Articles/November-2015/In-Search-of-Ibn-Battuta-s-Melon

WORKSHOP

Critchlow, James, and Paul B. Henze, 'Caravans and Conquests', *The Wilson Quarterly*, Vol. 16, No. 3, 1992 pp. 20–32.

Harvey, Janet, *Traditional Textiles of Central Asia* (Thames & Hudson, 1997).

Splendid Suzanis, archive.aramcoworld.com/issue/200304/splendid.suzanis.htm

BASE CAMP

Middleton, Robert and Thomas, Huw, *Tajikistan and the High Pamirs*, (Odyssey Publications, 2012).

Zanca, Russell, *Life in a Muslim Uzbek Village: Cotton Farming After Communism CSCA*, (Cengage Learning, 2010).

Obituary of Anatoli Boukreev *The Times* (24th January 1998).

TENT

Schmidt, Matthias, and Andrei Doerre, 'Changing Meanings of Kyrgyzstan's Nut Forests from Colonial to Post-Soviet Times', *Area* (2011) Vol. 43, No. 3.

Walnuts Through Time: Brain Food, Poison, Money, Muse, nationalgeographic.com/culture/food/the-plate/2015/09/29/walnuts-through-time-brain-food-poison-money-muse/

BAZAAR

Henryk, Alff, 'Trading for Change: Bazaars and Social Transformation in the Borderlands of Kazakhstan, Kyrgyzstan and Xinjiang' in *The Art of Neighbouring: Making Relations Across China's Borders* (Amsterdam University Press, 2017), pp.95–119.

Poirier-Bures, Simone, 'A Visit to the Dordoi', *Explorations in Nonfiction* (Michigan State University Press, 2001), Vol. 3, No. 2.

Spector, Regine A., *Order at the Bazaar: Power and Trade in Central Asia* (Cornell University Press, 2017).

DACHA

McReynolds, Louise, *Russia at Play: Leisure Activities at the End of the Tsarist Era* (Cornell University Press, 2002).

Koenker, Diane P., *Club Red: Vacation Travel and the Soviet Dream* (Cornell University Press, Reprint edition, 2017).

Miller, Arthur, 'Issyk-Kul: A Conversation with Gorbachev', *Aperture* (1987), No. 108: Witness to Crisis.

Gorsuch, Anne E., 'Tourism and Travel in Russia and the Soviet Union', *Slavic Review* (Cambridge University Press, Winter, 2003), Vol. 62, No. 4.

OPERA HOUSE

How do you say potato?, theguardian.com/books/2002/aug/17/featuresreviews.guardianreview2

Demolishing Dushanbe: how the former city of Stalinabad is erasing its Soviet past, theguardian.com/cities/2017/oct/19/demolishing-dushanbe-former-stalinabad-erasing-soviet-past

Tajikistan Discovers New Giant Buddha, cais-soas.com/News/2001/June2001/04-06.htm

BOTANICAL GARDEN

'Islamist gunmen' kill 23 soldiers in Tajikistan, bbc.co.uk/news/world-asia-pacific-11367069

Rasht Valley and Jafr Botanical Gardens, caravanistan.com/tajikistan/center/rasht/

Looking for Enemies in Tajikistan's Rasht Valley, eurasianet.org/looking-for-enemies-in-tajikistans-rasht-valley

SANATORIUM

Omidi, Maryam, *Holidays in Soviet Sanatoriums* (FUEL, 2017).

Gorsuch, Anne E., 'Tourism and Travel in Russia and the Soviet Union', *Slavic Review* (Cambridge University Press, Winter, 2003), Vol. 62, No. 4.

CITADEL

Bernard Lagan and David Sanderson, 'Alexander the grape was just too much of a seasoned campaigner', *The Times* (13th January 2014).

307

ACKNOWLEDGEMENTS

It has been a privilege to write this book and to travel through the places recounted within these pages. *Red Sands* is a series of journeys but it is really an anthology of the stories, anecdotes and memories shared to me by people in Central Asia over the course of six months, and in the years preceding them. My debt to them is incalculable and I wish I could name everyone here. I would, however, like to thank the following people: Rahat Ahmet, Yerlan Ashimov, Jakhongir Azimov, Marinika Babanazarova, Shokhinakhon Bakhromova, Serik Dyussenbayev, Boris Golender, Zukhra Iakupbaeva, Otabek Khojimatov, Dilfuza Kurolova, Abdu Samadov and Shuhrat Sharipov. I would also like to thank Jonny Bealby and Michael Pullman at Wild Frontiers and Annie Lucas at MIR. Back home in Scotland, I am grateful to Sara and Robert Stewart for insights into Ella Christie's time in Central Asia.

A heartfelt thanks to Theodore Kaye who shot the location images for this book and my last book *Black Sea*. I am grateful for his ideas, general brilliance and his willingness to always go the extra mile through these lands of fans and furs. It was a treat to travel together.

I drew more than a measure of inspiration from travellers who have gone before me, to name a few: the authors of the *Odyssey Guide to Uzbekistan*, Bradley Mayhew and Calum MacLeod and its publisher Magnus Bartlett, Hamid Ismailov, Giles Whittell, Lucy Kelaart, Bijan Omrani, Huw Thomas and Robert Middleton. Thank you also to the brilliant Boris Dralyuk for his help with Edi Ognetsvet's evocative poem Uzbek Sky.

I owe a great debt and special thanks to Sarah Lavelle at Quadrille who is brave and brilliant, and a dream to work with. Likewise I am hugely grateful to my super-agent Jessica Woollard at David Higham Associates for her guidance, friendship and navigational skills. To Tamsin English, who copy-edited this book, I salute you and am grateful for such a sensitive, thorough and painstaking job. A massive thanks to Dave Brown for his design wizardry, I am lucky to work with you, Dave. I am most grateful to Ola O. Smit for her creative and brilliant photographic talents in the studio, to Tabitha Hawkins for her incomparable prop design and positive energy (this is our third book together). Thanks must also go to the unflappable and kind-hearted Pip Spence for her styling and cooking, and her assistants Libby Silbermann and Jake Fenton. Many thanks to Giverny Tattersfield, my patient friend in Glasgow, who has had the deeply unenviable task of helping test my recipes. Also to Ivana Zorn for the brilliantly original maps and illustrations. Huge thanks also to Ruth Tewksbury who is never short on energy or excellent ideas. Working together with the Quadrille team is an absolute pleasure.

I am grateful to several editors who have commissioned pieces while I was working on this book: John Scott at *Cornucopia*, Isabel Choat and Jane Dunford at the *Guardian*, Catharine Morris at *The Times Literary Supplement* and Alexander Gilmour at the *Financial Times*.

Special thanks to Diana Henry who has supported me with generosity and great kindness right from the start. I'd also like to thank Eleanor Ford who has taught me tricks for making non bread, plov and samsa at home, some methods of which have been included here. I am enormously grateful, too, to Judith and Duncan at Langcliffe who look after my beloved beagle Darwin when I'm away. I couldn't leave the UK without you both, I am hugely thankful for everything you do.

As a former bookseller, I cannot let this opportunity pass without thanking the following bookshops who've hosted me and who have so generously supported my books in recent years: Golden Hare Books, Topping & Company Booksellers, Daunt Books, Stanfords and John Sandoe Books.

During the course of my writing this book, I sadly lost some friends. Bruce 'Aziz' Wannell, an expert traveller and linguist specialising on Iran, Central Asia and Afghanistan, was a great inspiration to me. When Bruce and I edited a guidebook on Iran together many years ago in London's East End, he would always supply us with mid-morning treats, usually cheese and good wines. My favourite memory of Bruce was wandering together through an exhibition on Persia at the British Museum. Fluent in the Persian language, among at least eight others, including Arabic and Urdu, he knew much about Islamic epigraphy and calligraphy and as a result we attracted a train of followers in the museum on that afternoon, each person in the chain hanging on his every word. Bruce died of pancreatic cancer aged 67. Renée Senogles, the publicity manager for Hardie Grant and Quadrille in the USA who worked with me on my last book, *Black Sea*, died far too young from a rare form of cancer, uveal melanoma, while I was writing this book. Renée is very much missed and will always be remembered.

My final thanks must go to family. I am forever grateful to my dad, David Pink, for his cheer, optimism and moral support. And I am eternally thankful to my husband, James Kilner, without whom none of this would have been possible. He is the first to hear of ideas, the first to read my work and is an endless source of fun, support, love and encouragement. This book is for him.

Caroline Eden is a writer contributing to the travel, food and arts pages of the *Guardian*, the *Financial Times* and *The Times Literary Supplement*.

Her last book, *Black Sea: Dispatches and Recipes Through Darkness and Light*, was published in 2018 by Quadrille. It won the prestigious 2020 Art of Eating Prize, and several awards including the John Avery Award at the André Simon Awards, Best Travel and Food Book of the Year at the Edward Stanford Travel Writing Awards and Best Food Book at the Guild of Food Writers Awards 2019.

Her first book, *Samarkand: Recipes & Stories from Central Asia & the Caucasus*, was published by Kyle Books in 2016. It won the Guild of Food Writers Food and Travel Award in 2017 and was a *Guardian* Book of the Year 2016.

She lives in Edinburgh. Twitter and Instagram: @edentravels •